WITH WARMTH, WIT, AND A TOUCH OF NOSTALGIA, popular food blogger Renée Kohlman offers more than 100 of her favourite recipes—including 60 new ones that have never appeared on her blog— guaranteed to make your mouth water.

Renée provides a practical list of pantry essentials, recommendations for useful tools and equipment, and lots of variations for those who bake gluten or sugar free.

Teeming with inspiration for bakers of all abilities, this collection features the stunning photography, heartfelt anecdotes, and engaging food writing that her readers have come to know and love.

ALL THE SWEET THINGS

ALL THE
SWEET THINGS

BAKED GOODS AND STORIES
FROM THE KITCHEN OF
Sweetsugarbean

RENÉE KOHLMAN

TOUCHWOOD EDITIONS

TouchWood Editions
103–1075 Pendergast Street
Victoria, BC v8v 0A1
TouchWoodEditions.com

The information in this book is true and complete to the best of the author's knowledge.
All recommendations are made without guarantee on the part of the author or the publisher.

Editing by Lesley Cameron
Proofreading by Claire Philipson
Cover and interior design by Tree Abraham
Photography by Renée Kohlman

Sugar-Coated Cake Doughnuts on page 224 is inspired by a doughnut recipe originally published
in *The Heritage Collection of Home Tested Recipes* (Chatelaine™, 1968). Used with permission of Rogers Media Inc.
All rights reserved.

Sticky Toffee Pudding on page 188 is from *High Plains: The Joy of Alberta Cuisine*
by Cinda Chavich (Fifth House Publishers, 2008).

Butterhorns with Vanilla Drizzle on page 244 is used with permission of *The Western Producer*.

LIBRARY AND ARCHIVES CANADA CATALOGUING IN PUBLICATION
Kohlman, Renée, author
All the sweet things : baked goods and stories from
the kitchen of Sweetsugarbean / Renée Kohlman.

Includes index.
Some of the recipes in the book have been previously published
on author's blog Sweetsugarbean.
Issued in print and electronic formats.
ISBN 978-1-77151-204-6 (hardcover).--ISBN 978-1-77151-206-0
(PDF).--ISBN 978-1-77151-205-3 (HTML)

1. Sweetsugarbean (Blog). 2. Desserts. 3. Baked products.
4. Confectionery. 5. Cookbooks. I. Title.

TX773.K64 2017   641.86   C2016-907694-6
                                        C2016-907695-4

We acknowledge the financial support of the Government of Canada through the Canada Book Fund
and the Province of British Columbia through the Book Publishing Tax Credit.

Canada

FOR MY MOM, MY HERO

*You'll never do a whole lot
unless you're brave enough to try.*

—Dolly Parton

CONTENTS

INTRODUCTION

FROM THE FARMHOUSE
TO THE LITTLE GREEN KITCHEN

IT IS 1977. I am four years old and standing on a chair in front of the sink in our small Saskatchewan farmhouse kitchen. I'm meant to be "helping" my mom do the dishes, but really I'm playing with the soapy bubbles, amazed at the shapes I can create in the sink and on my hands. I stand there, playing and enjoying my time at the sink until the water goes cold and the bubbles disappear. Perhaps it's a bit of foreshadowing: I would find my hands in plenty of soapy water over the next 40 years as I made a life for myself in kitchens, both professional and at home.

IT IS 1983. I am in our kitchen in Lloydminster, Alberta, creaming together butter and sugar in a large bowl with a hand mixer. My mom has trusted me with the task of baking chocolate chip cookies, from start to finish, and I watch the beaters go round and round, creating a creamy swath in their wake. I stop, stick my finger in the bowl of butter and sugar, and lick it with sheer pleasure. This is the beginning of my baking obsession. For one small moment, I find happiness in that mixing bowl.

My dad has been dead for three years, a profound and devastating shock to my mom, my three siblings and me. As the second-oldest child, I find ways to soothe the angst reeling inside of me. Sometimes it is by reading all the Laura Ingalls Wilder books I can get my hands on. Sometimes it is by watching all of those great afterschool '70s and '80s shows like *Happy Days, Beachcombers* and *The Facts of Life*. But most of the time it is by spending time in the kitchen, baking cookies and other simple treats for my family. Of course, I didn't know it at the time, but the repetitive motions of scooping, measuring, beating, stirring, waiting and watching are a sort of meditation and escapism. No kid should have to lose a parent so young and then be left to process the feelings of loss, with a hole in the heart that looms large and never, ever closes over. There's no doubt that learning to bake helped me get out of my head, at least for a little while. Warm chocolate chip cookies with milk diverted my attention to my belly instead.

IT IS 1993. I am sitting on my bed in a third-floor walk-up apartment in Montreal, opening a care package sent all the way from Saskatoon by my mom. It contains socks, tea, magazines and brownies carefully wrapped up in waxed paper. But the most treasured item is a letter penned in my mom's careful cursive. She tells of all the news from home—what the puppy, Dusty, has chewed to pieces, who my sister is dating, my little brother's basketball accomplishments and how she has finally put the garden to bed. Mom also tells me what she has been up to in the kitchen (our favourite topic) and goes on and on about a new brownie recipe—which she packed up and sent along to her first-born daughter, living halfway across the country in a massive city where English is the second language.

My eyes tear up as I read the letter over and over again. I feel the desperate pang of homesickness and would give anything to be in the kitchen with my mom. This isn't possible, so I do the next best thing. I whip up the brownie recipe she sent along to me, greasing the pan, melting the butter, measuring the flour and cocoa as per her instructions. I set the timer and fill the sink with suds, cleaning up while I wait. Soon the rich chocolate smell wafts throughout our large, drafty space; my roommates come out from behind their computers and we gather at the second-hand kitchen table, sip our tea, and devour the brownies. We are all missing home, and these late-night tea breaks offer comfort and a soothing reassurance. After the last crumbs are wiped from the table, we retreat to our respective bedrooms. In the dim lamplight, I see stacks of art history books and my portfolio of finished and unfinished art projects lingering in the corner. I call my mom and thank her for the parcel, choking back tears as I say goodbye and good night.

IT IS 1999. I am thrashing through the woods in Yukon, singing songs from U2 at the top of my lungs in hopes of scaring off any bears should they happen to be around. Seeing as I am alive to tell the tale, I guess my horrible out-of-tune shrieking worked. I love hiking on barely there trails, following the narrow paths forged by fellow former staff and wildlife alike. Sometimes I veer off and go my own way. In the cover letter of my resumé it states I have an adventurous spirit—I suppose I am living up to it.

Once again, I have moved to a different part of the country where I don't know anyone. I'm the staff cook at a fancy fly-in fishing lodge for the summer, and I'm having my only day off all week. It's also my first real cooking gig since graduating from the culinary program at the Northern Alberta Institute of Technology (NAIT) in Edmonton just a few months earlier. I love the wild, isolating beauty of Yukon, as well as the large and somewhat dysfunctional family vibe that can be camp life. I prepare hearty comfort foods like roast beef with mashed potatoes and all of the sides, including Yorkshire pudding with gravy. The meals I make are intended to be filling and nutritious. The guys are out on the lake working long days as fishing guides, or else doing physical labour around the lodge. The crew is mainly male, save a few girls hired to do housekeeping. The pastry chef, who is also the kitchen manager, is a fellow female. She's tough and talented. I'm both inspired by and a little bit afraid of her. The head chef is French-from-France. Kind, funny and cute, he's also a great teacher. I'm both inspired by and a little bit in love with him.

I like the role of being the one who feeds my friends. The faces gathered around the long rectangular table are my family for the summer, and for the most part, I've grown rather fond of them. When they're sick, I boil up pots of ginger tea; if there's a birthday, I bake a cake and garnish it with pansies grown in pots on the front porch.

Speaking of cake, when I was hired, my boss told me the guys like dessert, so I need to serve some sort of sweet thing after every meal. This is my favourite part of the job.

I bake up chocolate cake with buttercream, key lime pie with a graham cracker crust, apple crisp with ice cream, and pineapple upside-down cake. Their smiles of gratitude after a long day in the middle of Northern Nowhere make my day. If the food is good, the staff is happy. And when you're living remotely like we are, pie after dinner truly is what some of us look forward to. I take pride in working hard and being really good at something, and I know in my heart for the first time that following my love of food and cooking was the right path to take. I love this place so much, I go back for three more summers. Not yet 30, I already know this is one of the best things I will ever do in my life.

IT IS 2007. I am rolling out buttermilk scones in the basement kitchen of Rutherford House, a provincial historic site and home of Alberta's first premier, in Edmonton. It's early morning, and the other staff have yet to arrive. I like the quiet before the hustle and bustle of opening hours at this stately home. Better yet, I love the daily routine of rolling out these scones. This is my third year at The House, and I can almost make the recipe with my eyes closed. Roll, pat, cut, bake. Soon the scones will be just warm out of the oven and sent up to the restaurant alongside our famous raspberry butter that customers swoon over. We've become known as the place to go to in the city for High Tea. Daily, along with the scones, I prepare little tea sandwiches and other savoury items, cookies and bars and other sweet things, as well as hearty sandwiches and homemade desserts. Chocolate pot de crème is a staff favourite, as is the maple apple bread pudding. I'm the only cook, thus have my work cut out for me. I've made good friends with the staff, and seeing as I don't have any immediate family in Edmonton, they become like it. We have tea parties in the parlour whenever there is a birthday, a monthly knitting group guides me as I create my first scarf, and a gaggle of us girls go out for drinks on Whyte Ave after work. I don't know it yet, but in just a year I will be leaving them and the city I called home for 12 years. I will head east down the Yellowhead Highway, my small car full of boxes and two sleeping cats, and my heart aching for a fresh start and a return to family. I will go home.

IT IS 2012. I've been writing a food blog called Sweetsugarbean for just over a year. My sister and I are driving around Saskatoon trying to find a copy of April 14's *National Post* newspaper. I've just been listed as one of Canada's best food bloggers, and I'm dying to see the piece in print. But, no luck. The newspaper has no distribution in Saskatchewan, and I have to wait a few more days until copies arrive from family and friends in Alberta. When I first clap eyes on the full-page photograph of my breakfast tacos gracing the front of the Arts and Life section, I am trembling with pride and joy. I don't believe it. My name, written in the fine print under a photograph I snapped with my second-hand point and shoot camera, with my grandma's old wooden dresser as the backdrop, is in a national newspaper for all to see (unless you live in Saskatchewan).

I drive the two minutes to my mom's house and show her the front page and the pages inside, listing me along with other notable food bloggers. She's beaming. There in the top middle row is a small photograph of scones (made from the same Rutherford

House recipe from all those years ago), along with fresh lemon curd and berries. A small, detailed blurb outlines things like where I grew up, what kind of camera I use, what inspires me and how I got started blogging. That short phone conversation held with the *National Post* journalist just days earlier set in motion events that would change my life. No longer was I just a small blogger writing words I was certain only my sister and good friends read. There were bigger eyes, and more of them, on my site and new opportunities on the horizon just from being listed in that newspaper article. Just as I knew all those years ago in Yukon that I was on the right path, the publication of that piece tells me that I'm still on it. My writing and photography are being commented on and praised. Two skills I essentially taught myself, yet they are so innate I feel like I had them all along. I'm one year away from turning 40, and under profession (along with chef), I list food writer for the first time.

IT IS 2015. A cold February afternoon. I'm standing in my little green kitchen, looking out the window as large flakes of snow fly about. Days earlier, I gave my notice at a job I could no longer stand. Gravely unhappy and disillusioned, I took the chance of giving up a regular paycheque for the unknown. But sometimes the unknown is a lot more bearable than the present. While waiting for the water in the kettle to boil, I read an email on my phone from Taryn Boyd, the publisher at TouchWood Editions. She says that if I ever consider writing a cookbook I should contact her for a chat. I read the email again and again. The moment I've been waiting for all my life, though I hadn't realized it until now, has arrived.

FROM CHEF TO BLOGGER
TO COOKBOOK AUTHOR . . .

There is no real and surefire path to success. Certainly in my case, and likely for most everyone out there, the path has been winding and full of roadblocks. Detours and dead ends can
make you give up, but if there is anything I've learned in this short life, it is to always trust
your gut. Intuition and no doubt a little bit of good luck have been my blessings, and I nod
in gratitude to those people who came along when they did to get me to where I am today.
There is a Louisa May Alcott quote that I love: "There is not much danger that real talent
or goodness will be overlooked long." The author of one of my favourite books nailed it on
the head with those few words. She also penned these words for *Little Women*'s incorrigible
heroine, Jo March: "Write what you know." And so, with this cookbook, I am doing just
that. I know what it's like to be the daughter of a single mom. I know what it's like to move
to a new place, knowing no one. I know the thrill of adventure and the pain of heartbreak. I
know food and I know how to bake. Well. Baking is intrinsic to who I am. I've always been in
the kitchen. Ever since I was a kid, I've loved food with all my might. Cooking for my family,
cooking for my friends while away at university—food was always a primary part of my being.

NAIT's Culinary Arts program covered all of the bases, including meat cutting,
short-order cooking and fine dining, but I loved the two dessert classes best, although
I realized how important it was to have a good, well-rounded culinary education. When
I worked in Yukon as a camp cook that first summer, the other two chefs I worked with
gave me loads of knowledge and inspiration. I was a sponge, soaking it all up, and fortu-
nately, I was able to go back for three more summers. When the camp closed down in
September, I would fly back to Edmonton and work various jobs in the off-season. Bis-
tro and catering cook, pastry cook at a fancy private club, cook for a hot lunch program

at an inner city school. My experience was varied, which was a good thing. I became one of those cooks who can make killer pecan pies, as well as the best beef stroganoff you'll ever sink your teeth into. Given the temperamental employment market at the time, it was good to have a wide background of various cooking skills.

After I was hired on as chef at Rutherford House, I chose not to go back to Yukon. Instead, I stayed on at The House for four years. High Tea was our claim to fame among the ladies-who-lunch crowd, but we would get students coming in for just a bowl of soup or to share a decadent slice of pumpkin tiramisu and a delicious cup of tea served in fine bone china. Situated on the University of Alberta campus, the sprawling old mansion was a joy to work in, and with some of the best people I've ever known. Every time I go back to Edmonton, I pop in and see those fine ladies. We have tea in the parlour, just like old times. Moving back to Saskatoon in 2008 was never really in my plan, but when my brother offered to sell me his little house, I seriously considered it and thought to myself, *why the hell not*. I was 35, single and just out of a bad long-term relationship, and the thought of being close to my family again buoyed me up. It was time for a big life move, and I was ready to do it. I packed up my car, my two cats and my life and headed east.

Saskatoon was in the midst of an economic boom and the culinary scene was on the cusp of exploding. I figured I would find a cooking job without a problem. After a few weeks of settling in and unpacking, I worked at a few places before getting hired as a catering chef, preparing hot meals and appetizers. I did this for almost five years, and then I switched things up enormously by becoming a pastry chef at a gluten-free restaurant in the summer of 2013. Having no previous gluten-free baking experience, I welcomed the challenge. I enjoyed working with new-to-me ingredients—hello, quinoa flakes and buckwheat flour—but I also felt it was important to step out of my comfort zone and try something new. My experience here sharpened my baking skills and led me on to another adventure—as pastry chef at one of the most esteemed private clubs in the city, Riverside Country Club. Here, as part of a team of top culinary professionals, I would bake all sorts of sweet masterpieces, including 350 mocha mousse-filled cream puffs for Mother's Day 2015. I think my arm is still sore from all that piping and filling!

My professional career as a chef has twisted and turned. It hasn't always been easy or fun. The hours are long, the pay isn't the greatest and it's a job both physically and mentally taxing at times. But I wouldn't change a moment of it, even if I could. When I was just beginning my culinary career, an older female chef told me to work in as many places as possible. Learn from as many people as possible. Absorb that knowledge and experience. Follow your gut when it's time to leave. And she was right. Passing words at a party in Edmonton turned out to be some of the best bits of advice I've ever received.

In the fall of 2010, I didn't even know what a food blog really was, but my friends were adamant about me starting one. They were seeing all the photos of food I was posting on Facebook, and clearly thought I had something to offer the world of blogging. I thought I should at least check into it. To those bossy babes, I owe my endless gratitude. With limited computer skills, a second-hand Canon and a passion for creating, my food blog Sweetsugarbean went live on a frigid Saturday night in January 2011. The first recipe I posted was gingerbread waffles with caramelized pears, and I wrote about having break-fast with my family when we were kids. I also wrote about my love of pears and how if I ever got a tattoo, it would be of a pear . . . somewhere. And that's what started it all. A recipe for waffles, the sharing of personal stories, and some dim, blurry photos. I was certain that only my sister and friends would ever read it. But I was hooked. I loved taking and editing photographs, and playing around with lighting and editing software. I was happy to share recipes I was making in my little green kitchen with strangers all over the world. My garden became an inspiration. My notebooks and binders of recipes became an inspiration. My life experience became an inspiration. My blog became a journal I wanted people to read; it just happened to have recipes and photos along for the ride. This new-found creative outlet became my passion. I loved all the processes involved—cooking, styling, photographing, writing, editing. Pressing the little "publish" button always gave me a thrill (and still does). Reading those first comments from non-relatives amazed me. Strangers were reading my words and cooking my recipes! It was a marvelous feeling.

To this day, I'm still in awe that people outside of my immediate circle of friends and family read my blog. In its early days and months, Sweetsugarbean was a fun, creative place to hang out and nothing I took super seriously. All of that changed in April 2012, when I was featured in the *National Post*. I was soon offered media trips and swag. Lots of swag. My readership swelled, both abroad and here in Saskatchewan. Recipe writing contracts from all across Canada started coming my way. My blog also caught the eye of the publisher of the *Saskatoon StarPhoenix*. I was offered a restaurant review column (yes, they pay me to eat and write!) and then a recipe column and video series called *In Renée's Kitchen*. In September 2015, I took over as food writer for two weekly papers, *Bridges* and QC. I also write for Calgary-based *Culinaire Magazine*, in which my monthly Step-by-Step column has me making everything from gingerbread houses to corn dogs. None of this would ever have happened if it hadn't been for Sweetsugarbean and that *National Post* list. If you had told me, on that frigid January night in 2011 when I pressed "publish" for the first time, that all of this would come my way, I would have told you that you were crazy. It just goes to show that hard work and heart will almost always pay off.

ABOUT THESE RECIPES

If you've ever taken a look at my blog's recipe index, you'll know that I write about sweet things more than anything. All the sweet things. In the blog's beginning, my day job was heavy on the cooking of savoury items, but in my heart all I ever wanted to do was bake, and so I baked for Sweetsugarbean. Sure, there are soups, salads and snacky things thrown in on the blog for good measure, but writing about desserts is my favourite thing. And they're my favourite thing to photograph. I love capturing the ooze of a sour cherry tart or the crumbs left behind by a slice of cake. Even a stand mixer, with a bowl full of fluffy me-ringue, is a thing of beauty. Baking is simply a part of my identity, like the living Saskatch-ewan sky above me, and the solid strength that comes from having had a good mother. I've made my passion for food my life's work. You are holding it in your hands.

Some people find baking intimidating. I get that. But I don't want you to feel intimidated by these recipes. Think of me sitting at your kitchen table with a cup of tea, cheering you on. Maybe the Chocolate Marshmallow Pie (page 184) will be the first dessert you ever make for your boyfriend, or perhaps you'll break in your ice cream maker with my Salted Caramel Toffee Chip (page 290) recipe. Or maybe you'll make your daughter's wedding cake using my Classic Vanilla Cake with Cranberry Curd and Seven-Minute Frosting (page 150) recipe. I'll be your cheerleader the whole way. There are recipes here for every skill level. Whether you're a beginner baker or a seasoned pro who's been baking pies for 40 years, I know there are delicious things in this cookbook you will love and make your own. Some recipes are more sophisticated than others, yet all are doable. I've made sure of that. I've also tried to balance out the book with some recipes that are healthier than others, but I do believe a little indulgence goes a long way. Like Julia Child said, "A party without cake is just a meeting." Indeed. Butter, cream, sugar, they're all here. But so are coconut milk, quinoa flakes and cacao nibs. Even lentils. Yes, lentils. Trust me. I've also included some of my favourite gluten-free recipes, too. This cookbook is full of all the sweet things I've loved to bake over the years, and some new recipes I've recently tried and fallen in love with. Never stop learning or trying—I believe that. I'm hoping *All The Sweet Things* will pull you into the kitchen to bake, then back to the couch to curl up and read. I would love to hear of your baking triumphs! **Email me at renee@sweetsugarbean.com**

The Essential Baker's Pantry

The following are ingredients I like to have on hand to fulfill all of my baking needs, and most of them make an appearance in this cookbook. I bake a lot, so the list is long. Obviously, just purchase what you think you'll need to fulfill your own baking needs. Don't feel you need to have quinoa flour in the house if no one in your circle is eating gluten-free!

FLOURS & FLAKES

I use unbleached all-purpose flour most of the time, but have cake and pastry flour and either whole wheat or rye flour around, too. I keep those flours in the refrigerator or freezer, as I don't use them super often, but I like having them around in case I need them.

* UNBLEACHED ALL-PURPOSE FLOUR
* CAKE AND PASTRY FLOUR
* WHOLE WHEAT FLOUR
* RYE FLOUR
* SPELT FLOUR
* MULTIGRAIN FLOUR
* OAT FLOUR
* BUCKWHEAT FLOUR (gluten-free)
* MILLET FLOUR (gluten-free)
* QUINOA FLOUR (gluten-free)
* GLUTEN-FREE FLOUR BLEND
* LARGE-FLAKE OATS (not instant—you might know them as rolled oats)
* QUINOA FLAKES (gluten-free)

SUGAR & SWEETENERS

Most of these recipes were tested using good ol' granulated white as it's likely what most of you have in your cupboard. If I had won the lottery as I was testing these recipes, I would likely have used organic, fair trade cane sugar as that's what I use when I'm not writing a cookbook devoted entirely to sweet things. But the cost is quite hefty when I'm going through sugar like crazy. That being said, substituting cane sugar for granulated white should work well for most recipes—but for anything that involves meringue or marshmallows, the granules need to be small and white.

* GRANULATED WHITE SUGAR
* SUPERFINE SUGAR (or just grind some granulated in your food processor)
* DARK BROWN SUGAR (make your own, see page 20)
* COCONUT SUGAR
* CANE SUGAR
* ICING SUGAR (also known as powdered sugar or confectioner's sugar)
* COARSE SUGAR or TURBINADO SUGAR (for sprinkling)
* CANNED SWEETENED CONDENSED MILK
* PURE MAPLE SYRUP (no fake stuff, please)
* GOLDEN SYRUP
* LIGHT CORN SYRUP
* HONEY (raw unpasteurized and liquid)
* FANCY MOLASSES

CHOCOLATE

My favourite food group (next to cheese). I like to buy my chocolate in the bulk section of a large grocery store. It carries Bernard Callebaut, which I buy in chunks and large pieces that I chop up whenever I need to melt it. I also buy bars of good-quality dark chocolate, especially when they're on sale after the holidays. By dark chocolate, I mean bars that list the cocoa content as being around 70 percent. I chop these up for cookies, for ganache, for bark, for pretty much everything. I only use chocolate chips in cookies, but if I have chunks on hand, I'll use those instead. Chocolate chips contain stabilizers, which help them keep their shape while melted. I like my chocolate to ooze in cookies, bars, breads, hence my preference in most of these recipes for chunks or the chopped bars.

* UNSWEETENED DUTCH PROCESS COCOA POWDER
* DARK CHOCOLATE CHUNKS
* SEMI-SWEET CHOCOLATE CHIPS
* BARS OF GOOD-QUALITY CHOCOLATE WITH 70% COCOA SOLIDS, for chopping and melting
* WHITE CHOCOLATE CHUNKS
* WHITE CHOCOLATE PIECES, for chopping and melting
* SKOR TOFFEE BITS
* CACAO NIBS

VANILLA & OTHER EXTRACTS

Use only pure vanilla extract, please. The artificial stuff is full of ingredients you'd be better off not putting in your body. The price of the good stuff is worth it for the quality. If you're using paste, just use the same volume as you would for extract.

* PURE VANILLA EXTRACT
* VANILLA BEAN PASTE (this can be found in specialty stores and is well worth the cost)
* VANILLA BEANS
* PURE ALMOND EXTRACT
* ROSEWATER ESSENCE

SPICES & OTHER DRIED AROMATICS

I have a giant shelf in my kitchen with jars of all sorts of spices on it. I like to buy small quantities at a time to keep them as fresh as possible. These are the ones I primarily use when baking.

* GROUND ALLSPICE
* GROUND CARDAMOM
* WHOLE GREEN CARDAMOM PODS
* GROUND CINNAMON
* CINNAMON STICKS
* GROUND CLOVES
* WHOLE CLOVES
* GROUND GINGER
* GROUND NUTMEG
* WHOLE NUTMEG
* WHOLE STAR ANISE
* BAY LEAVES
* GROUND CHIPOTLE or CHILI POWDER
* DRIED LAVENDER FLOWERS (culinary quality)
* GROUND TURMERIC
* COFFEE BEANS
* ESPRESSO POWDER
* CHAI AND EARL GREY TEA

DRIED FRUIT, ETC.

* DRIED CRANBERRIES, BLUEBERRIES, CHERRIES, RAISINS, APRICOTS
* MEDJOOL DATES
* CANDIED/CRYSTALLIZED GINGER
* UNSWEETENED and/or SWEETENED SHREDDED COCONUT

NUTS, SEEDS, ETC.

I like to keep whatever nuts and seeds I don't use frequently in the freezer to help maintain their freshness.

* WHOLE, SLICED, BLANCHED or SLIVERED ALMONDS
* BRAZIL NUTS
* HAZELNUTS
* UNSALTED ROASTED PEANUTS
* PECAN HALVES
* PISTACHIOS
* WALNUT HALVES
* CHIA SEEDS
* FLAX SEEDS
* HEMP HEARTS
* POPPY SEEDS
* RAW PUMPKIN SEEDS
* SESAME SEEDS
* UNSALTED SUNFLOWER SEEDS
* POPPING CORN
* GREEN LENTILS
* ALL-NATURAL PEANUTS-ONLY PEANUT BUTTER (kept in the refrigerator)
* TAHINI PASTE

RANDOM BITS & BOBS & BOOZE

* OIL: OLIVE, CANOLA (Canola is my preferred cooking oil, but you can use your neutral-tasting cooking oil of choice) and COCONUT (solid at room temperature)
* VINEGAR: BALSAMIC, APPLE CIDER and WHITE
* SALT: FLAKY (such as Maldon), FINE SEA SALT and KOSHER
* CANNED PUMPKIN PURÉE
* CANNED FULL-FAT COCONUT MILK
* APPLE SAUCE
* SPRINKLES
* GRAHAM CRACKER CRUMBS
* CHOCOLATE COOKIE CRUMBS
* CANDY CANES
* PUFFED WHEAT
* PRETZELS
* ARBORIO RICE
* WILD RICE
* LARD FOR PIE CRUST
* BAKING POWDER
* BAKING SODA
* CREAM OF TARTAR
* UNFLAVOURED POWDERED GELATIN
* ACTIVE and INSTANT DRY YEAST
* RYE WHISKEY, BOURBON, BRANDY, RUM, RED WINE

THE FREEZER

I like to keep phyllo and puff pastry on hand for a quick galette or rustic tart, especially in the summer. I also make big batches of pie dough and keep extra discs of the stuff in the freezer for whenever the pie mood strikes. Which is often. Be sure to let any pastry thaw in the refrigerator, not on the counter, before using. Berries are another freezer staple—either ones I pick in the summer and freeze myself or those from the store, preferably organic. Whenever I see a great deal on butter, I'll buy the allowed limit and throw a few extra pounds in the freezer. There's nothing worse than having no butter in the house!

* PASTRY: PHYLLO and PUFF
* FROZEN BERRIES (and other fruit)
* BUTTER

THE REFRIGERATOR

These recipes were tested using full-fat dairy products. I don't like to bake with or eat the low-fat stuff. If you decide to use low-fat dairy when baking, know that the results may not be as successful. For most recipes, I like to use room-temperature dairy (except whipping cream when I am going to beat it—it must always be cold). Leave the dairy out on the counter for one to two hours before you want to bake with it.

DAIRY

* WHOLE MILK
* BUTTERMILK (shake before using. It's best to use the real thing, but if you're stuck, make your own buttermilk by adding 1 Tbsp of lemon juice or white vinegar to a 1-cup measure and top with milk. Stir and let stand for five minutes.)

* WHIPPING CREAM
* HALF-AND-HALF CREAM (10%)
* FULL-FAT SOUR CREAM
* PLAIN YOGURT (at least 3%)
* FULL-FAT CREAM CHEESE (the stuff in the bricks)

* MASCARPONE CHEESE (make your own, see page 28)
* RICOTTA CHEESE (make your own, see page 48)

BUTTER

* These recipes were tested using unsalted butter, unless otherwise stated. If you only have salted, then simply reduce the amount of salt in the recipe by ¼ tsp for every ½ cup of butter. We won't even mention margarine. If the ingredients list in a recipe tells you the butter should be softened, leave it out on the counter to soften before you begin. If you're in a panic because you need softened butter RIGHT NOW, as a last resort you can microwave butter for a few seconds to help speed the process along. Just be sure you don't melt it!

EGGS

* I used large eggs when testing these recipes, and for the most part they were at room temperature. Leave them out on the counter for one to two hours before you want to bake. This is especially important when making anything with meringue. For meringues, you can either separate the eggs and leave just the whites on the counter and refrigerate the yolks, or you can leave the whole eggs on the counter. It's up to you. If you wanna bake right this very second but have only cold eggs, simply place them in a bowl of warm tap water for 10 minutes.

CITRUS

* I used fresh lemons and limes to test these recipes. Try to avoid the stuff out of the bottle if you can. (For one thing, you can't get zest from it.) If you must use bottled, try to get pure citrus juice, and use the same volume as you would with fresh.

Other Housekeeping Tidbits

These are just my ramblings about things you may find interesting or useful.

* ALWAYS READ THE RECIPE THROUGH before beginning. You may realize you're out of an ingredient halfway through, which is super frustrating. I know, because I've had to run to my nearest grocery store for pumpkin purée at nine o'clock at night in my pyjamas. Lesson learned!
* GATHER ALL OF YOUR INGREDIENTS before baking (see above).
* PREHEAT THE OVEN and prepare your pans when the recipe tells you to.
* CLEAN AS YOU GO. Like we learned in Home Ec back in 1989, have a sink of soapy water ready and then add your dirty dishes as they accumulate. When you get a second, give them a quick wash. This beats having to stand and wash a bunch of dishes at the end of a baking session. I don't have a dishwasher (I know! Who writes a cookbook without a dishwasher?!) and this little trick helped me lots.

Useful Tools and Equipment

I know not everyone can afford to buy—or has space to store!—every little thing I have listed here, so don't panic when you see this list. I simply find these tools useful. And if a recipe needs nine-inch pans but you only have eight-inch, don't be afraid to borrow from a friend. That's what I did! Thank you, dear Lindsay, for the nine-inch pans and the ice cream maker. I gave them back to you, right?

PANS & POTS

* 13×17-INCH RIMMED WITH ¾-INCH BAKING SHEETS (I have at least three and use them all the time)
* 9×13-INCH BAKING DISH
* 10-INCH ROUND BAKING DISH
* 9-INCH ROUND BAKING DISH
* 8-INCH SQUARE BAKING DISH
* ANGEL FOOD CAKE PAN
* BUNDT CAKE PAN
* 9-INCH SPRINGFORM PAN
* 9-INCH PIE PLATE
* 9-INCH ROUND CAKE PANS (at least two)
* 8-INCH ROUND CAKE PANS (at least two)
* MUFFIN PAN
* MADELEINE PAN
* DOUGHNUT PAN (for six regular-sized doughnuts, or two pans if you plan on baking lots of doughnuts)
* 10-INCH CAST IRON SKILLET
* CRÊPE PAN
* MEDIUM SAUCEPAN (at least two)
* SMALL SAUCEPAN
* DUTCH OVEN
* LARGE ROASTER
* LARGE and SMALL SKILLETS

UTENSILS, ETC.

* HEATPROOF SPATULAS (the more the merrier)
* WOODEN SPOONS (various sizes)
* TONGS
* SILICONE PASTRY BRUSH
* ROLLING PIN
* WHISKS (large and small)
* LARGE OFFSET SPATULAS (for spreading batters and decorating cakes)
* MINI OFFSET SPATULAS (these get in the corners of pans really well)
* PASTRY BLENDER
* MICROPLANE (for zesting citrus, grating nutmeg)
* CHEF'S KNIFE, SERRATED KNIFE, PARING KNIVES (keep them sharp!)
* ICE CREAM SCOOP (for scooping muffins and meringues, as well as ice cream—mine measures a little more than ¼ cup in volume)
* MEASURING CUPS and SPOONS
* CANDY THERMOMETER
* MIXING BOWLS (all sizes)
* CAKE WHEEL (for decorating cakes)
* HANDHELD BEATERS
* IMMERSION BLENDER
* PARCHMENT PAPER (best thing invented, ever)
* ALUMINUM FOIL, WAX PAPER, RESEALABLE PLASTIC BAGS
* PIPING BAGS (disposable or cloth, with assorted piping tips of various shapes and sizes)
* FINE MESH SIEVE
* CHEESECLOTH

THE BIG EQUIPMENT

* GAS STOVE. I have a gas stove, so the recipes in this cookbook were tested using that. It's always a good idea to check if your oven's temperature is accurate. If you're using a convection oven, be sure to reduce the temperature of the recipes by 25 degrees Fahrenheit, and to check the doneness of the item a few minutes early.
* STAND MIXER. I also used a KitchenAid stand mixer for testing these recipes. I'm so glad it didn't break down during the eight-month testing period! What a workhorse. If you don't have a stand mixer, then a handheld mixer should work just as well for most recipes. You WILL need a stand mixer for the Vanilla Bean Marshmallows on page 272, though. The mixture is so sticky and viscous that it needs the power of a stand mixer. Besides, who wants to hold a mixer for 10 minutes?
* BLENDER. I don't have a fancy Vitamix blender. I believe I got mine in a Boxing Day sale for $29.99. For the recipes in this book, a cheapo blender like mine will suffice nicely.
* FOOD PROCESSOR. A food processor comes in handy so often, I can't quite imagine my life without it. From making pie dough to crushing graham crackers, to making energy bars, it's a useful investment when it comes to kitchen equipment.

Recipes

DESSERT FOR BREAKFAST

GINGER PEACH CRISP

It seems only fitting that the first recipe in my cookbook should be one I've been baking for many years. Fruit crisp was a common dessert in our house when I was growing up, and I can see why—it's easy to throw together, feeds a crowd of hungry kids, is relatively inexpensive and is a way to use up fruit that's been on the counter too long. Plus, it's ever so delicious, especially with ice cream. When I first moved away from home, I would call my mom and ask her what the secret was to her crisp. Butter, she said. Make sure you use lots of butter in the topping. That's also the first nugget of wisdom in this book. Use enough butter. Thanks, Mom!

   Served cold and topped with a puddle of yogurt, it's a quite a lovely way to start the day. Use any fruit you have on hand for this (though I have a long-standing love affair with peaches). Stone fruits, berries, rhubarb, pears and yes, apples, on their own or in any combination, all work well.

SERVES 4–6

5 cups sliced fresh, ripe peaches
   (skin on or off–your choice)
¼ cup granulated sugar
1 Tbsp all-purpose flour
1 Tbsp fresh lemon juice
1 tsp ground ginger

½ cup + 2 Tbsp unsalted butter, softened
3 cups large-flake oats
½ cup packed brown sugar
½ tsp salt

❋ Preheat the oven to 350°F. Place the rack in the centre of the oven.

❋ Stir the peaches, sugar, flour, lemon juice and ground ginger together in a medium bowl. Scrape this into a 9-inch round baking dish. Dot with the 2 Tbsp butter.

❋ Use the same bowl the fruit was in (this saves on dishes) to mix together the oats and brown sugar with the ½ cup butter and salt. Use your hands to rub the butter evenly into the mixture. Sprinkle this evenly over the fruit. Bake for 35–40 minutes, until the topping is golden brown and the fruit is bubbling. Turn off the oven and let the crisp sit inside for 5 more minutes. Cool the crisp on a wire rack.

❋ Serve warm, with vanilla ice cream or whipped cream; or serve cold, with plain yogurt. The crisp keeps well, covered, in the refrigerator for up to 4 days.

NOTE

How to make your own brown sugar: *Say you're in the middle of a recipe and you reach for the canister of brown sugar only to find it empty. After a few curse words are exhaled, you can make your own. All you need is 4 cups of granulated white sugar and ¼ cup of molasses. Scoop the sugar into a large bowl and add the molasses. You can use a spoon to stir, but I find working the mixture with my hands works best. Work it until all of the molasses is incorporated with the granulated white and it looks like dark brown sugar. Place it back in the empty brown sugar canister and go ahead with the recipe. This also saves a little bit of cash, and it feels rather nice on the hands.*

Cherry Dutch Baby

I first became acquainted with Dutch baby when my friend Katey brought one to a breakfast pot-luck when I was working at Rutherford House in Edmonton. Essentially, a thick crêpe-like batter is poured into a screaming hot skillet that has been well coated in butter. The eggs in the batter make it puff up like crazy, the edges get crispy and then the whole thing collapses, waiting for whatever goodness you wish to fill it with. It's really quite a lovely thing to behold. Fresh, seasonal fruit is then scattered on top. And do give it a dusting of icing sugar for a fancy effect.

SERVES 1–2

2 large eggs, at room temperature
1/3 cup all-purpose flour
1/3 cup whole milk
2 Tbsp granulated sugar
½ tsp ground cinnamon
½ tsp ground nutmeg

¼ tsp salt
2 Tbsp unsalted butter, softened
1 ½ cups fresh cherries, pitted
3 Tbsp icing sugar

❄ Preheat the oven to 400°F. Place the rack in the centre of the oven.

❄ Place the eggs, flour, milk, sugar, cinnamon, nutmeg and salt in a blender. Blend on high until you have a smooth batter. Place the butter in a 10-inch cast iron skillet and put it in the oven. Remove the skillet from the oven once the butter has melted and then use a pastry brush to evenly coat the sides and bottom of the pan with the butter. Blitz the egg mixture for another 10 seconds then pour it into the prepared skillet. Bake for 15–20 minutes, until the Dutch baby is puffed and golden brown.

❄ Remove the skillet from the oven and let it cool on a wire rack for about 5 minutes. Cut the Dutch baby into 4, top with cherries and dust with icing sugar.

❄ Serve warm on your prettiest plates (because life is too short to keep them all alone in the cupboard), or if you're like me and live alone, go ahead and eat it out of the skillet. I won't tell anyone. Any leftovers can be kept, covered, in the refrigerator for up to 1 day.

NOTES

Top the Dutch baby with any seasonal fruit or berries, or fruit compotes. Even a squeeze of fresh lemon juice and icing sugar is sometimes all you need.

If you don't have a cast iron skillet, any 10-inch baking dish with sides at least 2½ inches high will do.

Angel Food Cake French Toast

French toast is one of my favourite breakfast foods. Good bread dipped in an eggy batter, fried in a little bit of butter and topped with fruit—what's not to love? I discovered this recipe quite by accident. I had a few pieces of angel food cake lingering on the counter (I know! How is that even possible?) and thought I'd see what happens when they're substituted for bread. The result? Pure magic. The sugars on the outside give the French toast a slight caramelization that is out of this world. Served with a generous helping of fresh berries and fruit, a dollop of whipped cream and a splodge of maple syrup, it really is breakfast perfection. This is a great recipe to bust out for Mother's Day, Easter or any other occasion when the table is set with fresh flowers, pretty plates and mimosas.

SERVES 3–4

3 large eggs, at room temperature
1 cup whole milk
1 tsp ground cardamom or cinnamon
1 tsp pure vanilla extract
¼ tsp salt
3–4 Tbsp unsalted butter, softened and divided

6 thick slices Angel Food Cake (page 126)
1 cup unsweetened whipped cream
2 cups assorted fresh berries and fruit
4 fresh mint sprigs
⅓ cup icing sugar
½ cup pure maple syrup

❄ Preheat the oven to 200°F.

❄ Whisk together the eggs, milk, cardamom, vanilla and salt in a large bowl. Melt 2 Tbsp of the butter in a large skillet over medium-high heat. Soak half of the cake slices in the egg mixture, being sure all sides are soaked. Remove the cake from the egg mixture and place it in the hot skillet. Fry the cake on all sides, being sure not to let it get too brown. If it's getting too dark too fast, turn down the heat to medium.

❄ When the French toast is golden, place the slices on an ovenproof platter and keep them warm in the oven. Melt the remaining butter in the skillet. Soak the remaining cake slices and then fry them in the hot butter.

❄ Serve warm, garnished with dollops of whipped cream, fresh fruit, a mint sprig, a dusting of icing sugar and a drizzle of maple syrup.

Strawberry Rhubarb Mascarpone Crêpes

Like Mulder and Scully, Tina and Amy, and Lucy and Ethel, strawberry and rhubarb are best friends, and their delicious combination is only made better by the creamy addition of mascarpone filling in these crêpes. Crêpes are one of my favourite things in the world, and every time I make them, I wonder why I don't more often. They may take a little longer than pancakes, but not *that* much longer, and they look so much sexier. You'll have to make one at a time, but it's no big deal—just stand at the stove, wait a couple of minutes, and flip them quickly. There's something almost meditative about making my small batch of crêpes. Pour, swirl, flip. Repeat. For the compote, all you do is simmer some strawberries and rhubarb in a little lemon zest and a bit of sugar. Easy, right? Leftovers are lovely on granola and yogurt in the morning.

STRAWBERRY RHUBARB COMPOTE
2½ cups (½-inch chunks) fresh rhubarb
2½ cups fresh strawberries, hulled and cut in half
½ cup granulated sugar
2 Tbsp fresh lemon juice
2 Tbsp grated lemon zest
¼ tsp ground cinnamon

MASCARPONE FILLING
1 cup whipping cream
1 tsp pure vanilla extract
½ cup mascarpone cheese, softened (see following page)
2 tsp granulated sugar

CRÊPES
4 large eggs, at room temperature
1 cup whole milk

1 cup water
2 cups all-purpose flour
¼ cup unsalted butter, melted
1 tsp pure vanilla extract
½ tsp salt
¼ tsp ground nutmeg
¼ cup canola or other cooking oil, divided
⅓ cup icing sugar

❋ To make the compote, combine all of the compote ingredients in a medium saucepan over medium-high heat and bring to a boil, turn down the heat and simmer, uncovered, on low heat for about 20 minutes until the compote thickens, stirring occasionally. Set aside to cool.

❋ To make the filling, place the cream and vanilla in a stand mixer fitted with a whisk attachment and beat on high speed until soft peaks form. Turn the speed down to medium and, with the mixer running, drop in the mascarpone 1 Tbsp at a time, beating well after each addition. While the last addition of mascarpone is being beaten in, add the sugar. Continue to beat to combine. Set the filling aside while you make the crêpes.

❋ To make the crêpes, place the eggs, milk and water in a large bowl. Beat well by hand with a whisk. Add the flour, a couple of tablespoons at a time, whisking well after each addition (this will prevent lumps—and no one likes a lumpy crêpe). Once all the flour has been whisked into the batter, add the melted butter, vanilla, salt and nutmeg. Whisk well.

❋ Preheat the oven to 200°F. Line a rimmed baking sheet with parchment paper.

❋ Preheat a 10-inch crêpe pan, or a large skillet, over medium heat. Add 1 Tbsp of the oil and swirl to coat the pan. Pour ¼ cup of batter into the pan, swirling to spread the batter. Don't worry if it doesn't spread to the edge of the pan. Cook for 1 minute, or until the top is dry, then flip and cook for 1 minute more. Flip the crêpes onto the prepared baking sheet and keep them warm in the oven until all the crêpes are made.

❋ To serve, spread the crêpes with compote and mascarpone filling. Fold each in half, then in half again. Drizzle with more compote and dust with icing sugar. Wrap any extra crêpes tightly in plastic and refrigerate for up to 4 days. The compote can be refrigerated in an airtight container for up to 1 week, and the mascarpone filling can be refrigerated in an airtight container for up to 10 days.

Homemade Mascarpone Cheese

I love mascarpone cheese. Just going to come clean right away. Several recipes in this cookbook use it, as you may have already noticed. What I don't love is the price tag. Good Lord. Around here, it's about $10 for a pound, or 2 cups. That's a lot of cash, especially if you're on a budget. Baking can be expensive—I'm not going to lie—so whenever I can cut costs, I will. And if I get to make cheese in the meantime, well, I might as well give myself a high-five right now. So, the thing with real mascarpone is that it's made in Italy from fresh cow's milk, and it'll make you lose your balance if you're not careful. It's that good. This version is an imposter, but it's sort of like being in that famous wax museum where all of the celebrities are. Sometimes it's hard to tell the difference between real George Clooney and wax museum George Clooney. Same with this cheese. It's super indulgent and knee-wobblingly good. And it has only three ingredients: cream, lemon juice and salt. Commercial mascarpone has fructose, guar gum and other thickeners and preservatives. No thanks. Once you've made a batch, you'll want to make it on the regular. Stir it into other baked goods, slather it on toast, dip fresh, seasonal fruit into it for a lovely dessert, whip some into pasta sauce. You get the idea. The one thing you do need is patience. But that's a small price to pay for all of the money you'll save.

MAKES ABOUT 1½–2 CUPS

4 cups whipping cream
2 Tbsp fresh lemon juice
Pinch of salt

❋ Heat the cream in a medium saucepan over medium-high heat. Bring it to the point where bubbles just begin to appear around the edges. If you have a thermometer, you'll see this will be around 185°F. Try not to boil the cream. A full-on boil could scald the cream, meaning you may have to discard it and start over again. Stir in the lemon juice and keep it simmering gently for 5–7 minutes, maintaining the temperature at 185°F. There's no need to stir. Remove the pan from the heat, cover it and let it rest for 30 minutes.

❋ Place a fine mesh sieve over a bowl and line it with a few layers of damp cheesecloth. I like to fasten my cheesecloth to the sieve with clothespins. Without stirring, gently pour the mixture into the lined sieve. Sprinkle a pinch of salt over the cream. Cover loosely with plastic wrap and place the whole thing in the refrigerator for 20–24 hours. The longer it sits, the thicker it gets. When it's ready, lift the cheesecloth out of the sieve. Scrape the cheese off the cheesecloth and into a bowl (discard the liquid in the bowl).

❋ This can be refrigerated in an airtight container for up to 2 weeks.

NOTE

This recipe can be easily doubled or cut in half, depending on your mascarpone needs.

Roasted Stone Fruit with Vanilla Bean and Star Anise

At the peak of summer, I'm at the Saskatoon Farmers' Market every weekend. There's this little fruit truck that hauls out fresh fruit from the Interior of British Columbia for us prairie folk. The cherries are the first to arrive, in June, followed by the peaches and nectarines, plums, grapes, pears and apples. I'm a bit of a glutton, loading up my shopping bag with all of this fantastic fare, because for the other eight months of the year, the fruit selection in Saskatoon is not this fresh or varied. As with most things in life, I make the most of what I have while I have it.

This is a great recipe that celebrates the loveliness of stone fruit bounty. I adore contrasting the sweetness of peaches with the tang of prune plums. Substitute cherries and nectarines, if you have those on hand. The star anise and vanilla add a bit of sophistication, and while the balsamic vinegar seems odd, it really accentuates all of the flavours. This is truly a dish for the senses—the colours and smell alone will grab you. But one taste and you'll be smitten.

SERVES 4

3 large, ripe peaches with their skin on,
  pitted and quartered
5 large prune plums with their skin on,
  pitted and halved
1 vanilla bean
1 cinnamon stick

5 whole star anise
2 Tbsp liquid honey
1 Tbsp unsalted butter, softened
1 Tbsp balsamic vinegar
Pinch of flaky salt, such as Maldon

❋ Preheat the oven to 400°F. Place the rack in the centre of the oven.

❋ Arrange the fruit in an 8-inch baking dish. Scrape the seeds of the vanilla bean onto the fruit and then add the pod. Nestle in the cinnamon stick and star anise. Drizzle the honey overtop and dot with the butter. Pour the balsamic vinegar over everything and add a generous pinch of flaky salt. Toss to coat. Roast, uncovered, for 20 minutes.

❋ Remove the dish from the oven and stir. Turn down the heat to 350°F and roast for another 10–15 minutes, until the fruit is soft and slightly caramelized.

❋ Serve warm over vanilla ice cream or cold over Greek yogurt. The roasted stone fruit keeps well in an airtight container in the refrigerator for up to 3 days.

NOTE

Try using the roasted stone fruits instead of strawberries in my Strawberry Basil Shortcakes recipe (page 136).

Coconut Chia Pudding with Blueberry Ginger Compote

Chia seeds are the darling of the health food world, and deservedly so. They're neat little guys, full of antioxidants, heart-healthy minerals, fibre and omega-3s, and they help regulate insulin levels in the blood. Chia good! They also absorb a tonne of liquid and don't really taste like much on their own, which makes them great to play around with when it comes to puddings.

This version is made with coconut milk and is gluten- and dairy-free. I've added lime juice and maple syrup as well as a dash of ground star anise, but you could easily substitute cardamom or cinnamon. Cooked down with a little bit of sugar and grated ginger, the blueberry compote has a little zing that complements the chia pudding. Chopped pistachios add more nutrition and texture, plus they just look pretty. I eat this for breakfast and a little afternoon snack, but it would make a fine dessert, too. Not a fan of blueberries? Substitute frozen cherries or strawberries. Strawberry Rhubarb Compote (page 26) would also be fantastic.

COCONUT CHIA PUDDING
1 (14 oz) can full-fat coconut milk
⅓ cup pure maple syrup
1½ limes, grated zest and juice of
1 tsp pure vanilla extract
½ tsp ground star anise, cardamom or cinnamon
Pinch of salt
½ cup chia seeds
¼ cup chopped pistachios

BLUEBERRY GINGER COMPOTE
2 cups frozen blueberries
2 Tbsp granulated sugar
1 tsp grated fresh ginger
1 Tbsp water

❀ To make the pudding, place all the ingredients except the chia seeds and pistachios in a blender. Blend until smooth. Place the chia seeds in a medium bowl. Pour the coconut mixture over the chia seeds and stir well. After 10 minutes, stir again (this helps prevent lumps). After another 10 minutes, stir again. Cover the bowl tightly with plastic wrap and refrigerate for about 3 hours before serving.

❀ Meanwhile, prepare the compote. Place all the compote ingredients in a medium saucepan over medium-high heat and bring to a boil. Turn down the heat to medium-low and simmer, stirring often, until the berries are slightly jammy, 10–12 minutes. Remove the pan from the heat and let the compote cool down to room temperature. Cover and refrigerate until needed. This can be refrigerated in an airtight container for up to 1 week.

❀ To serve, spoon the chia pudding into serving dishes and top with blueberry compote. Garnish with chopped pistachios. The chia puddings can be covered with plastic wrap and stored in the refrigerator for up to 4 days (but best to do this without the pistachio garnish).

THE FIRST TIME
I TASTED
CLAFOUTIS . . .

MY EYES WERE OPENED TO THE POSSIBILITY OF A CULINARY CAREER THAT DID NOT HAVE TO BE ABOUT LINE COOKING AND DEEP FRYING. COOKING COULD BE CREATIVE, INTUITIVE AND ARTISTIC. IMAGINE THAT!

FLASHBACK: 1997. Picture a young, rosy-cheeked Renée, fresh out of university with her shiny new Bachelor of Fine Arts degree . . .

I was beyond confused as to what to do with this expensive and seemingly impractical degree. After working in a coffee shop for a year, I knew I needed a skill and further education. The big and constant question at the time was what in the world I was to do with this life. I knew I had to study something I was passionate about, something that was creative, and something I loved to do.

Cooking had always been in my blood, so enrolling in Culinary School at NAIT in Edmonton seemed like the perfect fit. The first few classes were okay . . . lots of training on how to make soups and sauces, braise meat, prepare vegetables, that sort of thing. I was generally a little underwhelmed, but then I met Mr. Butler in my second semester and my eyes were opened to the possibility of a culinary career that did not have to be about line cooking and deep frying. Cooking could be creative, intuitive and artistic. Imagine that!

John Butler taught a class called International. His class went something like this: one day we would research and discuss food from a particular country, and the next day we would whip up the recipes we wanted to make. There were no guidelines other than the recipes had to be from that country and we had to style and plate the items so they looked beautiful. You can imagine how much I loved this class. Free rein to make whatever I wanted and make it look pretty! Yes! I made wild mushroom risotto, pork satay with peanut sauce, tortilla soup, mango fool and apricot raspberry clafoutis. All for the very first time.

This was my absolute favourite class, and Mr. Butler saw something in my keen eye for design (plus my food didn't taste half bad either). He encouraged me to think more about food styling and design, and his words stuck with me for the remainder of the program. All these years later (going on 20!), I still think about Mr. Butler and his class, and what his words of encouragement did for me. Not all teachers are created equal, and he was one of the best. Mr. Butler passed away shortly after I graduated, but if he could see these pages, I think he'd be pretty darn proud. Thank you, Chef.

Apricot and Raspberry Clafoutis

Clafoutis was developed in the Limousin region of France to showcase the area's spectacular cherries. Some recipes say to leave the pits inside the cherries, but I value my dental work too much, so whenever I make a cherry version of this dessert, I remove the pits. If you don't have a cherry pitter, you can do what I do and use a large piping tip to push them out. Just twist, and out they come like magic. You can use any fruit you like when making clafoutis except strawberries (too juicy!). Apricots and raspberries make a fine combo—one that just teeters on the edge of tartness.

Clafoutis only takes 40 to 45 minutes to bake, and it's fancy enough to serve to company, but you'll be grateful for leftovers, because it's a grand breakfast. The eggs make the batter puff up into golden gorgeousness. Almost breathtaking, really. Then there's the buttery crust and the fruit that almost melts into the velvety, flan-like centre.

SERVES 2–4

3 Tbsp unsalted butter, softened
3 large eggs, at room temperature
1 cup whole milk
¾ cup all-purpose flour
½ cup + 2 Tbsp granulated sugar, divided
2 tsp pure vanilla extract

½ tsp salt
5–6 ripe apricots, cut in half and pitted
½ cup fresh or frozen raspberries
2 Tbsp icing sugar

❋ Preheat the oven to 375°F. Place the rack in the centre of the oven.

❋ Place the butter in a 10-inch ovenproof skillet or baking dish and put it in the oven to melt. Remove the skillet from the oven and, with a pastry brush, coat the bottom and sides of the skillet with the butter. Place the eggs, milk, flour, ½ cup of sugar, vanilla and salt in a blender and blend on high speed for 30 seconds, until it's completely smooth. Pour the batter into the hot skillet.

❋ Arrange the apricots round side up on the batter and scatter the raspberries on top. Sprinkle with the remaining 2 Tbsp of granulated sugar. Bake for 40–45 minutes, until the clafoutis is puffed and golden brown and the middle is set.

❋ Remove the skillet from the oven, let it cool for about 5 minutes, then cut the clafoutis into wedges and dust with icing sugar. Any leftovers can be kept for up to 1 day in the refrigerator.

CHOCOLATE CROISSANT BREAD PUDDING

Decadent. Indulgent. Rich. These are just a few words to describe this bread pudding. I don't know if you'll love me or hate me after you try this, because on the one hand, it's so bad for you, but the other hand is happily spooning it into your mouth. So, the major players are buttery croissants, cream, eggs and chocolate. Like I said: decadent. But I don't want you rushing out to your nearest artisan bakery and purchasing those lovely $3/each croissants for this bread pudding. The cheap all-butter croissants from any grocery store will do just fine. We're going to let them get stale, then toast them in the oven with more butter and sugar so they get crispy and lightly caramelized around the edges. When the creamy liquid is poured over them, those crispy edges will prevent the bread pudding from getting too soggy and gummy, like some bread puddings can be. Because the bread pudding is so darn rich, be sure to pair it with whipped cream or, as one tester suggested, coffee ice cream. Heck to the yes. A small wedge will satisfy most, therefore a pan of this makes enough for 10 to 12 people—10 to 12 people who will love you forevermore.

9–10 medium-sized day-old, all butter croissants (you need 12 cups of sliced croissants)
¼ cup unsalted butter, melted, plus more for greasing the pan
⅓ cup + 1 Tbsp granulated sugar, divided
3 large eggs, at room temperature
3 large egg yolks, at room temperature
1 ½ cups whole milk

½ cup whipping cream
½ cup half-and-half cream
1 tsp pure vanilla extract
1 tsp salt
¼ tsp freshly ground nutmeg
1 ¼ cups dark chocolate chunks
Unsweetened whipped cream (optional)

✽ Preheat the oven to 350°F. Place the rack in the centre of the oven. Butter a 9-inch round baking dish or casserole dish.

✽ Slice the croissants in half vertically, then cut each half in half horizontally. Toss the croissants with the melted butter and 1 Tbsp of the granulated sugar on a rimmed baking sheet large enough to hold the croissants without crowding. Arrange them in a single layer and bake for about 10 minutes, or until toasted. Meanwhile, whisk the remaining ⅓ cup of sugar with the eggs, egg yolks, milk, whipping cream, half-and-half, vanilla, salt and nutmeg in a large bowl.

✽ When the croissants have finished toasting, remove them from the oven and let them cool on the baking sheet for 5 minutes. Arrange half of the croissants in the baking dish and scatter half of the chocolate on top of them. Arrange the remaining croissants on top of the chocolate and pour the egg mixture over everything, pressing down to submerge the croissants in the liquid. Cover tightly with aluminum foil and bake for 30 minutes. Remove the foil and bake for another 15 minutes. Remove the dish from the oven and scatter the remaining chocolate on top. Bake for another 10–15 minutes, until the bread pudding is puffed, set and golden. Remove the dish from the oven and let it cool for 15 minutes on a wire rack before serving.

✽ Serve with whipped cream or ice cream. Cover any leftover bread pudding with plastic wrap and refrigerate for up to 4 days.

Be certain to buy plain all-butter croissants, and not those fancy chocolate ones.

Buttermilk Scones with Raspberry Butter

When I worked at Rutherford House in Edmonton, I made two dozen of these scones daily for four and a half years. That's a lot of scones! Scone making was the first thing on my morning prep list and there was something about the gentle kneading and patting and cutting out rounds that eased me into my busy day. The scones, along with our famous raspberry butter, were the centre-pieces of the dessert plates that we served for High Tea. Occasionally, bold customers would knock on the kitchen door and ask for the recipes—that's how good this combination is. The scones are light and fluffy, thanks to the eggs and buttermilk. I'm especially fond of these on Sunday morn-ings, with a good cuppa tea and the whole day ahead of me.

MAKES 1 DOZEN (3-INCH) SCONES

BUTTERMILK SCONES
3 cups all-purpose flour
1½ tsp baking powder
½ tsp baking soda
½ tsp salt
⅓ cup granulated sugar
½ cup cold, unsalted butter, cubed
3 large eggs

¾ cup cold buttermilk
¼ cup cold whipping cream
½ tsp pure vanilla extract
Coarse sugar (optional)

RASPBERRY BUTTER
½ cup salted butter, softened
½ cup good-quality raspberry jam

* Preheat the oven to 375°F. Place the rack in the centre of the oven. Line a baking sheet with parchment paper.

* To make the buttermilk scones, combine the flour, baking powder, baking soda and salt with the sugar in a large bowl. Cut in the butter using a pastry blender, being sure to leave some pea-sized bits behind.

* In a medium bowl, beat the eggs then add the buttermilk, whipping cream and vanilla. Whisk well to combine.

* Add the wet ingredients to the dry ingredients and stir with a wooden spoon just to combine. Shape the dough into a ball and gently knead it a few times on a floured surface. It's quite a wet batter, so be sure your countertop is well dusted with flour. Pat it into a ¾-inch thickness and cut out rounds using a 3-inch cookie cutter or water glass. Place the scones on the prepared baking sheet, spacing them about 1 inch apart. They like to be snug as they bake. Sprinkle the tops with coarse sugar if you like. Bake for 20–25 minutes, until the scones are lightly golden brown.

* Store the scones in an airtight container for up to 1 day, or freeze for up to 1 month. Simply warm them before eating them.

* To make the raspberry butter, in a stand mixer fitted with a paddle attachment, mix the butter and jam together on high speed until light, creamy and well incorporated, about 2 minutes, scraping down the sides of the mixer once or twice. Scrape the raspberry butter into a serving dish and serve it with the scones.

* You can refrigerate the raspberry butter in an airtight container for up to 2 weeks.

NOTES

For the raspberry butter, feel free to substitute any jam or jelly for the raspberry jam. Blueberry and cherry are also delicious! Jars of this make a lovely gift and the recipe doubles easily.

Raspberry butter is also delicious on toast, waffles and pancakes.

Sour Cherry and Mascarpone Perogies with Farmstand Cream

Homemade perogies are nothing like the ones in the freezer section of your supermarket. They are plump and tender and have an excellent filling-to-dough ratio. Plus, you know exactly what's in them. I've been lucky—I grew up with real perogies. When I was a little girl, I'd pull up a chair and help my mom pinch them shut. Christmas, Easter and Thanksgiving were prime perogie times, and even now, I marvel at how my mom can make these with her eyes practically closed. Stirring, kneading, rolling, cutting. She's got the rhythm down pat after 40-some years of being the perogie queen. Her filling has always been mashed potato and green onion, made the day before so the flavours have time to mingle. Topped with sour cream, fried bacon, fried onions, and sometimes cubes of bread fried in butter, it's not hard to see why perogie night was always my happy place. In honour of this happy place, and all those afternoons I spent pinching perogies with my mom, I've made a sweet perogie with sour cherries and mascarpone cheese. Hallelujah! These are so good. Once the perogies have boiled, I toss them in hot butter to crisp up the edges and add more flavour. Served with a sweet, tangy cream, they are a joy to eat for a late brunch. Yes, homemade perogies take a little bit of time and effort, but the end result is well worth it. Invite your friends over to help you pinch (and eat!), because there's nothing quite like a perogie party.

MAKES ABOUT 30 PEROGIES

SOUR CHERRY COMPOTE
4 cups pitted sour cherries (frozen can be used)
1⅓ cups granulated sugar
3 Tbsp balsamic vinegar
Pinch of salt

FILLING
1 batch Sour Cherry Compote
2 cups mascarpone cheese, softened (see my recipe on page 28)

PEROGIE DOUGH
2 large eggs, at room temperature
½ cup water
½ tsp salt
3 cups all-purpose flour (approx.)
2 Tbsp salted butter, softened, plus more if needed (for frying)

FARMSTAND CREAM
1½ cups sweetened whipped cream (about ¾ cup unwhipped whipping cream)
1 cup full-fat sour cream

❈ To make the sour cherry compote, combine the sour cherries, sugar, balsamic vinegar and salt in a medium saucepan over medium-high heat. Bring to a boil, turn down the heat and simmer, uncovered, until reduced and slightly thickened, 30–35 minutes. It will firm up as it cools.

❈ The compote can be refrigerated in an airtight container for up to 2 weeks.

❈ To make the filling, stir together the chilled compote and the mascarpone cheese in a medium bowl until smooth. You likely won't use all of the filling for the perogies, but it's also excellent on toast, scones, pancakes, waffles, etc.

❈ The leftover filling can be refrigerated in an airtight container for up to 5 days.

❈ To make the dough, beat the eggs, water and salt together in a large bowl. Add the flour 1 cup at a time until a firm yet soft and workable dough forms. Add more flour if need be. The dough should be pliable enough to roll out, almost like a pasta dough.

❈ Turn the dough out onto a lightly floured work surface and knead it until smooth, about 5 minutes. Shape the dough into a ball and allow it to rest under an overturned bowl on the counter for 20

minutes. Roll the dough out to about ½-inch thick (very thin) like you would for pasta dough. Cut the dough into circles using a 3-inch cookie cutter or water glass. Reroll any scraps and repeat the cutting-out process.

❊ Have a small bowl of cold water nearby, and use your fingers to dab water around the edges of the perogie rounds. Spoon 1 Tbsp of filling into the middle of each round and fold the dough over. Pinch the edge shut with your fingers and crimp with a fork to seal. Place the filled perogies on a countertop or table that has been lightly dusted with flour. Flip the filled perogies over at least once, so they don't stick to the surface. Repeat the process until all of the perogies have been filled.

❊ Bring a large pot of salted water to a boil over high heat. Add about 10 perogies at a time and boil them for 8–10 minutes. They will float to the top early on, but leave them in so the dough cooks and isn't too chewy.

❊ Heat a large non-stick skillet with 2 Tbsp of butter over medium-high heat. Remove the perogies with a slotted spoon, shaking off as much water as you can, and put them directly into the hot butter. Fry in an even layer over medium-high heat until golden and crispy, 2–3 minutes per side. Continue cooking this way until all of the perogies are fried. If need be, add more butter to the skillet. Serve warm with farmstand cream.

❊ Alternatively, skip the frying process entirely and just boil for 8–10 minutes, drain and serve with farmstand cream.

❊ These perogies are best eaten the day you cook them, but any leftovers can be gently reheated the next day in a frying pan over medium-low heat with 1 Tbsp of butter or in the microwave for a couple of minutes. I advise against freezing, as the texture of the filling changes and the perogies seem to expand and burst open more easily when they're being boiled.

❊ To make the Farmstand Cream: Fold together the sweetened whipped cream (sweeten it to taste) and sour cream in a medium bowl. Serve with warm perogies. The farmstand cream can be refrigerated in an airtight container for up to 2 days.

| NOTE | *Blueberries or fresh blackcurrants can be substituted for the sour cherries. The dough works well for savoury fillings as well.* |

Fancy Toast with Strawberries and Homemade Ricotta Cheese

Fancy toast is all the rage lately. And as a long-time toast lover, it's a trend I can fully support. Keep in mind that this isn't your usual peanut butter and jam on toasted white bread, though. The bread is important, so buy French bread or a baguette from your favourite bakery. And use homemade ricotta. I know you're looking at me like I'm crazy, but making your own cheese is easy, promise. This may seem over the top for toast, but if you dislike really early mornings like I do, something as tasty as this will make you jump out of bed a whole lot faster. I won't make you make cheese if you don't want to—the stuff from the store will suffice—but I do encourage you to try it one day. It might just blow your mind!

MAKES 6 SLICES

6 slices French bread or baguette
1 cup Homemade Ricotta Cheese (page 48)
2 cups fresh, sliced strawberries
⅓ cup liquid honey
¼ cup finely chopped pistachios

※ Preheat the oven to 375°F. Place the rack in the centre of the oven.

※ Place the bread in the oven and toast it for about 3 minutes. Remove the bread from the oven and slather each slice with ricotta. Heap on strawberries, then drizzle with honey and scatter pistachios on top.

※ Serve immediately.

NOTE

The recipe can be halved or doubled easily.

Homemade Ricotta Cheese

You could, of course, buy ricotta. But what fun would that be when you can easily make your own and save a few bucks, too? Plus, it's like a tasty science experiment, and science is always fun when you can eat your assignment in the end.

The basic ingredients are simple: whole milk, whipping cream, salt and lemon juice. Use this ricotta recipe as your jumping-off point, and have fun with other tasty creations. Spread it on pizza, layer it in lasagna, or spread it on crostini then dollop your favourite jam or tapenade on top for a tasty appetizer. Homemade ricotta is also quite lovely when beaten with eggs and chives for divine scrambled eggs. The cool thing about making your own cheese is that you can make as much or as little as you need. Plus, it tastes super fresh and creamy. I'm never going to buy it again. Never, I tell you. I'm spoiled for good.

MAKES 1 CUP

4 cups whole milk
½ cup whipping cream
¼ tsp salt
3 Tbsp fresh lemon juice

❋ Line a large sieve with a couple of layers of cheesecloth. Place it over a large bowl and fasten with 6 clothespins. In a large saucepan, bring the milk, cream and salt to a rolling boil over high heat. This is important. Make sure the liquid is boiling hard—just be sure to watch it closely. Stir occasionally to prevent scorching. Slowly stir in the lemon juice, turn down the heat to low and simmer, stirring occasionally, for 5 minutes, until the mixture curdles. Pour the mixture into the lined sieve and let it rest on the counter for 30-60 minutes. The longer it drains the thicker it will get. Scoop out the ricotta and put it in a small bowl (discard any liquid—the whey—sitting in the bottom of the bowl or use it in place of milk in smoothies, baking, pancakes, bread, etc.).

❋ The ricotta can be refrigerated in an airtight container for up to 3 days.

NOTES

This recipe can be doubled easily.

I know this isn't the "real" ricotta made with whey from a previous cheese-making session. That stuff sounds great too, but seeing as most folks don't have whey in the house, I'm making mine with milk and cream. Yes, it's more like a farmer's cheese or cottage cheese, but it's pretty darn close to the real thing.

RECIPES

COOKIES AND BARS

Chocolate Matrimonial Cake

Out on the Canadian prairies, date squares were called matrimonial cake because they were packaged up, tied with ribbon in the couple's "colour" and given out as wedding favours. I can still remember my Auntie Lou's wedding in 1982. My cousin and I were decked out in matching peach and white seersucker dresses. My mom had also given me a Toni home perm, so you get the picture. My cousin and I sat at the guest book signing table, which also came equipped with a basket of matrimonial cake squares, wrapped in baby blue ribbon, as a gesture of gratitude from the happy couple. Well, that and an open bar.

These are not your grandma's date squares. Yes, hers may be perfectly lovely, but traditional date squares have a bad rap for being a bit *boring*. What makes these date squares different from those of yesteryear is that they have chocolate in them, and orange, and plenty of vanilla. The base is studded with walnuts and large-flake oats, almost like a chewy oatmeal cookie—rich, wholesome, but definitely not boring!

MAKES 24–32 PIECES

DATE FILLING
2 cups packed, pitted Medjool dates
½ cup water
½ cup golden syrup or dark corn syrup
¼ cup unsalted butter, softened
1 Tbsp grated orange zest
²/₃ cup chopped (½-inch pieces) dark chocolate

WALNUT CRUMB
¾ cup unsalted butter, softened
1½ cups packed brown sugar
2 large eggs, at room temperature
2 tsp pure vanilla extract
2 cups all-purpose flour
¾ tsp baking soda
1 tsp salt
2½ cups large-flake oats
1 cup chopped walnuts

❋ Preheat the oven to 350°F. Place the rack in the centre of the oven. Line a 9×13-inch baking dish with parchment paper overhanging the sides to use as a handle.

❋ To make the date filling, place the dates, water, syrup, butter and zest in a medium saucepan over medium heat. Cook, stirring often, until the mixture is soft and jammy, 10–12 minutes. Remove the pan from the heat and stir in the chocolate until it's melted. Let this sit while you make the crumb.

❋ To make the walnut crumb, in a stand mixer fitted with a paddle attachment, cream the butter with the sugar until fluffy, about 2 minutes. Add the eggs and vanilla. Beat on medium-high speed for 2 more minutes, stopping once or twice to scrape the bottom and sides of the bowl.

❋ In a medium bowl, combine the flour, baking soda and salt. Add this to the butter mixture. Mix on low speed until just combined. Slowly stir in the oats and nuts until well blended.

❋ Press two-thirds of the oat mixture into the prepared baking dish, using your hands to pack it down. It will be sticky. Use an offset spatula to even it out. Spread the date mixture on top. Crumble the remaining oat mixture on top of the dates. Don't worry if the dates aren't completely covered—just dollop the mixture on as best you can.

❋ Bake the matrimonial cake for 22–25 minutes, until the top is golden brown. Remove the pan from the oven and set on a wire rack to cool for 30 minutes. Grip the edges of the parchment and lift the cake from the pan.

❋ Cool the cake completely before cutting into 24–32 evenly sized pieces. Store them in an airtight container in the refrigerator for up to 5 days, or freeze for up to 2 months.

Double Peanut Butter and White Chocolate Chunk Cookies

I would be remiss to not include a recipe for peanut butter cookies in a cookbook that is about sweet things. I know many people whose favourite cookie in the whole world is peanut butter. This cookie is for you! I've switched things up a bit and added chunks of white chocolate and roasted peanuts, just because I love the texture and flavour combo. You can use either natural peanut butter (smooth or crunchy—you choose) or the stuff you don't have to keep in the refrigerator. Both yield excellent results, though I do prefer the natural peanut butter as it doesn't have any wonky ingredients. Either way, these cookies are delicious and crowd-pleasing, especially with that little sprinkling of flaky salt. Keep in mind that if you like cookies with soft, chewy centres, you should take them out of the oven just when they are set and light brown around the edges. They'll continue to cook for a bit on the baking sheet. For this reason, it's important to set your timer!

MAKES ABOUT 30 COOKIES

1 cup unsalted butter, softened
2 cups peanut butter (smooth or crunchy), at room temperature
1 ½ cups granulated sugar
1 cup packed brown sugar
2 large eggs, at room temperature
2 Tbsp 2% or whole milk
2 tsp pure vanilla extract

2 ½ cups all-purpose flour
1 ½ tsp baking soda
1 tsp baking powder
½ tsp salt
¾ cup chopped (½-inch pieces) white chocolate, or white chocolate chips
⅓ cup chopped peanuts
Flaky salt, such as Maldon, for sprinkling

❋ In a stand mixer fitted with a paddle attachment, cream the butter with the peanut butter and both sugars. Beat on high speed for 2 minutes, scraping down the sides of the bowl once or twice. Add the eggs, milk and vanilla and beat on high for another 2 minutes, until light and fluffy, scraping the sides and bottom of the bowl once or twice again.

❋ Place the flour, baking soda, baking powder and salt in a medium bowl. Stir well. Add this to the butter mixture and mix on low speed just until combined, scraping the sides and bottom of the bowl. Stir in the white chocolate and peanuts by hand, just until the dough is smooth and incorporated. Cover the bowl with plastic wrap and chill for 30 minutes.

❋ Preheat the oven to 350°F. Place the rack in the centre of the oven. Line 2 baking sheets with parchment paper.

❋ Use an ice cream scoop (mine is about ¼ cup in volume) to portion out the cookies. Place them about 3 inches apart on the prepared baking sheets. Flatten the cookies with your hand, so they are about ½ an inch high. Use a fork to lightly make a cross-hatch pattern on top of the cookies. Sprinkle with flaky salt. Bake 1 baking sheet at a time for 8–10 minutes, until the middle is set and the edges are lightly browned. Remove the pan from the oven and let the cookies cool completely on the pan on a wire rack.

❋ Keep the cookies in an airtight container on the counter for up to 2 days, or freeze for up to 1 month.

NOTE

If you want to bake 1 dozen cookies and freeze the rest of the dough, you can do so by scooping cookie dough balls onto a parchment-lined baking sheet and putting them in the freezer until frozen solid. Afterwards, portion them into resealable freezer bags and keep them in the freezer for up to 1 month. When it's time to bake, place them on a parchment-lined baking sheet, let them thaw completely, then bake as above.

Puffed Wheat Cake

If you grew up on the Canadian prairies, chances are you cut your teeth on puffed wheat cake. If you didn't, you're probably going, "Puffed wheat what?" You are in for a treat. Puffed wheat cake has roots that date back decades, mainly to rural kitchens in Alberta, Saskatchewan and Manitoba. Back then you could purchase large bags of puffed wheat, which made it a fairly inexpensive ingredient to mix together with the staples of butter, sugar, corn syrup and cocoa that most cooks had on hand to bake with. My mom's mom made it for her when she was growing up in the 1950s, and it was a regular treat in our house, too. Not all versions are created equal, though. I'd go to some kids' houses after school and their puffed wheat cake wouldn't be as chewy or chocolatey as my mom's, which I came to know as far superior to what many of my friends were eating. So, it's official: my mom gets the trophy for the best puffed wheat cake. I love seeing new generations of eaters tuck into this chewy, chocolatey square. When I asked my niece Maggie what she loved most about PWC, she said, "Everything." And there you have it.

MAKES 12–16 BARS

1¼ cups packed brown sugar
1 cup light corn syrup
½ cup salted butter
⅓ cup + 1 Tbsp unsweetened cocoa powder
1 tsp pure vanilla extract
10 cups puffed wheat cereal

❋ Butter a 9×13-inch baking dish.

❋ Combine the brown sugar, corn syrup, butter and cocoa in a large saucepan over medium-high heat. Bring the syrup to a boil, stirring often. Let it boil hard for 1 minute, then remove the pot from the heat. Stir in the vanilla and then the puffed wheat. Stir well to make sure the cereal is evenly coated in the chocolate syrup.

❋ Scrape the puffed wheat into the prepared pan and use damp hands (have a bowl of cold water nearby) to press it down evenly. Let it rest at room temperature for 3 hours before cutting.

❋ Store the puffed wheat cake in an airtight container for up to 5 days. This doesn't freeze well.

Rosemary Oatmeal Shortbread

I first tasted these cookies in 1999, when I was working in Yukon at a fancy fly-in fishing lodge. The pastry chef baked up a batch for the guests, and after my first bite, I was like, *Hello, what do we have here?* This was the pastry chef's grandmother's recipe, and she graciously shared it with me that summer. I've been baking it up at Christmastime every year since to rave reviews from friends and family. It's a woodsy/savoury/sweet/buttery superstar of a cookie that pretty much smells of Christmas. Folk will wander into your kitchen asking what in the world you are up to. And then they'll wait to see the cookie magic come out of the oven. (Get them to load the dishwasher while they're loitering.) Don't be scared off by the 2 cups of butter in this recipe. This recipe makes a giant batch of cookies—enough for you to share and share some more.

MAKES ABOUT 75 COOKIES

2 cups salted butter (if using unsalted, add about
   1 tsp salt), softened
1⅓ cups granulated sugar
2 Tbsp finely chopped fresh rosemary
2¾ cups all-purpose flour,
   plus more for the counter
2½ cups large-flake oats
½ cup icing sugar

❊ Preheat the oven to 350°F. Place the rack in the centre of the oven. Line two baking sheets with parchment paper.

❊ In a stand mixer fitted with a paddle attachment, cream together the butter and sugar until light and fluffy, 2–3 minutes. Beat in the fresh rosemary. With the mixer running on low speed, add the flour and oats. Mix until well incorporated. On a lightly floured surface, shape the dough into a ball and then flatten it and roll it out to about ⅛-inch thickness. Dust the rolling pin with flour to prevent it from sticking to the dough.

❊ Cut the dough into your desired shapes, about 2½ inches in diameter, and place the cookies 2 inches apart on the prepared baking sheets. Bake for 8–10 minutes, or until the edges start to turn light brown. Remove the baking sheet from the oven and let the cookies cool on the baking sheet on a wire rack. Repeat with the remaining dough. Once the cookies have cooled down, dust them with icing sugar.

❊ You can store these in an airtight container for up to 4 days, or freeze them for up to 1 month.

NOTES

Cut the dough into any shape that catches your fancy—stars, diamonds, squares, circles, trees. Be as festive as you like! For smaller cookies, decrease the baking time. For example, for cookies 1½ inches in diameter, bake for 6–8 minutes. For cookies 2 inches in diameter, bake for 8–9 minutes. For cookies 3 inches in diameter, bake for 10–11 minutes.

To speed up the baking process, you can place racks in the upper and lower thirds of the oven and bake the cookies for 4 minutes, then rotate the pans and bake for another 4–6 minutes until the cookies are light brown around the edges.

Chocolate Tahini Cookies

I'm really proud of this cookie. It's gluten-free and it's glorious. When I was a pastry chef at a gluten-free/nut-free restaurant, I knew I wanted to create a kickass cookie within the parameters I was given. Just because some folks can't have gluten doesn't mean they shouldn't have a killer cookie. Thus, the birth of these babies. I used millet and quinoa flours, so the cookies are protein-packed as well as fabulously tasty. If you are intolerant to oats as well, quinoa flakes make a wonderful substitution. I love all the seeds (seriously, did I leave any out?) and the tahini adds a wonderful semi-nutty flavour without any nuts being used. Chewy, kinda healthy (they still have butter and sugar!) and super safe for those who are allergic to gluten and nuts, these cookies taste so good even those who can eat gluten love them.

MAKES 3 DOZEN COOKIES

1¼ cups + 2 Tbsp unsalted butter, softened
1½ cups granulated sugar
½ cup tahini
1 Tbsp pure vanilla extract
4 large eggs, at room temperature
1½ cups millet flour
1¼ cups quinoa flour
1½ cups large-flake oats (or quinoa flakes)
2 tsp baking soda

1½ tsp salt
2 cups semi-sweet chocolate chips
¾ cup pumpkin seeds
¾ cup sunflower seeds
¾ cup flax seeds
¾ cup dark raisins
½ cup hemp hearts
2 Tbsp sesame seeds

❄ In a stand mixer fitted with a paddle attachment, cream the butter with the sugar on high speed until fluffy, about 2 minutes. Scrape down the bottom and sides of the bowl. Add the tahini and vanilla and beat on medium speed for about 1 minute. Add the eggs, one at a time, beating well after each addition. Scrape down the bowl once or twice. The mixture should be pale and creamy.

❄ In a large bowl, stir together the flours, oats, baking soda and salt. Add this to the butter mixture. Mix on low speed until it's incorporated. In another bowl, mix together the chocolate chips and all of the seeds. Add this to the bowl and beat on low speed until you have an even dough. The mixer will be full. If you need to, remove the bowl from the mixer and stir in the chocolate chip/seed mixture by hand. Cover the bowl with plastic wrap and chill the dough for at least 1 hour, but no more than 3 hours.

❄ Preheat the oven to 350°F. Place racks in the upper and lower thirds of the oven. Line 2 baking sheets with parchment paper.

❄ Scoop out the dough using a ¼-cup ice cream scoop. If you don't have an ice cream scoop, the mounds should be approximately 2 inches wide and 1½ inches tall. Space the cookies about 2 inches apart. Bake for 4 minutes then rotate the pans from top to bottom. For a chewy cookie, bake for another 4–5 minutes, until the edges are lightly browned and the middle is set. If crispy cookies are more your style, bake them for a total of 10–11 minutes. The cookies will continue to bake on the baking sheet once they've been removed from the oven. Let the cookies cool completely on the baking sheet on a wire rack. Repeat this process until all of the cookies have been baked.

❄ These cookies keep well in an airtight container on the counter for up to 2 days and can be frozen for up to 1 month.

If you want to bake 1 dozen cookies and freeze the rest of the dough, you can do so by scooping cookie dough balls onto a parchment-lined baking sheet and putting them in the freezer until frozen solid. Afterwards, portion them into resealable freezer bags and keep them in the freezer for up to 1 month. When it's time to bake, place them on a parchment-lined baking sheet, let them thaw completely, then bake as above.

Millet, quinoa flour and quinoa flakes can be found at health food stores.

I have not tried making these cookies with all-purpose flour. My educated guess is to swap the millet and quinoa flours for 2 cups of all-purpose flour. If the batter seems too wet, add more all-purpose flour, ¼ cup at a time.

AN HEIRLOOM RECIPE

For as long as I can remember, I've been eating Jam Jams at Christmas. Every year, my mom puts these on her baking list, which, as the years go on, gets shorter and shorter. Jam Jams remain there, firmly in place, because not only are they a delicious cookie, they are also a tie to the past. This recipe is my mom's grandmother's, and it came with her from Russia, almost a century ago. My mom grew up eating these cookies, too.

Jam Jams are flavourful, simple cookies with sweet jam in the middle. Mom said they're an old German cookie (my ancestors came from a German-speaking part of Russia), and she remembers going to her grandmother's kitchen and watching her make them. Jam was either homemade or plenty cheap. Mom said you could get a huge can of jam for two dollars, with strawberry and raspberry being the flavours of choice. Originally, the recipe called for lard instead of butter, most likely because they raised their own pigs and would have rendered fat in the kitchen for daily use. Cost-effective and delicious, these cookies were always around at Christmastime. My great-grandmother has been gone a long, long time, and I never even got to meet my own grandmother as she passed away just months after my mom was married. While these are fabulous cookies, I know too that Mom makes these as a way of remembering her own mother, who died too soon, too long ago. For that, I cherish this heirloom recipe even more.

As with most of my mom's recipes, the steps are a little loosey-goosey. **Renée:** How much flour do I add? **Mom:** Just enough to make a soft dough. **Renée:** How thin do I roll them? **Mom:** Not too thin. **Renée:** How long do I bake them? **Mom:** Until they're done.

Oh, mama. Good thing I've got everything nailed down for you guys. The fun thing about this recipe is that it's good for small hands who want to help. Get the little people in your life cutting or jamming or sandwiching. I totally remember getting jam in my hair after helping out with these cookies. Jam Jams are great to bake ahead as they will last in the freezer for a few months, but if you're like me, you'll find them and wait a whole 30 seconds before biting into one. I love these cold (I take them out of the freezer and let them sit for a few minutes—delish!) with a glass of milk.

WHILE THESE ARE FABULOUS COOKIES, I KNOW TOO THAT MOM MAKES THESE AS A WAY OF REMEMBERING HER OWN MOTHER, WHO DIED TOO SOON, TOO LONG AGO.

Jam Jams

The dough is very simple and consists of butter (unless you have your own rendered pork fat kicking around), brown sugar, golden syrup (I prefer Roger's—it brings a nice toasty edge of sweetness), eggs, vanilla, baking soda and flour. All staples to be found in a kitchen in rural Saskatchewan circa 1930, 1962 and 1989. According to my mom, the dough is best if it's chilled for two hours or overnight. If you do the overnight thing, just remember to leave it out on the counter for about 2 hours before you want to roll it out, thin, but not too thin. Use whatever cutters you like. We grew up with Jam Jams being large and round, but cut-outs are particularly festive and ever so pretty. Be sure to work quickly when the cookies come out of the oven—they need to be filled with jam and sandwiched while still warm, otherwise they won't stick together quite as well.

MAKES ABOUT 4 DOZEN SANDWICH COOKIES

1 cup salted butter, quite soft
1 cup packed brown sugar
¼ cup + 2 Tbsp golden syrup
2 large eggs, at room temperature
1 tsp pure vanilla extract
2 tsp baking soda
3½ cups all-purpose flour (approx.),
   plus more for the counter
1½ cups good-quality seedless raspberry jam or jelly

❄ In a stand mixer fitted with a paddle attachment, cream together the butter and sugar until fluffy, about 2 minutes. Beat in the syrup for 1 minute, then the eggs and vanilla. Beat until light, about 2 minutes. Stir in the baking soda and, with the mixer running on low speed, gradually add the flour, 1 cup at a time. If it seems too wet, add a little more flour, 1 Tbsp at a time. According to Mom, the dough should be quite soft.

❄ Scrape the dough into a bowl, cover tightly with plastic wrap and chill for at least 2 hours or overnight.

❄ Preheat the oven to 350°F. Place the rack in the centre of the oven. Line 2 baking sheets with parchment paper.

❄ Lightly dust your work surface with flour. Roll the dough out to about ⅛ inch thick. Cut the dough into your desired shapes. You need an even number of cookies so that you can sandwich them. Place them on the prepared baking sheets. Bake for 7 minutes if the cookies are small (1¾ inches in diameter) or 9–10 minutes if they're bigger. The cookies should still be soft in the middle, but starting to brown around the edges. Remove the pan from the oven and immediately spread jam on one "base" side and top with a second cookie. Set the Jam Jams on a wire rack to cool and repeat the process until all the dough is rolled out and baked off.

❄ Store the cookies in an airtight container at room temperature for 3 days, or freeze them in a resealable freezer bag for up to 2 months.

NOTES

If you like, you can cut out a shape in the centre of half the unbaked cookies and use those as the top half of the cookie sandwiches so the jam is visible.

These will get softer as they sit in a container, so if you think you might have over-baked them, never fear, they will soften.

Feel free to use whatever jam and jelly you have on hand. I am partial to seedless raspberry myself, but the stuff with seeds works just as well.

Dark Chocolate and Cherry Energy Bars

This is my go-to snack when I need something to keep me energized for the day, be it at work or on a road trip. What? Driving can be exhausting! I love these bars because they're packed with nutrient-rich, tasty things like nuts, Medjool dates, dark chocolate, dried cherries and cacao nibs. Notice how there's no refined sugar in there? Awesome, right? Plus, they're gluten-free, if that's a concern for you. You'll need to use a food processor for these energy bars, as the dates and nuts are blended together with the melted chocolate to form a "dough."

MAKES 16 BARS

1½ cups coarsely chopped (½-inch pieces) dark chocolate
1½ cups unsalted pistachios, shelled
1 cup toasted slivered almonds
3 cups packed, pitted Medjool dates
1½ tsp pure vanilla extract
1 tsp ground cardamom

½ tsp salt
1 cup dried cherries
½ cup cacao nibs

❋ Grease an 8-inch square pan. Line it with parchment paper overhanging the sides.

❋ Melt the chocolate in a small saucepan over medium-low heat, stirring constantly. Remove the saucepan from the heat and let it cool to room temperature. Pulse the nuts in a food processor fitted with the steel blade until they're coarsely chopped. Add the melted chocolate, dates, vanilla, cardamom and salt. Add 3 Tbsp of warm water and mix on high until the mixture is smooth. You'll have to stop and start often, scraping down the bottom and sides of the bowl. You're looking for the consistency of a smooth cookie dough. Add more water 1 Tbsp at a time if need be.

❋ Mix in the dried cherries and cacao nibs until evenly incorporated. Press the mixture into the prepared pan, using a plastic bench scraper or your hands to smooth it out so the top is flat. You can also place a piece of parchment paper on top and press into this to flatten it out smoothly. Chill for at least 4 hours until firm.

❋ Cut into squares (an oiled knife works well) and store in an airtight container in the refrigerator for up to 5 days. (Confession: I've never experimented with freezing these.)

NOTE

Feel free to swap dried cranberries or raisins for the cherries, and pecans, salted peanuts or walnuts for the nuts. Make these your own!

Gingerbread Trees with Lemon Icing

Rolling out gingerbread dough and cutting it into perfect tree shapes is my idea of playing. And it reminds me of a little girl with a blonde head and a sweet tooth, by her mom's side, eating the gingery dough behind her back and peeking through the glass door of the oven, watching the cookies rise into stars and trees and pigs. I lived for those days before Christmas when the house smelled of butter and ginger and we got to decorate our cookies as we liked. Icing! Sprinkles! Sugar! The best part: biting off the limbs of the gingerbread man and saving the head for last. This gingerbread is what you want your house to smell like as you put that last star on the tree and finish addressing envelopes with the names of loved ones. The dough can be made the night before, so the next morning you just roll it out and cut it into your favourite shapes. The cookies only need to bake for about eight minutes if you like a softer cookie, or around 10 if you want your gingerbread to snap. The drizzle of lemon icing is a lovely complement to the smooth bite of ginger. I can't think of a better cookie to eat while curling up on the couch to watch *Love Actually* yet again. It never gets old. Nor does my fondness for these cookies.

MAKES 50–60 COOKIES

GINGERBREAD DOUGH
2½ cups all-purpose flour, plus a bit more
   for rolling
2 tsp ground ginger
1 tsp baking soda
1 tsp ground cinnamon
1 tsp salt
½ tsp ground cloves
1 cup unsalted butter, softened

¾ cup granulated sugar
1 large egg, at room temperature
¼ cup molasses

LEMON ICING
1⅓ cups icing sugar
2 Tbsp fresh lemon juice

TO FINISH
Coarse sugar (optional)

❆ To make the gingerbread, whisk the flour with the rest of the dry ingredients in a medium bowl. In a stand mixer fitted with a paddle attachment, cream together the butter and sugar on medium-high speed until creamy, about 3 minutes. Add the egg and molasses and beat to combine, scraping down the bowl as you need to. With the mixer running on low speed, gradually add the flour mixture and beat until combined. Remove the dough from the mixer and wrap it in plastic. Refrigerate until firm, about 1 hour or up to 3 days.

❆ Preheat the oven to 350°F. Place the rack in the centre of the oven. Line 2 baking sheets with parchment paper.

❆ On a lightly floured work surface, roll out the dough to approximately ⅙ inch thick and use cookie cutters to cut out your favourite shapes. My trees measure 2 inches wide and 3½ inches long. (My mom still uses the cutters from when we were kids. I love the pig!) Or you can use a sharp knife and cut the dough into triangles about 2 inches in diameter. Arrange the cookies on the prepared baking sheets, and bake until firm and golden, around 8 minutes for chewy, 10 minutes for snappy. If your cookies are smaller, reduce the baking time by 1 minute. If they are larger, increase the time by 1–2 minutes. Let the cookies cool completely on the baking sheets on wire racks.

❆ To make the lemon icing, sift the icing sugar into a medium bowl and whisk in the lemon juice. It takes a little while for it to come together. Add more lemon juice if it's too thick. I put the icing into a small plastic freezer bag and cut one corner to make a tip. Drizzle the icing onto the cooled cookies and sprinkle with coarse sugar.

❆ Store these in an airtight container for up to 1 week, or freeze for up to 1 month.

MIDNIGHT SUN
MEMORIES

Do you have food memories? Where all it takes is one bite of something and you are instantly transported back in time? As someone who loves food, I have many, many food memories, but one of the strongest is triggered when I eat these Chewy Peanut Butter Granola Bars. I first made them when I was working in Yukon. Right off the bat I fell in love with the crispy edges, the chewy peanutty goodness, and all the healthy stuff added to keep guests and staff fortified for long days of northern adventure. If there was one thing I had to keep around the kitchen for the four summer months I was up North, it was these bars. They would be packed into lunches for the guests and guides on fishing trips and heli-hikes. They would be stuffed into packs for those traversing over the tundra. They would be nibbled on during intense Yahtzee tournaments at the long kitchen table in the staff room. More often than not, they'd be eaten in the cozy confines of our rustic cabins, where my roommate and I would crimp each other's hair, talk about family and friends back home, and yes, play even more Yahtzee.

I've never made such intense friendships before or after my Yukon adventure. Perhaps it was the isolation, or the wild spirit of the North, or the spectacular scenery that made me forge bonds that I still have today with some of my fellow adventurers. We have shared experiences of listening to wolves howl outside our cabin doors. It is a haunting sound—one that makes even the bravest people shake under their sleeping bags. We have shared experiences of being so cold in the early mornings of September that we would get dressed under the covers and stumble down the path to the lodge, the darkness lit up only by the beams of our flashlights. Bears were around occasionally, which meant the adrenaline was pumping and I was always glad to get to the lodge unscathed. We have shared experiences of being in fishing boats in the middle of July at 1:00 a.m., still being able to see where we were going. We have shared experiences of getting mail once a week (if we were lucky), our only communication from loved ones back home. We have shared experiences of knocking on each other's cabin doors in the middle of the night when the Northern Lights were out. We'd jump out of bed, throw on our coats and hats and stand under the green and blue and sometimes red swirls of wonder lighting up the night sky. I would shiver from the cold, but also from the sheer amazement of how I found myself in that spectacular place at that moment. I still get the shivers thinking about it. There we stood, faces skyward, huddled together among the spruce trees, all at once feeling very small and very lucky. When the lights would move on, so would we; back to our down-filled sleeping bags and whatever dreams awaited.

The camera I had at the time (I think it was a Pentax point and shoot with a zoom lens) used film, so I would take the shots I wanted and then put it away. There was no editing and swiping and updating. It was point, shoot, okay, done. One of the first things I did when I got back to civilization was drop the film off at the drugstore and wait to get it developed. Do you remember that feeling of anticipation, ripping open the packages and seeing shots you'd forgotten you'd taken, of people you wish you still had close to you? Everything was unedited and unfiltered. It was what it was. For weeks after leaving Yukon, I would be so homesick for the people and the place. I'd mail photos to the friends I knew would appreciate them, and they did the same for me. Some of my favourite photographs are framed and hanging on the walls of my house—reminders of the time I was brave and adventurous and took a chance and it all turned out majestically.

For four months out of the year, this was my family. And like when all good things come to an end, saying goodbye at an airport or on a dock does nothing short of rip your heart apart. Now, when I make these granola bars, I think of singing out loud and off-key to the Counting Crows with Chyanne, of hiking on mountaintops with Anita, of playing Yahtzee with Candus in our tiny cabin while the rain drummed down on the roof, and of crowded, noisy cabin parties with boxed white wine and young men hanging from the rafters. I think of those who spent their summers with me, enriching my life more than they ever could have known. And I think of me, being so far from home and living each moment like it was my last. At the end of it all, I don't think I can ask for anything more.

Chewy Peanut Butter Granola Bars

This recipe is very versatile and you can make it your own with a variety of nut/seed/dried fruit combos. I dislike coconut, so I add whatever chopped nuts I have on hand. But if you like coconut, feel free to use it. I think we can still be friends. Sometimes, if I'm in one of those moods, I add just the chopped chocolate and omit the dried fruit. I know—rebel, right? I love how this granola bar is chewy and full of peanut butter flavour, and with all of the fun add-ins, it's not dry and boring like some granola bars can be. If I see another recipe for a granola bar, chances are I will give it a go, but I have a feeling I'll always come back to this one. If not for the deliciousness of it, then for the memories it conjures up.

MAKES 24 BARS

1 cup packed brown sugar
⅔ cup natural peanut butter (smooth or crunchy)
½ cup salted butter, softened
½ cup honey or dark corn syrup
2 tsp pure vanilla extract
3 cups large-flake oats
1 cup chopped (½-inch pieces) dark chocolate
   or chocolate chips

½ cup sweetened shredded coconut
   (or chopped nuts)
½ cup sunflower seeds or pumpkin seeds
⅓ cup flax seed or wheat germ
3 Tbsp sesame seeds
½ cup dried fruit such as raisins
   or chopped apricots (optional)

❋ Preheat the oven to 350°F. Line a 9×13-inch baking dish with aluminum foil and lightly grease it with your choice of cooking oil.

❋ In a medium saucepan over medium-low heat, melt the brown sugar, peanut butter, butter and honey, stirring often. Once it's smooth and completely melted, remove the pan from the heat and stir in the vanilla. Let it cool until it's lukewarm. Combine the remaining ingredients in a large bowl. Pour the peanut butter mixture over the dry ingredients and stir well. Scrape the mixture into the prepared pan and press it in evenly. I find moistening my hands with cold water first helps.

❋ Bake the granola bars for 20–22 minutes, until the edges are golden. Remove the pan from the oven and let it cool completely on a wire rack. It will firm up as it cools.

❋ Cut into evenly sized bars. Keep the granola bars in an airtight container for up to 5 days, or freeze them for up to 2 months.

CHOCOLATE ESPRESSO CRACKLE COOKIES

Everyone needs a one-bowl cookie recipe and this is mine. All you need is a large saucepan and a little willpower to keep your fingers out of the dough, because it's so good. I added espresso powder to the melted chocolate because I tend to have it on hand for baking, or for when there is a no-coffee-in-the-house-emergency. You've been there, right? If you don't happen to have espresso powder on hand, you can omit it for equally excellent results. These are one of my favourite cookies to make around the holidays. The dough can be prepared in the evening, then next morning you can put on your favourite Christmas songs (Wham!'s "Last Christmas," I'm looking at you) and bake these off. Soft, with lovely fudgy centres, their crackled beauty adds a little drama to the cookie plate.

MAKES ABOUT 4 DOZEN COOKIES

¼ cup unsalted butter
1¼ cups dark chocolate chunks or chips
2 tsp instant espresso powder
¼ cup granulated sugar
2 large eggs, at room temperature
1 (10 oz) can sweetened condensed milk
1 tsp pure vanilla extract
2½ cups all-purpose flour

1 tsp baking powder
1 tsp salt
1½ cups dark chocolate chunks or chips
³⁄₄ cup icing sugar

❊ Melt the butter with the chocolate in a large saucepan over medium heat. Add the espresso powder, remove the pan from the heat and stir in the sugar and eggs, one at a time, with a wooden spoon, stirring well after each addition. Let the mixture cool for 5 minutes. Beat in the condensed milk and vanilla. Add the flour, baking powder and salt and then the chocolate chunks. Mix well to combine. The dough will be soft. Scrape it into a bowl and cover tightly with plastic wrap.

❊ Refrigerate it overnight, or for at least 3 hours.

❊ Preheat the oven to 350°F. Place the rack in the centre of the oven. Line 2 baking sheets with parchment paper.

❊ Sift the icing sugar into a shallow bowl. Between the palms of your hand, roll pieces of chilled dough to form 1¼-inch balls. Drop the balls into the icing sugar and toss lightly until well coated. Place the cookies on the prepared baking sheets about 2 inches apart and flatten just slightly. Bake each sheet separately for 8-10 minutes, until the cookies feel slightly firm in the centre. Let the cookies cool on the baking sheet on a wire rack for 5 minutes, then transfer them to the wire rack to cool completely.

❊ Store in an airtight container for up to 5 days, or freeze for up to 2 months.

White Chocolate Rosemary Cranberry Blondies

I make these blondies every year around the holidays, and with one bite, you'll know why. Rosemary adds a delicate, herbal punch that plays really well with the pops of tart, fresh cranberries. All is swaddled together in a deliciously dense blondie that doesn't shout white chocolate, but instead whispers it in the background. Whenever I add these blondies to platters of baked goods, they disappear quickly and are a hit even among the seven and under crowd. My nieces always tell me to bring more next time, so now I bake a double batch. With a festive dusting of icing sugar, these are one of my favourite things to nibble on while we play Uno in our pyjamas on Christmas Day.

MAKES 24 BLONDIES

1⅓ cups chopped (½-inch pieces) white chocolate
½ cup unsalted butter, softened and cubed,
   plus more for greasing the pan
¾ cup granulated sugar
2 tsp finely chopped fresh rosemary
3 large eggs, at room temperature
1 tsp pure vanilla extract
1½ cups all-purpose flour

½ tsp baking powder
½ tsp salt
1½ cups fresh cranberries
Icing sugar, for garnish

✳ Preheat the oven to 350°F. Place the rack in the centre of the oven. Line the bottom and sides of a 9×13-inch baking dish with parchment paper overhanging the sides. Butter the parchment.

✳ In a medium saucepan over low heat, melt the chocolate and butter together, stirring constantly until smooth. Remove the pan from the heat and stir in the sugar and rosemary. Mix until smooth. Pour this mixture into the bowl of a stand mixer fitted with a paddle attachment. Add the eggs and vanilla and beat on medium-high speed until smooth, about 2 minutes, scraping down the sides of the bowl. If it seems to split, that's fine. It will smooth out once the flour is added. Add the flour, baking powder and salt, and beat on low speed just until incorporated and no dry bits of flour remain. Fold in the cranberries and scrape into the prepared pan.

✳ Bake for 25–30 minutes, until the top is lightly golden and a toothpick inserted in the centre comes out clean. Cool completely in the pan on a wire rack before cutting into evenly sized bars.

✳ Dust with icing sugar before serving. Keep the bars in an airtight container in the refrigerator for up to 5 days, or freeze for up to 2 months.

Buckwheat and Olive Oil Molasses Cookies

Don't let the lengthy ingredient list frighten you. There are small amounts of aromatics here, but they really make these cookies quite fantastic. And yes, that includes the black pepper. My old friend Peter used to make me Knock Your Socks Off Cookies when I lived in Montreal, and I thought he was bonkers for putting pepper in baked goods. Turns out he was brilliant. These cookies are also dairy-free—something to keep in mind when baking for those who don't eat dairy. I really love how they sparkle with coarse sugar, and while they will surely light up any dessert platter at the holidays, promise me you won't confine them to just that time of year. Soft and chewy, with a wonderful pop of spice in each bite, these are meant to be enjoyed year-round. If you decided to fill them with spoonfuls of Mascarpone Soft Serve (page 300) and make the best ice cream sandwiches EVER, I'd jump up and down with joy.

1½ cups all-purpose flour
½ cup buckwheat flour
1¼ tsp baking soda
1½ tsp ground cinnamon
1 tsp ground ginger
¾ tsp ground cardamom
½ tsp salt
¼ tsp ground cloves
¼ tsp ground nutmeg
¼ tsp freshly cracked black pepper

1 large egg
½ cup extra virgin olive oil
⅓ cup granulated sugar
⅓ cup molasses
¼ cup packed brown sugar
1 tsp finely grated peeled fresh ginger
1 tsp grated orange zest
1 tsp pure vanilla extract
¼–½ cup coarse or raw turbinado sugar, for rolling

❄ Combine all of the dry ingredients (flour to pepper) in a large bowl and mix well. Whisk together the remaining ingredients (except the coarse sugar) in another large bowl and then stir in the dry ingredients until everything is combined. Cover the bowl with plastic wrap and chill for 1–3 hours.

❄ Preheat the oven to 375°F. Place racks in the upper and lower thirds of the oven. Line 2 baking sheets with parchment paper.

❄ Place the coarse sugar in a shallow bowl. Scoop out the dough with a soup spoon and roll it into 1 ½-inch balls. Roll the balls in the sugar and place them on the baking sheets about 2 inches apart. Bake for 4 minutes, rotate the pans from upper rack to lower rack, and bake for another 4 minutes, until the cookies are puffed up and cracked. Remove the cookies from the oven and let cool completely on the baking sheets on wire racks.

❄ Store the cookies in an airtight container for up to 4 days, or freeze for up to 2 months.

NOTE

You likely won't use all of the sugar when rolling. Save it for the next time you bake!

Brown Butter Spelt Brownies

I've been baking brownies since the days of big hair and bigger glasses—back when the AM radio station in my town played A LOT of REO Speedwagon. If I could go back in time, I would tell my 12-year-old self to brown the butter first. And also, life, music, your hair, it all gets better. She would no doubt look at me like I was crazy, because brown butter wasn't really a thing in 1985. But trust me. Brown butter adds a nutty richness that lingers and leaves you thinking you should brown all the butter all the time and add it to all the sweet things. (See what I did there?) These brownies are ever so fudgy, and because spelt flour has a much lower gluten content than all-purpose flour, the crumb is tender on the inside, yet has all of those desirable crispy edge pieces that we long to dunk into a glass of milk. Listening to "Can't Fight This Feeling" is entirely optional.

MAKES 16 BROWNIES

½ cup unsalted butter,
  plus more for greasing the pan
1¼ cups chopped (½-inch pieces) dark chocolate
¾ cup granulated sugar
¾ cup packed brown sugar
3 large eggs, at room temperature

¼ cup unsweetened cocoa powder
1 tsp flaky salt, such as Maldon
1 tsp pure vanilla extract
¾ cup spelt flour

❊ Preheat the oven to 350°F. Place the rack in the centre of the oven. Lightly butter an 8-inch square baking pan and line it with parchment paper, leaving an overhang on 2 facing sides. Butter the parchment paper as well.

❊ Heat the butter in a medium saucepan over medium-high heat. The butter will froth and bubble and then turn golden. (It's okay to give it a bit of a stir.) When it starts to brown and smell nutty, remove it from the heat and stir in the chocolate and both sugars until smooth. Using a wooden spoon, beat in the eggs one at a time, stirring well after each addition. The batter will be shiny. Stir in the cocoa powder, salt and vanilla. Mix in the spelt flour just until combined.

❊ Pour the batter into the prepared pan and bake until a toothpick inserted in the centre comes out with just a few crumbs clinging to it, 25–30 minutes. Let the brownies cool completely in the pan on a wire rack. Lift them out of the pan using the parchment paper. Cut the brownies into 16 squares.

❊ Store the brownies in an airtight container at room temperature for up to 3 days, or freeze for up to 1 month.

NOTE

If you can't find spelt flour, use ½ cup all-purpose flour and ¼ cup whole wheat flour.

Sticky Toffee Cookies with Dark Chocolate Chunks

Secrets. I've got them, you've got them. Some are big, some are little. Some are much harder to keep than others. Some secrets you tell people and then wish you hadn't, and others you wish you could tell, but can't bring yourself to go there. Holding on, letting go. It's what we do. I'm spilling the beans, or rather pulses, when I tell you *there are lentils in these cookies*. For real. And you would never have guessed if I didn't tell you. Because look at them. They look just like regular sticky toffee cookies with chocolate chunks, but they're bursting with the goodness of fibre and protein from the lentils. If you feel like sharing your secret, go for it. But if you want to sneak a little lentil action into your family's diet without them knowing, then by all means, keep this little doozy to yourself. They won't have a clue. And you can feel all proud of yourself. Go ahead, pat yourself on the back.

MAKES ABOUT 2 DOZEN COOKIES

½ cup unsalted butter, softened
½ cup packed brown sugar
¼ cup molasses
1 large egg, at room temperature
⅔ cup lentil purée (see below)
1 tsp pure vanilla extract
2 cups all-purpose flour

1 tsp baking soda
1 tsp salt
1 cup pitted Medjool dates, roughly chopped
¾ cup Skor toffee bits
½ cup dark chocolate chunks

❋ Preheat the oven to 350°F. Place the rack in the centre of the oven. Line 2 baking sheets with parchment paper.

❋ In a stand mixer fitted with a paddle attachment, cream together the butter, brown sugar and molasses on high speed until light and fluffy, about 2 minutes. Beat in the egg, lentil purée and vanilla until well combined.

❋ In a separate bowl, stir together the flour, baking soda and salt. Add this to the butter mixture. Mix on low speed until almost combined, and then add the dates, Skor bits and chocolate chunks. Beat on low speed until well combined. Roll the dough into 1½-inch balls and place them on the prepared baking sheets, about 2 inches apart. Bake each baking sheet separately for 12–14 minutes, until the cookies are lightly golden around the edges but the middle is still quite soft. Transfer the baking sheets to a wire rack and let the cookies cool completely.

❋ Store the cookies in an airtight container at room temperature for up to 3 days, or freeze for up to 1 month.

LENTIL PURÉE
Makes about 3 cups

1 cup green lentils, picked over for stones and rinsed well
3 cups water

❋ In a small saucepan, bring the lentils and water to a boil over high heat. Turn down the heat to medium, cover and simmer until the lentils are tender, 25–30 minutes. Drain the lentils, return them to the pot and let them cool until barely warm. Place the lentils in a blender or food processor with about ½ cup cold water and process on high speed. You want a fairly thick, smooth purée, about the same consistency as canned pumpkin purée. Let it cool completely before adding ⅔ cup of it to the cookie batter.

❋ Leftover lentil purée can be refrigerated for up to 5 days or frozen for up to 1 month.

Cinnamon Twists

Cinnamon Twists—another classic cookie from my mom's recipe book —may not sound flashy and glamorous, but they're definitely no slouch in the flavour department. This cookie ranks high as one of my all-time favourites, thanks to its subtle sweetness and rich, buttery flavour. My niece Olivia, who loves her sweet things as much as yours truly, told my mom that cinnamon twists are her favouritest thing in the whole world. Apparently she likes them more than her cats, or that *Frozen* movie. Amazing! These cookies trump it all for that seven-year-old. And because they're small, eating two or three cinnamon twists at a time doesn't seem unreasonable. Made with basic pantry ingredients, the neat thing about this cookie is its crispy outside and tender middle. Yes, we have the large amount of butter to thank for that. The dough itself doesn't have any sugar, but it's rolled directly in the cinnamon sugar mixture on your counter, and this is what gives the twists that lovely crispness that kids of all ages adore. This makes a rather large batch of cookies, but they freeze extremely well, giving you a head start on holiday baking, school bake sales or any other occasion when a large amount of baked goods is required. I quite enjoy these with tea in the afternoon or after dinner, but they've also been known to make an appearance at a second breakfast with strong coffee.

MAKES 64 TWISTS

5 cups all-purpose flour, plus more for dusting
2 tsp baking powder
2 cups salted butter, softened and cubed
2 large eggs, at room temperature
1 cup whole milk, at room temperature

1½ cups granulated sugar
1½ Tbsp ground cinnamon

❄ Preheat the oven to 375°F. Place the rack in the centre of the oven. Line 2 baking sheets with parchment paper.

❄ Mix together the flour and baking powder in a large bowl. Cut in the butter using a pastry blender until it's evenly incorporated and no large bits remain. Beat together the eggs and milk in a medium bowl. Pour this into the dry ingredients and stir to make a soft dough. It will be similar to pie dough. Dump the dough onto a lightly floured work surface and shape it into a ball. Cut it in half, then cut each half into quarters. Shape each piece into a ball (you'll have 8 dough balls).

❄ Stir together the granulated sugar and cinnamon in a medium bowl. Sprinkle some of this onto your work surface. Roll out a ball of dough on top of the cinnamon sugar to a circle approximately ⅛ inch thick. Cut the circle into 8 triangles. Pinch in the wide corners of each triangle and roll from the wide end to the narrow end, forming a crescent. Press the seam end in a little so it seals. Roll the twists in the cinnamon sugar to evenly coat. Place them on a baking sheet 2 inches apart, seam side down. Repeat with the remaining dough. Bake each sheet separately for 18–20 minutes, until golden brown. Remove the baking sheet from the oven and place it on a wire rack to let the twists cool completely.

❄ Store the cinnamon twists in an airtight container at room temperature for up to 5 days, or freeze for up to 1 month.

NOTES

If you only have unsalted butter, add 1 tsp salt to the flour and baking powder mixture.

You may have some sugar/cinnamon mixture left over. Use it up on oatmeal, etc.

Chocolate Chip Cookies with Flaky Salt

The very first recipe I ever made on my own was the one for chocolate chip cookies on the back of the Hershey bag. I was probably 10 years old, and I embraced the delicious chemistry of beating together butter, sugar and eggs and stirring in some flour and chocolate chips. Glory be. I ate so much cookie dough. Now that I'm a grown-up, my consumption of raw dough has decreased, but my love for really good chocolate chip cookies has not. These aren't the cookies of my youth. For one thing, I use brown butter—which elevates them right there—and I finish them with flaky salt. The result is a soft, chewy middle with just enough crispy edges and craggy tops to make your heart sing. You don't need to brown the butter—melted would work just fine—but the flavour is that much better if you do. Every good baker needs to have a stellar chocolate chip cookie recipe up their sleeve—it's like our super power. This one is mine.

MAKES ABOUT 2 DOZEN COOKIES

1 cup unsalted butter
3 cups all-purpose flour
1½ tsp baking soda
1 tsp salt
1¼ cups packed brown sugar
1 cup granulated sugar
3 large eggs, at room temperature

1½ tsp pure vanilla extract
2 cups dark chocolate chunks or chopped
 (½-inch pieces) chocolate
Flaky salt, for garnish

❋ Preheat the oven to 375°F. Place the rack in the centre of the oven. Line 2 baking sheets with parchment paper.

❋ Heat the butter in a medium saucepan over medium-high heat. The butter will froth and bubble then turn golden. (It's okay to give it a bit of a stir.) When it starts to brown and smell nutty, remove it from the heat. Let it cool down so it's barely warm.

❋ Mix together the flour, baking soda and salt in a medium bowl. In a stand mixer fitted with a paddle attachment, beat the liquid butter with both sugars on high speed for 2 minutes. Scrape down the sides of the bowl. Beat in all the eggs at once on high speed for 1 minute. The mixture should be thick and creamy. Add the vanilla. With the mixer running on low speed, add the flour mixture, just until it's incorporated. Be sure to scrape the bottom and sides of the bowl. Stir in the chocolate chunks.

❋ If you have time to wait, chilling the dough for 30 minutes ensures a crispy edge and a still-gooey middle, but it's not essential.

❋ Using a ¼-cup ice cream scoop, drop mounds of cookie dough onto the prepared baking sheets 3 inches apart. Lightly flatten the tops a little with your hand and sprinkle with flaky salt. Bake the first sheet of cookies for 7-9 minutes, until the cookies are puffed and lightly browned around the edges. They will continue to bake once they are out of the oven. These are best when chewy, but if you prefer a crispy cookie, bake them for a total of 10-11 minutes. Let the cookies cool completely on the baking sheet on a wire rack. Repeat with the remaining cookie dough.

❋ The cookies keep well in an airtight container for up to 3 days at room temperature. The cookie dough can be kept in an airtight container in the refrigerator for up to 1 week, and frozen cookie dough balls can be kept in the freezer for up to 1 month. See the peanut butter cookie recipe on page 54—the same principle of freezing cookie dough balls applies here.

RECIPES

MUFFINS AND QUICK BREADS

Like any grandmother would,
she sent me home with care packages of food—most
welcome when I was a poor student.

AUNT HELEN

Aunt Helen is my mom's aunt, my grandma's sister, who I got to know well when I lived in Edmonton. She was the only family on my mom's side who I was close to, and in a way she became my surrogate grandma. I never knew my Grandma Clara, as she passed away before I was born, but Aunt Helen would tell me about her, and I loved that. Through her, I would connect to a bit of my history, finding out what my grandma was like as a kid—stories I never heard from my mom. We'd sit in Aunt Helen's living room and drink Earl Grey tea while she gave me a glimpse into the past and where I come from. She would tell me that I looked just like my grandma when she was my age, and this lit me up from within.

I spent a lot of time with my aunt, hitting up yard sales (she was great at spotting deals), driving out to the country to pick saskatoon berries in the summer, going to movies where she almost always fell asleep and going out for Chinese food, ordering lemon chicken and egg rolls. We were kindred spirits, she and I. Not having had an easy life, she was tough and brave—a fighter who took on cancer and won. And she was a fantastic cook. Her Sunday dinners weren't complete without her famous Caesar salad, one of my favourite things in the whole world. She was generous with advice and hugs, and I would almost always leave her house feeling way better than when I got there. Like any grandmother would, she sent me home with care packages of food—most welcome when I was a poor student. Her bran muffins were a "regular" item (couldn't resist) in those packages. I'm so glad she shared the recipe with me, so I can now share it with you.

Aunt Helen's Big Batch Buttermilk Bran Muffins

Let's face it. There is absolutely nothing sexy about bran muffins. Nothing at all. But that doesn't mean they can't be delicious. The great thing about this recipe is that the batter can be kept in the refrigerator for two weeks and you can bake the muffins as you need them. Freshly baked muffins daily if you like! They're full of all kinds of good things like bran (of course), ground flax seed and large-flake oats, but you could even stir in a cup of raisins if you're so inclined. Unlike some bran muffins that can be dry dry dry, these are super moist thanks to the buttermilk. I reduced the amount of sugar from the original recipe and even sprinkled various seeds on top, just for fun—because if you can't be a sexy muffin, you might as well be a fun one.

MAKES ABOUT 3 DOZEN MUFFINS

2 cups boiling water
2 cups natural wheat bran
4 large eggs, at room temperature
1 cup canola or other cooking oil
1¾ cups packed brown sugar
½ cup molasses
4 cups buttermilk, at room temperature
4½ cups all-purpose flour

4 cups large-flake oats
½ cup ground flax seed
4½ tsp baking soda
1 tsp salt
1 tsp ground cinnamon
2 Tbsp each sunflower seeds, poppy seeds, flax seeds and sesame seeds

❋ Preheat the oven to 350°F. Place the rack in the centre of the oven. Line a muffin pan with papers or grease well with your preferred cooking oil. (You don't need to bake up all the batter in one session.)

❋ Pour the boiling water over the bran in a medium bowl and stir. Let it rest, uncovered, while you prepare the rest of the ingredients. It should be room temperature when you stir it into the batter.

❋ Meanwhile, in another medium bowl, whisk the eggs and then add the oil, brown sugar, molasses and buttermilk in this order. In a large bowl, place the flour, oats, flax seed, baking soda, salt and cinnamon and stir well. Pour in the egg mixture, stir a little to combine, then add the wet bran. Stir just until the batter is moistened. Portion out the batter using an ice cream scoop so the cups are three-quarters full. In a small bowl, stir together the seeds and sprinkle some of the mixture on top of the muffins. Reserve any remaining seed mixture for the next time you bake some of these muffins.

❋ Bake for 20-30 minutes, depending on the size of your muffins. They're done when a toothpick inserted in the centre comes out clean and they spring back when lightly touched. If your finger leaves an indentation, leave them to bake a little longer. Let the muffins cool in the pan on a wire rack for 5 minutes then remove them from the pan and let cool completely on the rack. Continue with the remaining batter.

❋ The bran muffins keep well in an airtight container for 3 days and can be frozen in an airtight container for up to 1 month. The batter will keep well in an airtight container in the refrigerator for 2 weeks.

NOTE

The batter bakes up best when it sits overnight before baking the first time.

Dark Chocolate Banana Rye Muffins

Dark chocolate and rye flour seems an odd combination to me—and maybe to you, too. But trust me when I say it's a fantastic match of flavours. The list of ingredients for this recipe deserves a good glance over, but don't be put off by the length of it. These are pretty great muffins, with no refined sugar or dairy. Rye and spelt flours are high fibre and good for you. Cocoa and dark chocolate are excellent antioxidants. Coconut milk adds richness and moisture. I like the fruity, earthy taste olive oil gives to baking—it seems to go well with chocolate, too. And because there is just a little maple syrup and mashed banana action, these muffins are not too sweet and yet are highly indulgent. Chunks of good chocolate melt into little puddles, a highly desirable quality when biting into one of these while it's still warm. Don't forget the light sprinkling of flaky salt. That dark chocolate/sea salt combo never gets old.

MAKES ABOUT 1 DOZEN LARGE MUFFINS

1 cup rye flour
1 cup spelt flour
1½ tsp baking powder
1 tsp baking soda
1 tsp coarse salt
¼ cup + 2 Tbsp unsweetened cocoa powder
3 large eggs, at room temperature
2 medium bananas, mashed
1 cup full-fat coconut milk
$\frac{1}{3}$ cup pure maple syrup

$\frac{2}{3}$ cup extra virgin olive oil
1 tsp pure vanilla extract
1 cup coarsely chopped (½-inch pieces) dark chocolate
Flaky salt, such as Maldon, or coarse salt if that's all you have, for garnish

❊ Preheat the oven to 375°F. Place the rack in the centre of the oven. Line a muffin pan with papers or grease well with your choice of oil or butter.

❊ Combine all of the dry ingredients in a large bowl, sifting in the cocoa. Stir well to combine. In a separate bowl, beat the eggs until light, about 1 minute. Whisk in the mashed banana, coconut milk, maple syrup, olive oil and vanilla. Stir the wet mixture into the dry, then stir in half of the chopped chocolate, being careful not to overmix. Scoop the mixture into the muffin cups so they're three-quarters full. Sprinkle the remaining chopped chocolate on top and bake for 18–21 minutes, depending on the size of your muffins. They're done when a toothpick inserted in the centre of a muffin comes out clean and they spring back when lightly touched. If your finger leaves an indentation, leave them to bake a little longer. Sprinkle with flaky salt while they're still hot. Let the muffins cool in the pan on a wire rack for 5 minutes, then remove them from the pan and let cool completely on the rack.

❊ Store the muffins in an airtight container for up to 3 days, or freeze for up to 1 month.

NOTE

If you don't have spelt flour, substitute all-purpose flour. If you don't have rye flour, substitute whole wheat flour.

MAPLE, OAT AND APPLE BREAD

I really, really adore maple syrup, which likely stems from my love of all things Quebec. It's a dream of mine to one day go to a maple farm during sugaring-off season, just to see how the syrup goes from the tree to the bottle. I'm currently accepting any and all invitations, but in the meantime, I'll have to be content with this lovely loaf. With notes of maple syrup, cinnamon and apple, it's a hearty, substantial quick bread that makes a smashing breakfast, especially when slathered with a wee bit of butter. Buttermilk and applesauce make it quite tender, while the whole wheat flour and oats bring along healthy amounts of our friend fibre.

MAKES 1 (9×5-INCH) LOAF

1¾ cups all-purpose flour
¾ cup whole wheat flour or multigrain flour
1½ tsp baking soda
½ tsp baking powder
1½ tsp ground cinnamon
1 tsp salt
½ tsp ground nutmeg
½ tsp ground ginger
¾ cup large-flake oats
2 large eggs, at room temperature

1 cup buttermilk, at room temperature
½ cup unsweetened applesauce
½ cup pure maple syrup
½ cup melted unsalted butter
⅓ cup packed brown sugar
1 tsp pure vanilla extract
1 tsp grated lemon zest
1 cup peeled, small-diced apple
   (any type of apple)

❋ Preheat the oven to 350°F. Place the rack in the centre of the oven. Line a 9×5×3-inch loaf pan with parchment paper overhanging the sides.

❋ Stir the flours, baking soda and baking powder with the cinnamon, salt, nutmeg and ginger in a large bowl. Stir in the oats. Make a little well in the centre. In another bowl, beat together the eggs, buttermilk, applesauce, maple syrup, butter, brown sugar, vanilla and lemon zest. Pour the wet ingredients into the well in the dry ingredients and stir just until combined. Stir in the diced apple. Scrape the batter into the prepared pan and bake for 45–55 minutes, until the bread is golden and risen with a few cracks on top and a toothpick inserted in the centre comes out clean. Let the bread cool in the pan on a wire rack for 20 minutes, then remove from the pan and discard the parchment paper. Let the bread cool completely on the rack before slicing.

❋ The bread will keep well for up to 2 days at room temperature when wrapped in plastic or a resealable freezer bag. It can also be frozen for up to 1 month.

Lemon and Cream Cheese Muffins

If you're looking for the best muffin to curl up with as you read the Sunday paper with your favourite mug of tea (and favourite person), look no further. With their gentle punch of lemon, these light and lovely muffins are exactly what you need to wake up to on the weekend. Cream cheese is cut into the dry ingredients, so you know what that means—you bite into little nuggets of cream cheese gold with every bite. The best part, though, is the lemon and sugar syrup, brushed over the muffins as soon as they're pulled from the oven. Heavenly stuff. This is another recipe from my Yukon days, passed down to me from the pastry chef who worked there that first summer. I've used it a lot over the years, carting the muffins off to birthdays and baby showers, often not allowed to leave until I've shared the recipe with the attendees.

MAKES ABOUT 10 MUFFINS

1¼ cups all-purpose flour
⅔ cup + 2 Tbsp granulated sugar, divided
1½ tsp baking powder
½ tsp salt
½ cup cream cheese, softened
1 large egg, at room temperature
⅓ cup canola or other cooking oil

½ cup whole milk
4 Tbsp fresh lemon juice, divided
1 Tbsp grated lemon zest

❄ Preheat the oven to 375°F. Place the rack in the centre of the oven. Line a muffin pan with 10 papers or grease well with your preferred cooking oil. Pour some water into the empty muffin cups to stop them from burning.

❄ Combine the flour, ⅔ cup of sugar, the baking powder and salt in a large bowl. Cut the cream cheese into ¼-inch cubes and work it into the dry ingredients, using a pastry blender or your hands, until small and large chunks of cream cheese remain. Beat together the egg, oil, milk, 2 Tbsp of the lemon juice and the lemon zest. Stir this gently into the dry ingredients until just combined.

❄ Scoop the batter into the prepared muffin pan so the cups are about three-quarters full, and bake for 20-25 minutes, until the tops are golden, the tops spring back when lightly touched and a toothpick inserted in the centre of a muffin comes out clean. Stir together the remaining 2 Tbsp of sugar and remaining 2 Tbsp of lemon juice in a small bowl. Use a pastry brush to brush this mixture on top of the hot muffins. Let them cool in the pan on a wire rack for 5 minutes, then remove them from the pan and let cool completely on the rack.

❄ Store the muffins in an airtight container for 1 day, or freeze for up to 1 month.

Double Chocolate Zucchini Olive Oil Bread

I'm almost certain that zucchini was invented just for the purpose of turning it into delicious baked goods. Come fall, I know all too well the conflict of the zucchini bounty. You love that you have them, but you hate having just so many of them. Unsuspecting neighbours find the squash on their doorsteps or stuffed into mailboxes. And the zucchinis seem to multiply in the garden overnight. If you find yourself in such a situation, don't freak out. Just go ahead and bake them into bread. And if you love chocolate, know that this has the one-two punch of both cocoa and dark chocolate chunks. A glass of cold milk is the perfect accompaniment.

MAKES 1 (9×5-INCH) LOAF

1 cup all-purpose flour
½ cup unsweetened cocoa powder
¾ tsp baking soda
¼ tsp baking powder
½ tsp salt
½ tsp ground cinnamon
½ tsp ground cardamom
2 cups shredded zucchini, skin on

½ cup dark chocolate chunks or chips
2 large eggs, at room temperature
½ cup granulated sugar
½ cup packed brown sugar
½ cup extra virgin olive oil
¼ cup buttermilk, at room temperature
2 tsp pure vanilla extract

❊ Preheat the oven to 350°F. Place the rack in the centre of the oven. Line a 9×5×3-inch loaf pan with parchment paper overhanging the sides. Lightly butter the paper.

❊ Sift together the flour, cocoa, baking soda and baking powder into a large bowl with the salt, cinnamon and cardamom. Stir in the zucchini and chocolate chunks. Whisk together the eggs, sugar, brown sugar, olive oil, buttermilk and vanilla in another bowl. Pour this into the zucchini mixture and stir just until combined.

❊ Scrape the batter into the prepared pan and bake for 50–60 minutes, until the bread has risen and a toothpick inserted in the centre comes out clean but with a few crumbs clinging to it. Let the loaf cool in the pan on a wire rack for 20 minutes, then remove the loaf from the pan and let cool completely on the rack.

❊ Store the zucchini bread in an airtight container at room temperature for up to 3 days, or freeze for up to 2 months.

NOTE

If the shredded zucchini is full of moisture, squeeze it dry in a clean dishcloth before adding to the batter.

Pumpkin Chai Chocolate Muffins

Come September, it seems like everyone wants to eat and drink pumpkin everything—from lattés to pies to muffins. And deservedly so—there's something quite fantastic about our favourite squash when it's combined with all of those warm, aromatic spices we associate with it. I first made these as gluten-free muffins when I was a pastry chef at a gluten-free restaurant in Saskatoon. They were a hit among the staff and the customers, with some not quite believing they were free of gluten. I've adapted that recipe to make them with all-purpose flour and oats, and I love them just the same, if not more. These are good year-round, not just for when you're wearing your favourite boots and scarves. They're also dairy-free—something to keep in mind if that's a consideration for you.

MAKES 1 DOZEN MUFFINS

2 large eggs, at room temperature
1 cup canned pumpkin purée
¾ cup packed brown sugar
½ cup canola or other cooking oil
⅓ cup apple juice
2 tsp pure vanilla extract
1½ cups all-purpose flour
½ cup large-flake oats
1½ tsp baking powder

1 tsp baking soda
½ tsp salt
1 tsp ground cinnamon
1 tsp ground ginger
½ tsp ground cloves
½ tsp ground nutmeg
¼ tsp ground cardamom
½ cup semi-sweet chocolate chips
¼ cup pumpkin seeds

❋ Preheat the oven to 350°F. Place the rack in the centre of the oven. Line a muffin pan with papers or grease well with your choice of oil or butter.

❋ Whisk together the eggs, pumpkin purée, brown sugar, oil, apple juice and vanilla in a large bowl until smooth. In another large bowl, stir together the flour, oats, baking powder, baking soda, salt and spices. Stir in the chocolate chips. Add these wet ingredients to the dry ingredients and stir just until incorporated. Scoop into the muffin cups so they're about three-quarters full and sprinkle with pumpkin seeds.

❋ Bake for 18-22 minutes, until the tops spring back when lightly touched and a toothpick inserted in the centre of a muffin comes out clean. Let the muffins cool in the pan on a wire rack for about 5 minutes, then remove the muffins from the pan and let cool completely on the rack.

❋ The muffins keep well in an airtight container for up to 3 days on the counter, or can be frozen for up to 2 months.

NOTE

To make these muffins gluten-free: Omit the flour and oats. Instead use ½ cup brown rice flour, ½ cup tapioca starch, ½ cup sorghum flour, ¾ tsp xanthan gum, ½ tsp psyllium flakes and ½ cup quinoa flakes. Proceed with the recipe as directed.

Brown Butter Buttermilk Banana Bread

You'll have to excuse the alliteration. I couldn't help myself. I also can't help myself when I tell you this is the banana bread of my dreams. Moist. Delicious. Rich, with toasty, nutty notes of caramel, thanks to the brown butter and brown sugar. I have a bit of a love-hate relationship with bananas. To me, they are only edible when they have a little bit of green on them and are super firm. Once they turn soft and spotty, forget about it. In other words, I pretty much buy bananas for the sake of baking. My freezer almost always has bananas tucked away for days when I have a banana bread emergency—you know *those days* when the only baked good that will do is banana bread? Yeah, you get where I'm coming from. This recipe is a blank slate. I know some of you are quite particular as to what should and shouldn't be in banana bread, so feel free to gussy it up with toasted nuts and chunks of chocolate. A swirl of Nutella would not be out of place. A thick slice with a slather of salted butter really is one of the best things in this life.

MAKES 1 (9×5-INCH) LOAF

½ cup unsalted butter,
   plus more for greasing the pan
½ cup granulated sugar
½ cup brown sugar
2 large eggs, at room temperature
¼ cup buttermilk, at room temperature
2 tsp pure vanilla extract

2 cups all-purpose flour
1 tsp baking soda
½ tsp salt
3 very ripe medium bananas, mashed
½ cup toasted, chopped nuts and/or
   semi-sweet chocolate chips (optional)

❊ Preheat the oven to 350°F. Place the rack in the bottom third of the oven. Line a 9×5×3-inch loaf pan with parchment paper overhanging the sides. Lightly butter the paper.

❊ Heat the butter in a medium saucepan over medium-high heat. (It's okay to give it a bit of a stir.) The butter will froth and bubble then turn golden. When it starts to brown and smell nutty, remove it from the heat and let it cool to room temperature. Whisk together the brown butter and both sugars in a large bowl. Using a wooden spoon, beat in both eggs together until smooth, then beat in the buttermilk and vanilla. In a medium bowl, stir together the flour, baking soda and salt.

❊ Add the dry ingredients to the wet and use a spatula to stir just until everything is almost incorporated. Gently stir in the mashed bananas and stir to combine. If you're using nuts or chocolate, add them now.

❊ Scrape the batter into the prepared pan and bake the bread for 55–60 minutes. The banana bread is done when it's golden, the top springs back when lightly touched and a toothpick inserted in the centre comes out clean, but do check it around the 50-minute mark just in case it finishes early. If the top is getting too dark, lay a sheet of aluminum foil on top. Remove the banana bread from the oven and let it cool in the pan on a wire rack for 15 minutes. Remove it from the pan and let cool completely on the rack before slicing.

❊ Wrap the banana bread in plastic or place in a resealable plastic bag. It keeps well at room temperature for up to 5 days and can be frozen for up to 1 month.

NOTES

Substitute half of the all-purpose flour with whole wheat, rye or multigrain flour. Or swap one-third of the all-purpose flour for spelt flour, oat flour or ground flax seed.

To make muffins, line a muffin pan with papers and fill each cup three-quarters full. Makes 10–12 muffins. (Pour some water into empty muffin pan cups to stop them from burning.)

Orange-Glazed Cranberry Cream Cheese Bread

Everyone who tasted a corner of this bread while I was testing the recipe hunted me down afterwards and asked what in the world was in it. When I said cream cheese, all was clear. Cream cheese works magic in baked goods, adding fat and moisture as well as that signature bit of tang. Combined with cranberries and a pretty orange glaze, this bread is wonderful to serve over the holidays and makes a delicious edible gift. The sweet orange glaze not only looks attractive, but also camouflages any parts that may get overly brown. I prefer this bread the next day, after the flavours have melded and mingled, and it goes just smashingly with a cup of tea.

MAKES 1 (9×5-INCH) LOAF

1 cup unsalted butter, softened,
   plus more for greasing the pan
1 cup cream cheese, softened
1½ cups granulated sugar
1½ tsp pure vanilla extract
4 large eggs, at room temperature
1 Tbsp grated orange zest

2 cups all-purpose flour
1½ tsp baking powder
½ tsp salt
2 cups fresh or frozen cranberries
1¼ cups icing sugar
2 Tbsp fresh orange juice
Pinch of salt

❄ Preheat the oven to 350°F. Place the rack in the bottom third of the oven. Line a 9×5×3-inch loaf pan with parchment paper overhanging the edge. Lightly butter the paper.

❄ In a stand mixer fitted with a paddle attachment, beat the butter, cream cheese, sugar and vanilla on high speed until creamy, about 3 minutes. Beat in the eggs, one at a time, being sure to scrape down the sides and bottom of the bowl after each addition. Beat in the orange zest. Combine the flour, baking powder and salt in a medium bowl. Turn the mixer to low speed and slowly mix the flour mix into the batter until just combined. Fold in the cranberries by hand.

❄ Scrape the batter into the prepared loaf pan and bake for 60–75 minutes. The bread will likely get quite brown, so cover it with aluminum foil at the 50-minute mark, or sooner if you notice it getting dark. The bread is done when a toothpick inserted in the centre comes out clean and the top is puffed and golden brown. Remove the pan from the oven and let the bread cool in the pan on a wire rack for 15 minutes before removing it from the pan to cool completely on the rack before glazing.

❄ To make the orange glaze, whisk together the icing sugar, orange juice and salt in a medium bowl until smooth. Slowly drizzle the glaze over the bread and let it firm up before slicing.

❄ The cranberry orange bread keeps well refrigerated for up to 4 days when wrapped in plastic or in a resealable plastic bag. You can also freeze it without the glaze for up to 2 months.

Blueberry Turmeric Muffins with Oats and Honey Streusel

Before you turn the page thinking I'm a total weirdo for putting turmeric in my muffins, hear me out. This golden, earthy spice has healing anti-inflammatory powers. As do blueberries. That's why they are a gorgeous combo in this delicious muffin that has very little refined sugar and a healthy dose of fibre-filled oats. The turmeric lingers in the background, but you know it's there thanks to the lovely colour that complements the deep purple of the blueberries. It loves to stain clothing and countertops, though, so do take care when handling this spice.

MAKES 16–18 MUFFINS

MUFFINS
1½ cups multigrain, rye, oat or whole wheat flour
$^2/_3$ cup + 1 Tbsp all-purpose flour, divided
½ cup large-flake oats
1 Tbsp ground turmeric
1 Tbsp lemon zest
1½ tsp baking powder
1 tsp ground cardamom
1 tsp ground ginger
½ tsp baking soda
½ tsp salt
3 large eggs, at room temperature
2 large bananas, mashed
$^2/_3$ cup buttermilk, at room temperature

$^1/_3$ cup canola or other cooking oil
¼ cup pure maple syrup
1 cup fresh or frozen blueberries

STREUSEL
½ cup large-flake oats
2 Tbsp salted and roasted sunflower seeds
2 Tbsp butter, softened
1 Tbsp liquid honey
2 tsp all-purpose flour
½ cup fresh or frozen blueberries, for garnish

❋ Preheat the oven to 375°F. Place the rack in the centre of the oven. Line a muffin pan with papers or grease well with your preferred oil or butter. (You'll need to bake these in batches. Pour some water into empty muffin pan cups to avoid burning.)

❋ To make the muffins, stir together the multigrain flour, $^2/_3$ cup of the all-purpose flour, the oats, turmeric, lemon zest, baking powder, cardamom, ginger, baking soda and salt in a large bowl. In another large bowl, whisk together the eggs, mashed bananas, buttermilk, oil and maple syrup. Stir these wet ingredients into the dry ingredients just until combined. In a small bowl, toss together the blueberries with the remaining 1 Tbsp flour and then stir them into the batter until just incorporated. Try not to overmix the batter.

❋ To make the streusel, combine all the streusel ingredients, except the blueberries, in a medium bowl. It should be buttery and crumbly. Use an ice cream scoop to fill the muffin cups so they are three-quarters full, then sprinkle the tops of the muffins with about 3 blueberries each and a bit of the streusel.

❋ Bake for 20–22 minutes, until the muffins are golden, the tops spring back when lightly touched and a toothpick inserted in the centre of a muffin comes out clean. Let the muffins cool in the pan on a wire rack for about 5 minutes, then remove them from the pan and let cool completely on the rack.

❋ Store the blueberry muffins in an airtight container at room temperature for up to 2 days, or freeze for up to 1 month.

White Chocolate and Ginger Irish Soda Buns

I have a little love affair happening with Irish soda bread. Not only is it simple to throw together and fun to shape, it bakes up all rustic and pretty, too. Plus, it looks like you worked way harder than you actually did to produce such a lovely gluten-filled specimen. The only thing is, sometimes it's just so big, and if you're like me, living solo with just the kitties, a large loaf of bread can be just too much to handle. So, I've made wee buns out of the batter—dilemma solved! With a moist, tender crumb, veering towards scone-like territory, these buns don't even need butter. Yeah, I can't believe I just said that either. Someone check to see if hell might have just frozen over. With lovely pockets of melted white chocolate and the delicate bite of candied ginger, these buns are perfectly acceptable to serve at brunch or with tea in the afternoon. Give them a quick warm-through in the oven so you can best enjoy the melted white chocolate experience.

MAKES 12–16 BUNS

2 cups all-purpose flour
1 cup rye flour or whole wheat flour
½ cup granulated sugar
2 tsp baking powder
1 tsp salt
1 tsp ground ginger
½ tsp baking soda
½ cup cold unsalted butter, cubed

1¼ cups white chocolate chunks or chopped (½-inch pieces) white chocolate
¼ cup chopped (½-inch pieces) candied ginger
1 large egg, at room temperature
1¼ cups buttermilk, at room temperature
1 tsp pure vanilla extract
2 Tbsp half-and-half cream or milk, for brushing the tops

※ Preheat the oven to 375°F. Place the rack in the centre of the oven. Line a baking sheet with parchment paper.

※ Whisk the first 7 ingredients together in a large bowl. Add the butter and rub it in with your fingers until the mixture resembles coarse meal. Stir in the white chocolate and candied ginger. Whisk the egg, buttermilk and vanilla together in a medium bowl then add to the dry ingredients, stirring just until a soft dough forms.

※ Turn the dough out onto a floured work surface and knead gently until it comes together, about 5 turns. It's a sticky dough, so be sure to have enough flour on the counter. Form the dough into a square, about 1 inch thick. Using a sharp knife (I like to dust it with flour before each cut), cut the dough into 12–16 squares, depending on how large you'd like them.

※ Transfer the buns to the prepared baking sheet, spacing them about 2 inches apart, and brush the tops lightly with the cream. Bake for 20–22 minutes for small buns, or 22–25 minutes for larger buns. The buns will be golden on top and, if you pick one up to look, golden underneath. Rotate the baking sheet 180 degrees halfway through the baking time so that the buns bake evenly. Remove the baking sheet from the oven and let the buns cool completely on the baking sheet on a wire rack.

※ The buns can be kept for up to 2 days in an airtight container at room temperature, or can be frozen for up to 1 month.

Parsnip and Cardamom Muffins with Brown Butter Cream Cheese Icing

I love most fruits and vegetables. The list of those I won't eat is a very short one (rutabaga, I'm looking at you) and for the longest time, parsnips were on that list. I think it had something to do with their texture, or perhaps how I just wanted them to be carrots. I've since wised up to their elegant, herbal sweetness and now find myself roasting them whenever I get the chance. Parsnips are also fantastic in baked goods—yes, just like their cousin the carrot. In these muffins, they're grated and stirred into a fragrant cardamom-laced batter that's lightened with buttermilk. My recipe testers commented on what a clever use this was for this humble, underrated vegetable, and I couldn't agree more. Once they're slathered with a little brown butter cream cheese icing the muffins officially land in cupcake territory, but no matter. Seeing as they contain vegetables, go ahead and have one for breakfast.

MAKES 1 DOZEN MUFFINS

1 cup all-purpose flour
1 ½ tsp ground cardamom
1 tsp baking powder
½ tsp baking soda
½ tsp salt
2 large eggs, at room temperature
½ cup packed brown sugar
½ cup canola or other cooking oil

⅓ cup buttermilk, at room temperature
1 tsp pure vanilla extract
2 cups peeled, grated parsnip
½ recipe Brown Butter Cream Cheese Icing
   (page 140)

❊ Preheat the oven to 350°F. Place the rack in the centre of the oven. Line a muffin pan with papers or grease well with your preferred cooking oil.

❊ Whisk together the flour, cardamom, baking powder, baking soda and salt in a medium bowl. In a large bowl, whisk together the eggs, brown sugar, oil, buttermilk and vanilla. Stir in the grated parsnip. Stir the flour mixture into the parsnip mixture just until combined.

❊ Scoop the batter into the muffin cups so they're about three-quarters full and bake for 18–22 minutes, until the muffins are golden and spring back when lightly touched, and a toothpick inserted in the centre of one comes out with just a few crumbs clinging to it. Remove the pan from the oven and let the muffins cool in the pan on a wire rack for 10 minutes then remove from the pan and let cool completely on the rack before icing.

❊ Spread a generous amount of the icing on each muffin. These will keep unfrosted for up to 4 days in an airtight container at room temperature and will keep frosted for up to 4 days in the refrigerator in an airtight container. They can also be frozen, without frosting, for up to 1 month.

Recipes

CAKES AND MORE CAKES

Mocha Bundt Cake with Dark Chocolate Ganache

If you don't already own a Bundt pan, you'll want to buy (or borrow one) for the sole purpose of baking this cake. And once you taste it, I have a feeling this Bundt will be in your baking rotation for both special occasions (birthdays, Mother's Day, Christmas) and also for days when you just want a really good chocolate cake (every day in my life). Prized not only for its photogenic properties, it's one of my favourite chocolate cakes ever—it's swaddled in dark chocolate ganache and has a damp, dense texture and notes of coffee and chocolate shining through. I dare you not to lick the plate. I've shared this recipe on my blog and had fan mail for it. I'm not the only one in love!

SERVES 10–12

CAKE
1¼ cups hot, strong brewed coffee
¾ cup unsweetened cocoa powder,
  plus more for dusting the pan
2¼ cups granulated sugar
2½ tsp baking soda
1½ tsp salt
2 large eggs, at room temperature
1 large egg yolk, at room temperature
1¼ cups + 2 Tbsp buttermilk, at room temperature

½ cup + 2 Tbsp canola or other cooking oil
½ cup olive oil
2 tsp pure vanilla extract
2 cups + 2 Tbsp all-purpose flour
½ cup rye (or all-purpose) flour

GANACHE
1 cup chopped (½-inch pieces) dark chocolate
1 cup whipping cream

❋ Preheat the oven to 350°F. Place the rack in the lower third of the oven. Butter a 10-inch Bundt pan generously and dust it with cocoa powder.

❋ To make the cake, place the coffee and cocoa in a small saucepan and bring it to a boil over medium-high heat, whisking constantly. Remove the pan from the heat and let it come to room temperature.

❋ Place the sugar, baking soda and salt plus the eggs and egg yolk in the bowl of a stand mixer fitted with a paddle attachment. Beat on low speed for 1 minute. Scrape down the sides. Add the buttermilk, canola oil, olive oil and vanilla and mix on low speed for another minute. Add the flours and mix on medium speed for 2 minutes. Add the cooled cocoa mixture and mix on medium speed for 3 minutes. Don't forget to scrape the sides down after each addition. The batter will be thin.

❋ Pour the batter into the prepared pan and bake for 1 hour, or until a toothpick inserted in the centre comes out clean and the cake springs back when lightly touched. Let the cake cool in the pan on a wire rack for 30 minutes, then invert it onto the rack and let cool completely before drizzling with ganache.

❋ To make the ganache, place the chocolate in a medium bowl. Heat the whipping cream in a small saucepan over medium-high heat. Let it come just to a boil and then pour it over the chopped chocolate. Let it rest for 5 minutes. Stir well, until the ganache is perfectly smooth.

❋ Refrigerate, uncovered, for 20–30 minutes, stirring every 10 minutes. You want the glaze to drizzle over the Bundt cake, not slide off it. If the glaze gets too thick, gently reheat on low heat then drizzle onto the cake.

❋ Store the cake in an airtight container in the refrigerator for up to 5 days. The cake can also be frozen, without the ganache, for up to 2 months.

GIVING THANKS

Every day I give thanks. For little and big things, like the butter on my bread, and birthdays and big dreams. For the wet nose of an old grey cat. For the voice of my mom, reassuring and kind. For the squeaks and squeals of my wee nieces when I walk into the room. For the fit and feel of a sexy dress. For the sky above and the ground below and everything in between. For my hands and legs and knees and shoulders, who work so hard and are finally telling me to slow down. For belly laughs and brave hearts. For Bach and the Beatles. For coffee with cream and honey (I can't quit you). For a friend, cancer-free. For the warmth of wool, wrapped around my feet, and the arms of good friends, wrapped around me. It's these things that make my life full—though hardly perfect. There are concerns and complaints that bounce around, too. Sometimes I don't know how to deal with bumps in the road. Sometimes I just bake a cake and do the dishes. Sometimes I just pick up my fat orange cat and dance. (He likes it—honest!)

Thanksgiving is one of my favourite holidays. In fact, I think it is my favourite favourite holiday. There's great food and company without the crazy that comes with Christmas. Mom's house smells like sage and the kids run around dressed as princesses or pirates. We always talk about *that* time, long ago, when I came home from Edmonton for Thanksgiving weekend, and a huge blizzard snowed us in, making it impossible for me to get back on the Greyhound. We had one extra day together, my mom and I, and I still remember how happy I was that I could stay a little longer with her. Reality was put on hold for another day, as was the tearful goodbye at the bus station. We *still* talk about that Thanksgiving, 20 years later. Memories. I'm thankful for those, too.

SOMETIMES I DON'T KNOW HOW
TO DEAL WITH BUMPS IN THE ROAD.
SOMETIMES I JUST BAKE A CAKE
AND DO THE DISHES.

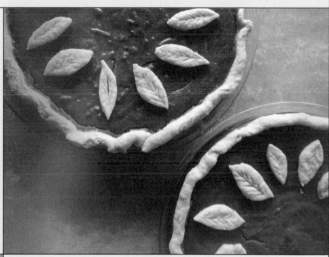

Maple Cream Cheese Pumpkin Roll

Pumpkin pie is a Thanksgiving staple, but every now and again it's good to switch things up. Enter the pumpkin roll. Once you get over the whole flipping-hot-cake-onto-an-icing-sugar-splattered-tea-towel thing you're good to go. It's just a simple pumpkin sponge cake, baked with all of those warm spices it's been known to party with. The maple cream cheese filling is a thing of beauty and complements the pumpkin sponge very well. Rich and indulgent, a small slice is perfectly satisfying, especially with a cup of coffee.

SERVES 10

PUMPKIN SPONGE CAKE
¾ cup all-purpose flour
½ tsp baking powder
½ tsp baking soda
2 tsp ground cinnamon
½ tsp ground nutmeg
¼ tsp ground cloves
¼ tsp allspice
¼ tsp salt
3 large eggs, at room temperature
1 cup granulated sugar

1 tsp pure vanilla extract
⅔ cup canned pumpkin purée
¼ cup icing sugar

MAPLE CREAM CHEESE FILLING
1 cup icing sugar, divided
¾ cup cream cheese, softened
¼ cup unsalted butter, softened
1½ Tbsp pure maple syrup
¼ tsp salt

❋ Preheat the oven to 375°F. Line the bottom and sides of a 13×17¾-inch jelly roll pan or rimmed baking sheet with parchment paper. Be sure the paper goes right up the sides. Lightly grease the parchment with canola oil or other cooking oil. Place the rack in the centre of the oven.

❋ To make the cake, place the flour, baking powder, baking soda, spices and salt in a medium bowl and mix to combine. In the bowl of a stand mixer fitted with a paddle attachment, beat the eggs, sugar and vanilla on high speed until thick. Add the pumpkin and mix to combine on medium speed. Stir in the flour mixture and beat on low speed just until it's smooth. Spread the batter into the prepared pan, trying to get it as even as possible. An offset spatula works well for this. Bang the pan on the counter a few times to release any air bubbles. Bake the pumpkin sponge for 13–15 minutes, until the cake is golden, a toothpick inserted in the centre comes out clean and the cake springs back when lightly touched.

❋ Sprinkle a clean tea towel with the icing sugar. Immediately loosen the hot cake from the pan and carefully invert it onto the prepared towel. Carefully peel off the parchment paper and then roll the cake and tea towel tightly together, starting with the narrow end closest to you. This will help it remember what to do when you roll it up with the filling. Cool the roll on a wire rack, seam side down.

❋ Make the filling. Sift ¾ cup of the icing sugar into the bowl of a stand mixer fitted with a paddle attachment. Add the cream cheese, butter, maple syrup and salt. Beat on high speed until smooth, stopping to scrape down the bowl occasionally. Don't fret if there are small lumps of cream cheese.

❋ Carefully unroll the cake and remove the towel. Spread the filling over the cake (you may have some filling left over) leaving a 1-inch border so no filling escapes. Carefully reroll the cake (without the help of the towel), tightly but gingerly, and wrap in plastic. Chill the pumpkin roll for at least 1 hour before cutting, but the longer it chills the better. Dust with more icing sugar, slice and serve.

❋ This will keep refrigerated in an airtight container for up to 3 days.

NOTE

For a lighter filling, whip 1¼ cups of whipping cream with 2 Tbsp of maple syrup. Spread on the pumpkin sponge and proceed as above.

PEACH UPSIDE-DOWN CAKE WITH GINGER AND VANILLA

The best of summer's peaches are combined with fall aromatics of cinnamon, ginger and vanilla. I've baked a lot of cakes in my little lifetime, but none have smelled quite like this one. And its aroma is going to waft throughout your neighbourhood, so be prepared for unexpected drop-ins. There are a couple of steps to this cake, but it is definitely worth the effort. Once you invert it onto a pretty platter and see the warm golden glow of the peaches you'll be happy you did.

SERVES 6

PEACHES
4 large ripe peaches, each pitted and sliced into 8
¾ cup packed brown sugar
3 Tbsp whiskey or apple juice
2 Tbsp unsalted butter
1-inch piece fresh, peeled ginger, sliced into
   thin rounds
1 vanilla bean, sliced in half lengthwise,
   seeds scraped out
¼ tsp salt

CAKE
½ cup unsalted butter,
   plus more for greasing the pan
1 cup all-purpose flour
1 tsp baking powder
1 tsp ground cinnamon
½ tsp ground ginger
½ tsp ground cardamom
½ tsp salt
¾ cup packed brown sugar
1 tsp pure vanilla extract
2 large eggs, at room temperature
⅓ cup buttermilk, at room temperature
2 tsp grated fresh ginger

❊ Preheat the oven to 350°F. Place the rack in the centre of the oven. Butter an 8-inch square baking dish.

❊ Stir together the peaches, brown sugar, whiskey, butter, ginger, vanilla bean seeds and pod and salt in a large skillet over medium-high heat until the juices thicken. If the peaches are quite soft and start to break up, remove them from the skillet and thicken the juices on their own. This takes about 12 minutes. Pour the peaches and their juices into the prepared baking dish.

❊ To make the cake, heat the butter in a medium saucepan over medium-high heat. The butter will froth and bubble and then turn golden. (It's okay to give it a bit of a stir.) When it starts to brown and smell nutty, remove it from the heat and let it cool to room temperature.

❊ Combine the flour, baking powder, cinnamon, ginger, cardamon and salt in another bowl and set aside.

❊ In a stand mixer fitted with a paddle attachment, beat together the brown butter, brown sugar and vanilla on high speed for 1 minute. Add 1 egg at a time, mixing on high speed and scraping the bowl between additions. On low speed, alternate adding the dry ingredients with the buttermilk, beginning and ending with the dry ingredients. Continue on low speed, mixing the batter until it's smooth and add the grated fresh ginger. Pour the batter on top of the peach mixture, smoothing the top with a spatula.

❊ Bake for about 30 minutes, until the cake is golden and a toothpick inserted in the centre comes out clean. Remove the cake from the oven and let it rest in the pan for 5 minutes on a wire rack. Carefully, using oven mitts, place a large platter on top of the skillet and quickly invert the cake onto it. Leave it for a minute or two. If any peaches stick to the dish, pick them off and place them on the cake.

❊ Serve with vanilla ice cream or whipped cream. This can be stored in an airtight container in the refrigerator for up to 4 days.

Angel Food Cake

If there's any cake that shouts "spring is here!" it's angel food cake. There's a lightness to it, which is kind of how I feel after toughing out another long, cold winter. As soon as the snow starts to melt, I let out a large sigh and get cracking eggs. Angel food cake has rules, but don't let that scare you. First off, you need a tube pan with a removable tube. Whatever you do, don't grease it. I know that goes against everything you've been taught about baking cakes, but angel food cake is special. The batter needs a dry pan to climb up as it bakes. If there's any fat, the batter can't climb and you'll have a flat, congealed, eggy mess on your hands. So, rule #1: don't grease the pan. Rule #2: use cake and pastry flour. All-purpose is too heavy. Buy a bag and keep it in your freezer if you don't use it that often. Rule #3: egg whites must be at room temperature (they don't beat as well when cold) and add a pinch of cream of tartar to get great volume. Rule #4: be sure both bowl and beaters are grease-free, otherwise the whites won't beat very well. So basically, keep all fat away from the cake. Once the cake is baking, try not to open the oven until the 30-minute mark. Angel food is also kind of neat in that it hangs out upside down while it cools.

SERVES 8–10

1½ cups granulated sugar, divided
1 cup cake and pastry flour
1¼ cups egg whites (about 10–12), at room temperature
1 tsp pure almond or vanilla extract
¼ tsp salt
1¼ tsp cream of tartar

* Preheat the oven to 375°F. Place the rack in the lower third of the oven.

* In a medium bowl, add ½ cup sugar to the flour and stir very well. Set aside. Place the egg whites, almond extract and salt in a stand mixer fitted with a whisk attachment. Beat on high speed until the whites are foamy. Add the cream of tartar and beat the whites on high speed to medium stiffness. Gradually, with the mixer on medium speed, add the remaining 1 cup of sugar, 1 Tbsp at a time. After all of the sugar has been added, beat on high speed until stiff, glossy peaks form, 2–3 minutes.

* Gently fold the flour/sugar mixture in by hand, using a rubber spatula—I do this in 4 batches—and pour the batter into the ungreased tube pan. Make about 4 slashes with a sharp knife to remove any air pockets and bake for 30–35 minutes, until the cake is golden and the top is dry to the touch. Invert the cake on the counter or a wire rack and let it cool completely inside the pan. Take a sharp knife and run it around the edge of the pan. Gently remove the cake.

* You can slice it and serve it as is, with heaps of whipped cream and berries, or stuffed with whipped cream and berries. Basically, any combination of cake/fruit/whipped cream is a winner. Store the angel food cake in an airtight container on the counter for up to 2 days.

NOTES

For a gluten-free version: Substitute the cake and pastry flour with a mixture of ¼ cup tapioca starch, ¼ cup potato starch, ¼ cup sweet rice flour and ¼ cup cornstarch. Bake as above.

If you happen to have a few slices left over, they make smashing French toast (see page 24).

Spiced Apple Skillet Cake with Streusel Topping

You totally need to have this skillet cake recipe in your back pocket. It comes together in under 15 minutes and bakes up like a dream in a cast iron skillet. It's simple and straightforward, with a tender crumb and a crispy edge. And guess what? I stirred in some cooked lentil purée and you can't even tell. No one will be able to tell. I promise. It adds protein and fibre, so really, this cake is practically health food. Go ahead and have two pieces. Enjoy it for breakfast. Pack it for picnics. Serve it at dinner parties and for afternoon coffee with old friends. Swap in other seasonal fruit as you like. Peaches and apricots would be lovely. Plums and nectarines, too. Rhubarb and raspberries can't be left out. This is a versatile, everyday cake that looks as good as it tastes. If you're afraid of putting legumes in your baking, dont be—just add pulses instead of legumes. This cake it turns out equally well when the lentils are omitted.

SERVES 6

CAKE
⅓ cup unsalted butter, softened,
  plus more for greasing the skillet
¾ cup granulated sugar
2 large eggs, at room temperature
2 tsp pure vanilla extract
1 cup all-purpose flour
1 tsp baking soda
1 tsp ground cinnamon
1 tsp ground nutmeg

1 tsp ground ginger
½ tsp salt
2 cups medium-diced peeled apples (any type)
½ cup lentil purée (see page 84)

STREUSEL
⅓ cup unsalted butter, softened
⅓ cup packed brown sugar
⅓ cup all-purpose flour
¼ tsp salt

❊ Preheat the oven to 350°F. Place the rack in the centre of the oven. Butter a 10-inch cast iron skillet.

❊ To make the cake, beat the butter with the sugar in a stand mixer fitted with a paddle attachment until light, about 2 minutes on high speed, scraping down the sides occasionally. Beat in the eggs and vanilla on high speed until fluffy, another 3 minutes. In a separate bowl, combine the flour, baking soda, spices and salt. Stir this into the batter on low speed, along with the chopped apples and lentil purée. Spread the batter into the prepared skillet.

❊ To make the streusel, place the butter, brown sugar, flour and salt in a medium bowl and rub the mixture together with your fingers until incorporated and clumpy. Evenly scatter the streusel on top of the cake and bake for 25–35 minutes, until the cake is golden and springs back when lightly touched and a toothpick inserted in the centre comes out clean. Remove the cake from the oven and let it cool in the pan on a wire rack.

❊ Serve the skillet cake warm, with ice cream or whipped cream, if you like. The cake keeps well refrigerated in an airtight container for up to 3 days.

NOTE

Substitute a 9- or 10-inch round baking dish for the cast iron skillet. If you're using a 9-inch dish, increase the baking time by 5–10 minutes to allow for the extra depth.

Chocolate Espresso Date Cake
with Dark Chocolate Coconut Ganache

Don't be scared when I tell you this cake is gluten-free and vegan. It's also dense and decadent, but with little refined sugar and no added fat, so it accommodates dietary restrictions without losing out on flavour. I developed this recipe when I was pastry chef at a gluten-free/nut-free restaurant. The learning curve was steep, but I enjoyed working with new-to-me ingredients and it was a pretty good feeling when something turned out delicious, like this cake. Medjool dates are a great source of natural sugar and a wonderful partner with chocolate and coffee. I've used coconut sugar, as it's less processed than other sugars and has lovely notes of caramel that hum along nicely with all of the other flavours. If you don't have coconut sugar, granulated white or cane sugar will work just fine. Coconut cream and dark chocolate form a vegan ganache, and as someone who swears "ganache" could be her middle name, I can promise you this one does not disappoint. With its deep, dark mocha flavour, a sliver of a slice is highly satisfying and best served with whipped cream—from either a coconut or a cow.

SERVES 10–12

CAKE
3 cups packed, pitted Medjool dates
2¼ cups very strong, hot brewed coffee
2 Tbsp pure vanilla extract
1½ cups unsweetened cocoa powder
1½ cups gluten-free flour blend
¾ cup coconut sugar
1½ tsp baking powder
¾ tsp xanthan gum
¾ tsp salt

DARK CHOCOLATE GANACHE
2 cups chopped (½-inch pieces) dark chocolate
1½ cups coconut cream (from two 14 oz cans of premium full-fat coconut milk)

❖ To make the cake, place the pitted Medjool dates, coffee and vanilla in a medium bowl. Let them rest, uncovered, for 30 minutes. Meanwhile, line the bottoms of two 9-inch cake pans with parchment paper. Grease the bottoms and sides with canola oil or coconut oil. Preheat the oven to 350°F. Place the rack in the centre of the oven.

❖ In a large mixing bowl, sift in the cocoa (to prevent lumps), then add the flour, sugar, baking powder, xanthan gum and salt. Stir well to combine. Pour the coffee/date mixture into the bowl of a food processor fitted with the steel blade. Process for 1 minute, then scrape the sides of the bowl. Process for another minute or until the mixture is completely smooth. Add the dry ingredients to the bowl and process until it forms a smooth batter. Remember to scrape the sides of the bowl occasionally. Divide the cake batter evenly between the prepared cake pans, smoothing the tops with a mini offset spatula.

❖ Bake for 30 minutes, until the cakes spring back when lightly touched and a toothpick inserted in the centre of one comes out clean. Remove the pans from the oven and let the cakes cool in the pans for 10 minutes on a wire rack. Remove them from the pans and let cool completely on the rack. Once they're cool, wrap them in plastic until you're ready to ice and assemble the cake. The cakes can be made 1 day ahead and refrigerated.

❖ To make the ganache, scrape the thick coconut cream (NOT the coconut milk liquid) from the cans into a medium saucepan—this should be about 1½ cups. Reserve the coconut water, as you may need it later. Bring the cream to a boil over medium-high heat. In a medium bowl, place the chopped chocolate. Pour the hot coconut cream over the chopped chocolate and let it rest

for a few minutes. Stir well, making sure it's very smooth with no lumps. Chill, uncovered, in the refrigerator for 1–2 hours, stirring every 30 minutes or so. You want the ganache to be thick enough to spread on the cake. If it gets too thick, place the ganache in the bowl of a stand mixer and beat it with a tablespoon or two of the reserved coconut milk. You want a nice, spreadable consistency (but you don't want it so thin it slides off the cake).

✴ Place 1 cake on a platter or cake stand. Smear some of the ganache on the platter or cake stand to help the cake stay in place while icing it. Spread a fair amount of ganache over the cake. Top with the second cake and completely cover the whole thing with ganache. Chill the cake for 2 hours before cutting. Garnish with fresh seasonal fruit and flowers if you're feeling fancy. Serve it with whipped coconut or dairy cream. The cake keeps well wrapped in plastic and refrigerated for up to 5 days.

NOTES

To make the cake using 8-inch round cake pans, increase the baking time to 35–40 minutes.

To make whipped coconut cream, chill 2 (14 oz) cans of premium full-fat coconut milk in the refrigerator overnight. Scoop off all of the thick, hard coconut cream into a stand mixer fitted with a whisk attachment. Reserve the coconut milk for another use. Add ¼ cup icing sugar and 1 tsp vanilla and beat on high speed until creamy. This keeps refrigerated in an airtight container for up to 3 days.

When I'm buying coconut milk, I shake the can. If I don't hear a sloshing sound, I know it has thick coconut cream inside. If I hear sloshing, I know it's not going to work for the ganache. Yes, I do get funny looks in the grocery store when listening to coconut milk, but whatever.

Be sure your gluten-free flour blend does not include xanthan gum.

THE STRAWBERRY PATCH

I'll never forget the first time I saw a strawberry patch. I was seven years old, and that summer my family moved away from our farm and into a small town. My dad had passed away in the spring, and to say I felt like a lost little girl is an understatement. Life for us was forever changed. Instead of running around on the farm, chasing cats and getting chased by turkeys, I was facing an uncertain future. Gone were the days of playing in the tree house my dad had built for us. Gone were the days of going for rides in the truck to check on the cows. Gone were the days that he had filled with his love. That summer, I spent a lot of time outside in our new backyard, which had lush, green grass and a strawberry patch by the back fence. I'd never seen strawberries grow before. What a delight to crouch down, turn back the leaves with my little fingers and find the sweet, red treasures that were trying to hide. Into my mouth they went, one after the other.

Whenever I pick strawberries now, I'm often struck by that intoxicating smell that brings back those sad, summer days. Grieving the loss of a parent never ends. It gets better, and you grow into a functioning, fairly well-adjusted human being, but it's still a scar that never quite heals. Now and then I'll meet someone who also lost their dad when they were very young. Once the stories are shared, we just give a little nod to each other—both unfortunate members of the Dead Dad Club. Not much more needs to be said after that. The eyes say it all.

WHENEVER I PICK STRAWBERRIES NOW, I'M OFTEN STRUCK BY THAT INTOXICATING SMELL THAT BRINGS BACK THOSE SAD, SUMMER DAYS. GRIEVING THE LOSS OF A PARENT NEVER ENDS. IT GETS BETTER, AND YOU GROW INTO A FUNCTIONING, FAIRLY WELL-ADJUSTED HUMAN BEING, BUT IT'S STILL A SCAR THAT NEVER QUITE HEALS.

Strawberry Basil Shortcakes

Strawberry shortcake is synonymous with summer, when the ripe, juicy berries are at their finest and all you want to do is sit at a picnic table with your favourite people. This is a pretty familiar set-up—biscuits, berries, cream—but I've added some fresh basil and cracked black pepper to the berries. Both make their flavour more alive, and your guests will be impressed that you thought of such a thing. I always have half-and-half cream in my house, but sometimes it goes a little sour before I can use it all—hence the birth of these biscuits. Sometimes I think I subconsciously stock up on large containers of cream just so I have to make biscuits. Sometimes I think I was a southern belle in my former life, given my biscuit addiction. I wonder if she would have stirred basil into her strawberries . . . I'm going to go with a yes, ma'am. This recipe makes a whole lotta strawberry shortcake, but I've never heard anyone complain that there's too many biscuits or strawberries in the house.

MAKES 8–10 SHORTCAKES

BISCUITS
4 cups all-purpose flour, plus more for the counter
¼ cup + 2 Tbsp granulated sugar
2 Tbsp baking powder
1 tsp salt
½ tsp baking soda
¾ cup cold unsalted butter, cubed
1½ cups cold soured half-and-half cream
(see Note), plus more for brushing the tops

STRAWBERRIES
2 cups sliced, ripe strawberries
1 Tbsp shredded fresh basil
2 tsp granulated sugar
Freshly ground black pepper

TO SERVE
2 cups whipping cream
2 Tbsp icing sugar, plus more for dusting
2 tsp pure vanilla extract

❋ Preheat the oven to 425°F. Place the rack in the centre of the oven. Line a baking sheet with parchment paper.

❋ To make the biscuits, combine the flour, sugar, baking powder, salt and baking soda in a large bowl. Use a pastry cutter to cut in the butter until only pea-sized bits of butter remain. Make a well in the flour mixture and pour 1½ cups of half-and-half in the centre; stir gently with a wooden spoon until it all comes together. Dump the dough onto a lightly floured work surface and pat it into a circle, about 1 inch thick. Cut the dough into circles using a 2- or 3-inch cutter. Place the biscuits on the prepared baking sheet, spacing them about 2 inches apart. Brush the tops with cream and bake for 12–17 minutes, depending on the size. They will be golden brown when done. The biscuits keep well in an airtight container for 2 days and freeze well for up to 1 month.

❋ To prepare the strawberries, stir together the sliced strawberries, basil, sugar and a grinding of black pepper in a medium bowl. These are best when used the same day.

❋ To make the whipped cream, in a stand mixer fitted with a whisk attachment, beat the whipping cream, icing sugar and vanilla on high speed until stiff peaks form.

❋ To assemble the shortcakes, slice the biscuits in half. Top each bottom half with a generous scoop of strawberries and another generous scoop of whipped cream and finish off by replacing the top half. Dust each serving with icing sugar, if you like.

NOTE

Make your own soured half-and-half cream by squeezing 1 Tbsp fresh lemon juice in 1½ cups half-and-half.

RASPBERRY AND ROSEWATER MERINGUE JELLY ROLL

I love seeing the transformation egg whites undergo when beaten with sugar. The boring, un-appealing white is lifted into lofty, glossy peaks of sweetness, thanks to our friend granulated sugar. Those clouds of meringue don't happen without some patience and skill, though. It may be tempting to rush the process and add the sugar too quickly—you'll know you did something wrong when the meringue falls flat. I know, because I've done this myself. It's hard being patient! This is a lovely cake to enjoy in the summer, when fruit is at its finest, and a light, not-too-sweet dessert is desired. It feeds a crowd especially well.

SERVES 10–12

2 tsp canola or other cooking oil
6 large egg whites, at room temperature
1⅓ cups granulated sugar, plus more for
 sprinkling
1 Tbsp cornstarch
1 tsp white vinegar
1¼ cups whipping cream
1 tsp rosewater
3 cups fresh raspberries

❋ Preheat the oven to 425°F. Place the rack in the centre of the oven. Line a rimmed 13x17¾-inch baking sheet with parchment paper, ensuring that it goes up the sides by a couple of inches. Brush the paper (including the sides) lightly with the oil.

❋ Put the egg whites in a stand mixer fitted with a whisk attachment and beat on high speed until light, fluffy and stiff peaks form. With the mixer still running, add the sugar gradually, about 1 Tbsp at a time. The whites should be glossy and very thick, and should hold their shape when lifted out of the bowl. Gently fold in the cornstarch and white vinegar. Use a rubber spatula to lightly spread the mixture onto the prepared baking pan, getting it as even as you can, right to the edges. Smooth the top so it is quite flat. An offset spatula works great for this.

❋ Place the pan in the oven and bake for 10 minutes. Turn down the heat to 325°F and bake for 15 minutes longer. The meringue should be golden on top. Place a sheet of wax paper on your countertop and sprinkle it generously with granulated sugar. Remove the meringue from the oven and carefully invert it onto the wax paper. Gently peel off the parchment paper and cover the meringue lightly with plastic wrap. Leave it to cool completely.

❋ In a stand mixer fitted with a whisk attachment, beat the whipping cream on high speed until thick. With the mixer running on low, beat in the rosewater. Remove the plastic wrap from the meringue and slather the surface with the whipped cream, leaving a 1-inch border around the edges. Scatter the raspberries all over the cream. Starting with the long edge closest to you, carefully roll the meringue up snuggly. Transfer to a long serving platter or cutting board and let it stand for 30 minutes before serving. Slice using a sharp serrated knife. The meringue roll is best eaten the day it is made, but leftovers can be stored in an airtight container in the refrigerator for up to 1 day.

NOTES

Rosewater can be found in large supermarkets in the international foods aisle or in Middle Eastern grocery stores.

The rosewater enhances the raspberry flavour, but vanilla or almond extract could be substituted.

The meringue roll is gluten-free.

Carrot Cake with Maple Pumpkin Seed Brittle and Brown Butter Cream Cheese Icing

That title is a rather large mouthful, is it not? Well, there's lots happening here, from the moist and aromatic carrot cake to the sweet and crunchy brittle in the middle to the delicious brown butter cream cheese icing that smothers the whole deal. If you love regular cream cheese icing, this recipe will make you downright giddy. It's smooth and creamy, with the lovely caramel nuttiness that brown butter is known for. The carrot cake is rather wonderful in its simplicity—no pineapple, raisins or nuts to be found here, just straight-up carrots. Feel free to make the cakes a couple of days ahead. They freeze well, too. The middle layer of crunchy brittle may feel like an extra step, but it's one you want to take. As my friend Lindsay said while testing this cake, the brittle makes it. This is an impressive cake. Bring it out on your prettiest cake stand, slice it at the table and be prepared to take a bow.

SERVES 12–14

CARROT CAKE
3 large eggs, at room temperature
1½ cups granulated sugar
½ cup packed brown sugar
1 cup canola or other cooking oil
¾ cup buttermilk, at room temperature
2 tsp pure vanilla extract
3½ cups lightly packed grated carrots
3 cups all-purpose flour
2 tsp baking powder
1 tsp baking soda
1 tsp salt
1 tsp ground cinnamon

1 tsp ground ginger
½ tsp ground nutmeg
¼ tsp ground cloves

BROWN BUTTER CREAM CHEESE ICING
1 cup unsalted butter, softened and divided
2 cups cream cheese, softened
1 tsp vanilla bean paste or pure vanilla extract
Pinch of salt
3–4 cups icing sugar
1 cup crushed Maple Pumpkin Seed Brittle
  (page 278)

❉ Preheat the oven to 350°F. Place the rack in the centre of the oven. Grease the bottoms and sides of two 9-inch round cake pans with your preferred cooking oil and line the bottoms with parchment paper.

❉ To make the carrot cake, whisk together the eggs, sugars, oil, buttermilk and vanilla in a large bowl. Stir in the grated carrots. In another large bowl, whisk together the flour, baking powder, baking soda, salt and spices. Add the dry ingredients into the carrot mixture and stir until well combined. Divide the batter evenly between the cake pans.

❉ Bake for 35–40 minutes, until the cakes are golden and spring back when touched lightly and a toothpick inserted in the centre of a cake comes out clean. Remove the pans from the oven and let the cakes cool in the pans on a wire rack for about 30 minutes. Run a knife around the edges of the cakes and carefully remove them from their pans. Let the cakes cool completely on the rack. The carrot cakes can be made a day or two ahead of time. Wrap them well in plastic and refrigerate until ready to assemble.

❉ To make the icing, melt ½ cup of the butter in a small saucepan over medium-high heat. The butter will froth and bubble then turn golden. (You can give it a bit of a stir.) When it starts to brown and smell nutty, remove the pan from the heat. Pour the butter into a small dish and let it cool for 5 minutes. Place it in the refrigerator, uncovered, and chill for 15 minutes.

❉ In a stand mixer fitted with a paddle attachment, place the chilled melted brown butter, remaining ½ cup butter and cream cheese. Beat the mixture on high speed until creamy and smooth. Scrape down the sides of the bowl a couple of times. Beat in the vanilla and salt. With the machine running

on low speed, add 1 cup of icing sugar and then increase the speed to high and beat it well. Add the remaining icing sugar in batches of 1 cup, 1 cup, ½ cup and then a final ½ cup if needed, stopping to scrape down the sides of the bowl a few times. I use about 4 cups of icing sugar, but if it's thick and creamy after 3½ cups, stop then. If you feel like you need more icing sugar to make a thick and creamy icing, then by all means add more icing sugar.

❄ To assemble the cake, smear a bit of icing on the bottom of a cake stand or platter. This will keep the cake in place as you decorate it. Set the bottom layer of cake on this smear of icing and then spread the cake layer generously with icing. Scatter the crushed maple brittle on top of the icing. Top with the second layer of cake. Using a large offset spatula, apply a thin layer of icing all around the cake. This is called "dirty icing" and it helps adhere those pesky crumbs to the cake. Chill the cake for 30 minutes.

❄ Remove the cake from the refrigerator and apply the remaining icing with an offset spatula. Use the back of a spoon to create swirls, if you so desire. Refrigerate the cake for 30 minutes before serving. The cake will keep wrapped well in plastic in the refrigerator for up to 5 days. Unfrosted carrot cakes can be wrapped well in plastic and frozen for up to 1 month.

| NOTE | *You can also bake this cake using 8-inch cake pans—and bonus, you'll have some batter left over for cupcakes, which will take 20-22 minutes to bake.* |

Chocolate Smartie Cake with Fudgy Cream Cheese Icing

One of the things I loved most about childhood was the birthday cakes. This shouldn't come as a shocker to those who know me well. My mom's cakes were simple, made from scratch and slathered with a thick layer of icing. Given all that she had to deal with when raising four kids by herself, she always tried to give us each a beautiful birthday cake. When we were very young, she would bundle up all sorts of coins in plastic wrap and stick them in the cake before she iced it. The lucky kid of the night got a quarter. Ideally this would be the birthday girl or boy, and if it wasn't, well, there may have been tears. Not naming any names or anything. My favourite was the chocolate Smartie cake, because cake covered in candy will always blow a kid's mind. In my version, beet purée adds moisture and a lovely earthiness that bounces around nicely with the espresso, chocolate and buttermilk. Not terribly sweet, the cake will stay moist for at least five days, so if you want to get a head start and bake the layers before assembling, you're in luck. The cream cheese icing isn't terribly cheesy, but it does have a lovely consistency that is perfect for spreading. I like triple-layer cakes because they add an air of majesty, which birthday girls and boys, young and old, always deserve.

SERVES 12–14

CHOCOLATE CAKE
2 Tbsp espresso powder
½ cup boiling water
2½ cups all-purpose flour
¾ cup unsweetened cocoa powder, sifted
1½ tsp baking powder
1½ tsp baking soda
1 tsp salt
1½ cups granulated sugar
½ cup canola or other cooking oil
2 large eggs, at room temperature
1 cup beet purée (see note)

2 tsp pure vanilla extract
1¼ cups buttermilk, at room temperature

FUDGY CREAM CHEESE ICING
1 cup cream cheese, softened
½ cup unsalted butter, softened
3 cups icing sugar
½ cup unsweetened cocoa powder
1 tsp pure vanilla extract
½ tsp salt
1 cup Smarties

⁂ Preheat the oven to 350°F. Place the rack in the centre of the oven. Grease the bottoms and sides of three 8-inch round cake pans with your preferred cooking oil and line the bottoms with parchment paper.

⁂ To make the cake, place the espresso powder in a small bowl and stir in the boiling water to dissolve it. Let it cool, then combine with beet purée.

⁂ Stir together the flour, cocoa, baking powder, baking soda and salt in a medium bowl. Place the sugar and oil in a stand mixer fitted with a paddle attachment and beat on high speed for about 2 minutes, scraping the bottom and sides of the bowl once or twice. Beat in the eggs, then the beet purée/espresso mixture and vanilla. With the mixer running on low speed, gradually beat in one-third of the flour mixture then add half of the buttermilk. Scrape down the bowl and repeat the additions, ending with the flour mixture, and then beat on medium speed for about 30 seconds. Divide the cake batter evenly between the cake pans. Bake for 20 minutes, or until a toothpick inserted in the centre of a cake comes out clean. Cool the cakes in the pans on a wire rack for about 20 minutes, then remove from the pans and cool completely on the rack before icing.

⁂ To make the icing, beat the cream cheese and butter together in a stand mixer with a paddle attachment until creamy, about 3 minutes. Sift in the icing sugar and cocoa. Mix on low speed until

combined then add the vanilla and salt. Scrape the bottom and sides of the bowl, and then beat on high speed for 2 minutes, until the icing is smooth.

✳ To assemble the cake, spread a small amount of icing on a cake stand or platter. This helps to keep the cake in place. Set the bottom layer of cake on this smear of icing and then spread a thin layer of icing on this layer of cake. Top with the second cake layer and spread a thin layer of icing on that. Top with the third layer of cake. Using a large offset spatula, apply a thin layer of icing all around the cake. This is called "dirty icing" and it helps adhere those pesky crumbs to the cake. Refrigerate for about 15 minutes, and then cover the cake completely in icing. Decorate with Smarties. Refrigerate for 1 hour before serving.

✳ This cake keeps well in an airtight container in the refrigerator for up to 5 days. The unfrosted chocolate cakes can be wrapped well in plastic and frozen for up to 1 month.

NOTES

If you don't have three 8-inch pans, you can make a double-layer cake with 9-inch pans. Just increase the baking time to 30–40 minutes. Or you can make about 2 dozen cupcakes. Bake them for 20–25 minutes, depending on how large they are.

If you don't have access to Smarties, any small chocolate candy will do, though it may not look as pretty depending on what you use.

Substitute ½ cup very strong coffee for the espresso powder and hot water.

Beet purée can be made from blending canned (NOT pickled) beets in a blender or food processor until smooth. Or you can roast/boil raw beets (about 3 medium) until they're tender. Peel them once they've cooled down, cut them into small pieces and purée them in the blender or food processor with a tiny bit of water, if need be. The consistency should be like pumpkin purée. Remember, you just need 1 cup of purée for this cake. Any leftovers can be refrigerated for up to 1 week or frozen for up to 1 month.

Pear Gingerbread

The baking of gingerbread, at least in my world, smells like winter, roaring fires, kisses on cold, rosy cheeks and the kind of magic you can't quite name but know is hanging in the air. This upside-down pear gingerbread cake is one of my all-time favourites. It's everything you want your gingerbread to be—spicy, tender, sweet but not *too* sweet—and does double duty as breakfast if you top it with Greek yogurt. I tell no lies! It's not super-duper low fat, but there is applesauce in it, which busts out some of the butter. And because there's a lovely coupling of butter and brown sugar in the base of the skillet, the edges get the crispy, caramelized treatment, which adds a lovely textural contrast, and the pears and crystallized ginger lend it a seasonal, sophisticated air.

SERVES 8–10

PEAR TOPPING
3 medium, ripe pears (Bosc or Bartlett)
1/3 cup unsalted butter, softened
2/3 cup packed brown sugar
2 Tbsp diced crystallized ginger

GINGERBREAD CAKE
1/4 cup unsalted butter, softened
1/2 cup packed brown sugar
2 large eggs, at room temperature
1 cup unsweetened applesauce

1/2 cup molasses
1 tsp pure vanilla extract
1 1/2 cups all-purpose flour
1 1/2 tsp ground ginger
1 tsp baking powder
1 tsp baking soda
1 tsp ground cinnamon
1/2 tsp ground cloves
1/2 tsp salt

❋ Preheat the oven to 350°F. Place the rack in the centre of the oven.

❋ To make the topping, peel and core the pears, cutting each into 8 slices. In the bottom of a 10-inch cast iron skillet, melt the butter over medium heat. Swirl the butter up the sides and stir in the brown sugar, mixing until it's smooth. Remove the pan from the heat. (If you don't have a cast iron skillet, you can pour the melted butter and brown sugar mixture into the bottom of a greased 10-inch baking dish, with sides at least 2½ inches high. Move the dish around to coat the sides.) Lay the pears on top of the butter/brown sugar in a circle, overlapping if necessary. Scatter the crystallized ginger on top.

❋ To make the cake, in a stand mixer fitted with a paddle attachment, cream the butter with the brown sugar, beating on high speed for 2 minutes. Add the eggs and then beat on high speed for another 2 minutes. Scrape the bottom and sides of the bowl. Beat in the applesauce, molasses and vanilla on medium speed. In a separate bowl, combine the dry ingredients and with the mixer running on low speed, mix them into the molasses mixture, beating until you have a smooth batter. Pour the batter over the pears, smooth the top with an offset spatula and bake for 30–40 minutes, until the cake is golden and springs back when lightly touched and a toothpick inserted in the centre comes out clean.

❋ As soon as the cake comes out of the oven, run a knife around the edge of the skillet and carefully invert it onto a serving platter. Let it hang out for a minute to let all of the topping dribble out. Carefully lift the pan off the platter. If any pear slices are stuck to it, use a spoon to lift them off and put them in their place.

❋ Serve the pear gingerbread warm with whipped cream or vanilla ice cream. Leftover cake keeps well in an airtight container in the refrigerator for up to 4 days.

CLASSIC VANILLA CAKE WITH CRANBERRY CURD AND SEVEN-MINUTE FROSTING

There is nothing new and fandangled about this vanilla cake. Like the name says, it's classic, like the recipe on the box of cake and pastry flour classic. There's a reason why the 1-2-3-4 cake has stood the test of time—it's darn tasty and relatively easy to throw together with pantry ingredients. I've gussied things up with a Cranberry Curd filling (page 190), but you could make a choco-late ganache for the filling or even just use your favourite jam like my mom would do when we were kids. I love the curd because it has a lovely pink colour and the bit of tartness it brings is a welcome contrast to the sweetness of the frosting—although the Seven-Minute Frosting makes this cake a real bombshell. (And yes, it only takes seven minutes!) You can make the curd up to a week in advance and the cake layers a day before. Assemble on the day of your party and away you go. The best part is creating those swoops and swirls with the back of a soup spoon. It's playing with your food in the very best way.

CLASSIC VANILLA CAKE
1 cup unsalted butter, softened
2 cups granulated sugar
4 large eggs, at room temperature
3 cups cake and pastry flour
2 tsp baking powder
1 tsp salt
1 cup whole milk, at room temperature
2 tsp vanilla bean paste or pure vanilla extract

SEVEN-MINUTE FROSTING
4 large egg whites, at room temperature
1 cup granulated sugar
¼ tsp cream of tartar
1 tsp pure vanilla extract

TO ASSEMBLE
Cranberry Curd (page 190)

❋ Preheat the oven to 350°F. Place the rack in the centre of the oven. Grease the bottoms and sides of three 8-inch round cake pans with your preferred cooking oil and line the bottoms with parchment paper.

❋ To make the cake, in a stand mixer fitted with a paddle attachment, beat the butter with the sugar on medium-high speed until light and fluffy, about 3 minutes. Be sure to scrape the bowl down once or twice. Add the eggs one at a time, beating on medium speed until each one is thoroughly mixed in and scraping the bowl down between additions. Sift together the flour, baking powder and salt in a medium bowl. Stir together the milk and vanilla in a small bowl. With the mixer running on low speed, slowly add one-third of the flour mixture to the butter mixture, then add half of the milk mixture. Repeat with the remaining flour and milk, ending with the flour and scraping the bowl between additions. Mix on low speed just until combined.

❋ Divide the batter evenly between the prepared pans, giving them each a few good taps on the counter to help release any air bubbles. Bake for 20–22 minutes, until the tops are golden, the sides come away from the sides of the pan and a toothpick inserted in the centre of a cake comes out clean. Cool the cakes in the pans on a wire rack for 20 minutes, then remove them from their pans and let cool completely on the rack before icing.

❋ To make the frosting, place the egg whites, sugar and cream of tartar in the bowl of a stand mixer. Place this bowl over a pot of simmering water, being sure that the water is not touching the bottom of the bowl. Whisk constantly until the sugar dissolves and the whites are warm to the touch, 2–3 minutes. Wipe dry the outside of the bowl and then place it in the mixer. Using a whisk attachment, beat the mixture on low speed, gradually increasing to high speed, until stiff, glossy peaks form, 4–5 minutes. Add the vanilla and mix until combined.

❋ To assemble the cake, spread a small amount of icing on a cake stand or cake platter. This helps to keep the cake in place. Fill a small piping bag with icing (or use a small resealable plastic bag, cutting a corner off once it's filled) and pipe around the outside edge of each cake. This will help create a dam and keep the cranberry curd inside. Place 1 cake layer on the cake stand and spread a good amount of cranberry curd in the middle. Top with a second layer and spread the cranberry curd in the middle. Top with the third layer of cake. Using a large offset spatula, apply a thin layer of icing all around the cake. This is called "dirty icing" and it helps adhere those pesky crumbs to the cake. Refrigerate the cake for about 15 minutes then cover it completely in frosting, decorating it with swoops and swirls. The back of a soup spoon works great for this. Refrigerate the cake for 30 minutes before serving.

❋ The cake keeps well in an airtight container in the refrigerator for up to 5 days. Wrap the unfrosted cakes well in plastic and freeze them for up to 1 month.

NOTES

If you don't have three 8-inch pans, you can make a double-layer cake with 9-inch pans. Just increase the baking time to 30–40 minutes. Or you can make about 2 dozen cupcakes. Bake them for 20–25 minutes, depending on how large they are.

You won't use all of the cranberry curd, but any leftovers are great on scones (page 40), toast, waffles or pancakes—or just out of the jar.

Instead of cranberry curd, fill the cake with your favourite lemon curd, or jam, or Brown Butter Cream Cheese Icing from the Carrot Cake (page 140), or Fudgy Cream Cheese Icing from the Smartie Cake (page 144) or even the Red Wine and Dark Chocolate Truffle filling (page 260). And then, please, invite me over for dessert!

Recipes

TARTS AND PIES

SEARCHING FOR SASKATOONS

If you ask anyone who grew up in rural or small-town Saskatchewan about saskatoon berries, they'll have a story to tell. I'm not talking about the conveniently cultivated U-Picks, where you park your car, grab your basket and head towards your allotted row. Oh no. I'm talking about *wild* saskatoons—those grown on bushes along river banks, in coulees and on hilly farmland across the Canadian prairies. For generations, the saskatoon berry has been a hardy prairie food source. Canada's First Peoples picked, dried and pounded the berry with dried bison meat to create pemmican, the preserved staple of their diet. Settlers too relied on this nutritious berry to provide essential vitamins. Fruit from the western species *Amelanchier alnifolia* resembles a blueberry, but anyone who has braved the prairie heat and countless mosquito attacks in July can tell you they taste nothing like each other. Saskatoons have a musky, almost almond-like sweetness. And their deep purple skins and juice stain the hands as you pick them off the gnarled bushes. When they're baked into juicy pies or preserved in jammy jars of the darkest purple, I swear you can taste their history in every bite.

I grew up picking saskatoons, as did my mom and her mom before her. In mid-July, we would get together with my Auntie Jean and my cousins and drive out to Where The Saskatoons Are. Finding wild saskatoon berries is largely a word-of-mouth process. Someone tells someone where there is good picking, and the directions go something like this: Go south down the gravel road until you cross a bridge, turn east at the old Miller place then go another two miles until you see a clump of trees.

It was always an adventure. We were stuffed into a minivan like sweaty sardines, Duran Duran on the radio. Once the berry bushes were spotted, we were sprayed heavily with bug repellent and each given a four-litre ice cream pail and told to pick, not eat. As if. More berries went into our gobs than our pails, proof being the purple teeth at the end of the day. We were then set free to run around and play, the chickadees cheering us on. Mom and Auntie Jean picked pail after pail while they chatted and laughed with each other. Auntie Jean had the best laugh. Loud. Goofy. Happy. From the depths of her belly, it would come out and grab you. Hers was contagious. And then it was gone. On a frigid January morning in 1988, the small airplane she was on crashed, leaving her children without a mother and my mom without her best friend. After the untimely passing of someone so dear, life is never the same. It goes on, but the absence of the departed lingers long after their light has gone out.

I don't recall picking many saskatoons after that. By then I was into my mid-teens, and summer afternoons were likely spent reading books and sunbathing. Fast-forward to my 20s and I was living in big cities, going to university, the dusty gravel roads a long distant memory. In my 30s, I picked a few times. Friends of a friend knew of a spot. Now, I live in the city named after the berry, and have happily, finally discovered where the wild saskatoons are. On hot, midsummer days, I park my car and walk towards the winding South Saskatchewan River, hoping to fill my pail. And then I spot them—the saskatoons hanging heavily in their deep purple glory. I'm pretty proud I've found such a treasure, doing what generations of prairie women before me have done. My hands, stained and sticky, slide the inky berries into the ice cream pail secured around my waist with a belt. If I listen closely, over the buzz of the mosquitoes, I hear the long ago echo of children playing and sisters laughing. The chickadees, cheering me on.

FRUIT FROM THE WESTERN SPECIES *AMELANCHIER ALNIFOLIA* RESEMBLES A BLUEBERRY, BUT ANYONE WHO HAS BRAVED THE PRAIRIE HEAT AND COUNTLESS MOSQUITO ATTACKS IN *JULY* CAN TELL YOU THEY TASTE NOTHING LIKE EACH OTHER.

Saskatoon Berry Pie with Lattice Crust

I'm glad I live in a land where saskatoon berries thrive (in a good year). There's nothing quite like the flavour of them in this pie—all cooked down in their deepest purple glory. If you close your eyes, you can taste a bit of summer and riverbank and feel the sun on your shoulders and the breeze lightly kissing your face. This is the kind of pie I grew up on, as did my mom and grandma. Paired with vanilla ice cream or a healthy dollop of whipped cream, oh man, it's heaven. The first thing to know about baking pie is that it doesn't have to be perfect. Once you take the pressure off yourself, it's amazing what good things can happen. Also, don't be intimidated by the lattice crust. It's just pieces of pastry woven together, like a basket. If you go under instead of over, don't fret. You've made pie! I love how the bottom crust is folded over the lattice edges to give a rustic look. It also traps the juices, keeping all that loveliness inside the pie instead of on the bottom of your oven. I know that saskatoon berries don't grow everywhere (I'm so sad for you!), but blueberries or sweet cherries make adequate substitutions.

SERVES 6

LARGE BATCH PASTRY
5½ cups all-purpose flour
2 tsp salt
1 cup cold unsalted butter, cubed
1 cup cold shortening, cubed
1 large egg
1 Tbsp vinegar
Ice-cold water

FILLING
5 cups saskatoon berries, fresh or frozen
½ cup + 1 Tbsp granulated sugar
3 Tbsp cornstarch
2 Tbsp unsalted butter, cubed
1 large egg, beaten with 1 Tbsp water

❋ Preheat the oven to 350°F. Place the rack in the lower third of the oven. Line a baking sheet with aluminum foil to catch drippings.

❋ To make the pastry, place the flour and salt in a large bowl. Mix well. Add the cubes of butter and shortening and mix them in (I like to use my hands to mix the fat into the flour, but you can use a pastry blender) just until it looks like coarse oatmeal with some pea-sized bits remaining. Place the egg in a 2-cup measure and beat it with a fork. Beat in the vinegar and just enough ice-cold water to bring it to the 1-cup mark. Stir this into the flour mixture, just until the dough clings together. I like to use my hands for this part as well, but a wooden spoon would also work. Try not to overmix it.

❋ On a lightly floured surface, gather the dough into a ball and divide it into 6 evenly sized portions. Shape each portion into a disc and wrap tightly in plastic. Chill 2 of these discs for 1 hour. Freeze the other 4 in a resealable freezer bag for future use. The pastry keeps well in the freezer for up to 2 months.

❋ On a lightly floured surface, roll out 1 disc of pastry into a 12-inch circle, or thereabouts. Place it in the bottom of a 9-inch pie plate, with the pastry overhanging the edges of the pie plate.

❋ To make the filling, place the saskatoon berries in a large bowl and stir in the ½ cup sugar and the cornstarch until well combined. Pour the berry mixture into the bottom of the pie. Dot with the butter. On a lightly floured surface, roll out the pastry in another 12-inch circle for the top crust. Use a ruler to guide you when cutting the pastry into 6 wide, long strips to keep the edges straight. Save the 2 end pieces in case you need to do any patching. I like wide strips, but if you like a thinner look, feel free to cut thin strips of pastry. Weave the pastry strips, going over and

under, making sure they connect with the edges of the pie crust. Fold over the edges of the bottom crust, tucking in the lattice ends. This will help to trap the juices and give a rustic look.

❄ If you prefer a cleaner, tidier look, you can trim the overhanging pieces and crimp the edges with a fork. Brush the top of the pie with the egg wash. Sprinkle with the 1 Tbsp sugar. Place the pie on the prepared baking sheet and bake it for about 90 minutes, until it's golden brown and bubbling. Remove the pie from the oven and place it on a wire rack to cool.

❄ Serve the pie warm or at room temperature with whipped cream or vanilla ice cream. This keeps well if covered with plastic and refrigerated for up to 4 days.

Rustic Peach Tart with Dulce de Leche

Peaches taste like summer, and sometimes in summer you don't want all the fuss and drama of pie, but you do want all of those flavours at the end of your fork. Enter the rustic tart. All you do is slice some peaches, toss them with a little sugar and cinnamon, and gently fold them in some pastry in a free-form, unfussy way. You'll want to hang out in the kitchen as the tart bakes, because the smell wafting from your oven is a thing of beauty. You'll eat the first slice while it's too hot and likely burn your tongue, because patience was never your virtue. The second slice is best served with ice cream on the front porch just as the stars begin to pop out of the night sky.

SERVES 4–6

PASTRY
2¾ cups all-purpose flour
½ cup cold butter, cubed
½ cup cold shortening, cubed
1 tsp salt
2 tsp vinegar
1 large egg yolk, cold and slightly beaten

FILLING
4 large peaches, each one peeled and sliced into 8
2 Tbsp granulated sugar
1 Tbsp all-purpose flour
1 tsp ground cinnamon
2 Tbsp dulce de leche (see note)
1 tsp salted butter, softened

❋ To make the pastry, in the bowl of a food processor fitted with the steel blade, place the flour, butter, shortening and salt. Pulse until the dough is crumbly. Place the vinegar and egg yolk in a ½-cup measure and enough cold water to fill. With the food processor running, add the liquid to the flour mixture. Then add a teaspoon or so more cold water. The dough should come together and be soft, not crumbly at all.

❋ On a floured surface, divide the dough into 3 evenly sized portions and form each into a disc. Wrap each tightly in plastic. Chill 1 disc in the refrigerator for an hour. Freeze the other 2 in a resealable freezer bag for future use. The pastry keeps well in the freezer for up to 2 months.

❋ Alternatively, you can leave the dough in the refrigerator overnight. If you do that, remove it from the refrigerator 30 minutes before you want to roll it out.

❋ Preheat the oven to 350°F. Place the rack in the centre of the oven. Line a rimmed baking sheet with parchment paper.

❋ Place the peaches, sugar, flour and cinnamon in a medium bowl and stir gently to combine. On a lightly floured surface, roll out 1 disc of dough, as you would for a pie, into a 12-inch circle. Place the pastry on the prepared baking sheet. Place the filling in the centre of the pastry, spreading it out, but leaving a 2-inch border around the edges. Gently fold the sides over the edge of the peaches. Melt the dulce de leche and butter in a small saucepan over medium heat. Pour this evenly over the peaches. Bake for 30–35 minutes, until the crust is golden and the peaches are fragrant. Remove the tart from the oven and cool on the baking sheet on a wire rack.

❋ Serve warm, with ice cream. Any leftovers can be covered with plastic wrap and refrigerated for up to 4 days.

NOTES

Dulce de leche can be found in the jam and jelly spreads section of the supermarket. Once you have a jar in the refrigerator, you'll use it in lots of ways. And it keeps for a decent length of time as well.

Substitute nectarines, apricots, plums or apples for the peaches.

Raspberry and Dark Chocolate Ganache Tart

I'm fortunate to have not one, but two thriving raspberry patches in my backyard. On summer mornings I'm out there, picking some for my morning parfait with granola and yogurt. Often I'll pad out barefoot, because I love the feel of the dewy grass under my feet. I'll check them later in the evening, just as the sun is thinking about going down, and grab a few (still warm from the sun) for a bedtime snack. With copious berries on hand, I freeze many to use during winter, when I need a reminder that the weather will get better. I also turn the fresh, juicy raspberries into delicious desserts, like this tart. Raspberries and chocolate are gorgeous together, but you already know that. This tart has it all going on—a buttery, flaky crust, a truffle-like filling and fresh, juicy berries. It's a looker, too. You should also know it makes a dandy breakfast with good, strong coffee to accompany it.

CRUST
1½ cups all-purpose flour
½ cup + 3 Tbsp cold butter, cubed
3 Tbsp icing sugar
2 large egg yolks, cold
1 Tbsp vinegar
1 Tbsp + 2 tsp ice-cold water

FILLING
1 cup whipping cream
2 cups chopped (½-inch pieces) dark chocolate
1 Tbsp Kahlúa liqueur or strong coffee
1 tsp pure vanilla extract
4 cups fresh raspberries, lightly rinsed and laid
  to dry on a tea towel
3 Tbsp seedless raspberry jam
Sweetened whipped cream, for garnish

❋ To make the crust, combine the flour, butter and icing sugar in a food processor fitted with the steel blade and pulse until crumbly. In a small bowl, beat the egg yolks with the vinegar and water. With the food processor running, add this to the flour mixture to make a soft dough. Dump the dough onto a lightly floured surface. Shape it into a disc, wrap it in plastic and chill for 30 minutes. Roll out the dough and place it in a 9-inch tart pan with a removable bottom. Trim the edges. With a fork, poke a few holes in the bottom of the crust. Freeze, uncovered, for 20 minutes.

❋ Preheat the oven to 350°F. Place the rack in the centre of the oven. Bake the crust for 20–25 minutes, until golden brown. Let it cool completely on a wire rack.

❋ Meanwhile, make the filling. Heat the whipping cream in a heavy saucepan over medium-high heat until it comes to a boil. Remove the pan from the heat and add the chocolate. Let it stand for 3 minutes then stir until the chocolate is completely smooth. Add the Kahlúa and vanilla. Let it cool at room temperature for 15 minutes.

❋ Remove the cooled crust from the tart pan, place it on a platter and pour the chocolate filling into it. Refrigerate, uncovered, until firm, about 40 minutes, then top with the raspberries. In a small saucepan over medium-low heat, melt the raspberry jam with 1 Tbsp of water until it's smooth, then brush it over the berries. Chill for at least 1 hour.

❋ Remove the tart from the refrigerator 30 minutes before you wish to serve it. Slice it into wedges and serve with sweetened whipped cream. The tart keeps well in an airtight container in the refrigerator for up to 2 days.

Sour Cream Rhubarb Pie with Oatmeal Streusel

Rhubarb grows freely across many a backyard on the Canadian prairies. It's a hardy thing, able to withstand the deep freeze that locks us in for five months of the year, and it returns every spring like a trooper. I know that winter truly is over when I see the dark green leaves starting to unfurl from the ground. I usually give a little dance and text my friends "the 'barb is back!"—which isn't odd at all. Rhubarb is called the Pie Plant for a reason—it makes gorgeous pies. The tartness needs to be cut with sugar, and often other fruit, and here I subdued it even more with a good amount of sour cream. Pie really is best when it's shared. When I bake this one especially, I like to gather together some of my friends who I haven't seen all summer, and we sit in the shade of my tall, tall trees eating glorious pie and ice cream. What better way to spend a summer afternoon?

SERVES 6–8

PASTRY
1 disc of Rustic Peach Tart pastry
(page 162)

FILLING
2¾ cups chopped (½-inch
    pieces) fresh rhubarb
1 apple (any type), peeled,
    cored and diced
1 cup full-fat sour cream
¾ cup granulated sugar
2½ Tbsp all-purpose flour
1 tsp pure vanilla extract
Pinch of salt

STREUSEL
1 cup large-flake oats
½ cup packed brown sugar
⅓ cup all-purpose flour
⅓ cup salted butter, softened

❋ Roll out the pastry on a lightly floured surface, drape it over a 9-inch pie plate. Trim and flute the edges. Set aside at room temperature.

❋ Preheat the oven to 375°F. Place the rack in the centre of the oven. Line a baking sheet with aluminum foil.

❋ To make the filling, combine all the filling ingredients in a large bowl and pour them into the prepared pie shell. Place the pie on the baking sheet and bake for 30 minutes. While the pie is baking, combine the streusel ingredients in a large bowl. Remove the pie from the oven and sprinkle the streusel on top. Return the pie to the oven and bake for 25 minutes longer, until golden. Remove the pie from the baking sheet and let it cool completely on a wire rack before cutting into slices.

❋ Serve with vanilla ice cream. This keeps well covered with plastic in the refrigerator for up to 3 days.

NOTE

This pie is best made with fresh rhubarb rather than frozen.

Tarte Tatin

Legend has it that in 1898, one of the Tatin sisters who owned a hotel in France left apples cooking too long on the stove. They were ruined for pie, but she covered them in pastry anyway, baked them even longer and then turned the whole concoction upside down for a tart. Customers were overjoyed by this "mistake," and the rest is history. You'll need to plan a day or two ahead for this, as the apples work best if you peel them and let them dry out in the refrigerator. You'll also need a 10-inch cast iron skillet for the recipe. With just a few ingredients involved, the real measure of this dessert is in the technique. You've got this, but you must be brave! Flipping hot, caramelized apples upside down requires a bit of gumption, but the end result will be worth it. The apples are completely soaked with butter and caramel, rendering them almost toffee-like. Don't forget the vanilla ice cream, as it pools with the caramel of the apples and you'll want to use your fork to scrape up every last bit from your plate.

SERVES 6–8

10 Gala, Golden Delicious or Granny Smith apples, or a combination
1/3 cup salted butter, softened
2/3 cup granulated sugar
8 oz (½ pkg) pre-rolled frozen puff pastry,
    thawed in the refrigerator

※ Peel, core and quarter the apples. Place them, uncovered, in the refrigerator for 24–48 hours to dry out. Don't worry about the apples browning—this will help them not get too juicy when they bake.

※ Spread the butter on the bottom and sides of a well-seasoned 10-inch cast iron skillet with sides at least 2½ inches high. Sprinkle the sugar evenly over the butter on the bottom of the skillet. Arrange the apple slices in a flat, concentric circle, squishing them in and completely filling the skillet. Pack them in tightly—they'll shrink as they cook. Place the skillet over medium heat and cook for 30 minutes.

※ Preheat the oven to 375°F. Place the rack in the centre of the oven.

※ When the apples start releasing their juices around the 20-minute mark, begin basting them with the juices for the remaining 10 minutes. They should be a light caramel colour at this point. If they're caramelizing too much, turn down the heat. Place the skillet in the oven, bake for 10 minutes, and then increase the heat to 425°F while the tart is inside and bake for 5 more minutes.

※ Meanwhile, remove the puff pastry from the refrigerator and cut it into an 11-inch diameter circle. Remove the tart from the oven and carefully place the pastry on top of the apples, tucking it under the outer ring of apples. Bake for 18–20 minutes, until the pastry is golden. Remove the tart from the oven and let it cool for 5 minutes. Take a deep breath. Using oven mitts, place a large serving platter on top of the skillet and quickly flip the tart onto the platter. Let it hang out here, with the skillet sitting on top, for 1 minute before removing the skillet. If any apples remain in the skillet, pick them off with a fork and place them back in the tart.

※ Serve the tarte tatin warm, with vanilla ice cream or whipped cream. Any remaining slices can be wrapped in plastic and kept in the refrigerator for up to 2 days.

NOTES

Be sure to use a serving platter larger than the skillet when flipping the tart over.

Cold leftovers are delicious with Homemade Ricotta (page 48).

Plum and Nectarine Hazelnut Galette

I like to make this dessert just as summer is fading and fall is waiting in the wings. It's a photogenic, rustic tart that reminds me of fallen leaves—and it tastes as good as it looks. The not-too-sweet stone fruits bake into jammy goodness, and the hazelnuts offer a nice textural contrast. I love this whole wheat pastry because I figure I'm getting more fibre, hence this tart is essentially health food. You're with me, right? *Galette* is just another word for rustic tart, but it sounds all fancy-pants. Nothing could be simpler, though. Just roll, sprinkle, fill, fold and bake. If a little juice escapes, all the better. It's rustic, remember.

WHOLE WHEAT PASTRY
1½ cups all-purpose flour
¾ cup whole wheat flour
1½ tsp salt
½ cup cold butter, cubed
1 large egg, cold
¼–½ cup ice-cold water
1 Tbsp white vinegar

FILLING
5 ripe prune plums, pitted and sliced
(skin on or off—your choice)

5 ripe nectarines, pitted and sliced
(skin on or off—your choice)
⅓ cup + ¼ cup + 1 Tbsp granulated
sugar, divided
1 tsp pure vanilla extract
¼ cup ground hazelnuts
3 Tbsp all-purpose flour
1 tsp ground cinnamon
½ tsp ground cardamom
½ tsp salt
3 Tbsp unsalted butter, softened

❋ To make the pastry, combine the all-purpose flour, whole wheat flour and salt in a large mixing bowl. Cut in the cold butter with a pastry blender so that only pea-size amounts of butter remain. Beat the egg, ¼ cup ice water and vinegar together in a small bowl. Pour this over the dry ingredients and stir together until it forms a dough. I like to use my hands, but a wooden spoon would also work. If it's too dry, gradually add more ice water, 1 tsp at a time. Dump the dough on a lightly floured surface and shape it into a disc. Wrap it in plastic and refrigerate for at least 1 hour.

❋ Preheat the oven to 375°F. Place the rack in the centre of the oven. Line a baking sheet with parchment paper.

❋ To make the filling, stir together the fruit, ⅓ cup of the sugar and vanilla in a large bowl. Let this stand for 5 minutes. In a small bowl, stir together the ground hazelnuts, ¼ cup of the sugar, flour, spices and salt.

❋ If your pastry has chilled for longer than 1 hour, let it sit at room temperature for a few minutes before you try to roll it.

❋ On a lightly floured surface, roll out the pastry into a circle about 12 inches in diameter and about ⅛ inch thick. Carefully move this onto the prepared baking sheet. Sprinkle the hazelnut mixture on the surface, leaving a 2-inch border. Dump the fruit in the centre, carefully moving it out to the edges, keeping the 2-inch border intact. Fold the dough over the edge of the fruit—not all of the fruit will be covered with pastry—and dot with butter. Sprinkle the remaining 1 Tbsp sugar over the crust, avoiding the fruit.

❋ Bake for 50–60 minutes, rotating the pan 180 degrees halfway through, until the crust is golden and the fruit is tender (test it with a knife). Remove the tart from the oven and let it cool on the baking sheet on a wire rack before slicing.

❋ Serve with vanilla ice cream or whipped cream. Any remaining slices can be wrapped in plastic or put in an airtight container and stored in the refrigerator for up to 3 days.

Flapper Pie

What an odd name for a pie, you're probably thinking to yourself. Essentially, a creamy custard is poured into a graham cracker crust and a lid of meringue is carefully swooped on top. After a brief visit to the oven, the pie emerges with beautiful, browned meringue and you feel all proud of yourself for building something so pretty. It's a prairie classic, this pie, with origins that go back to the 1920s—that's where the flapper part comes in. Flapper pie was served in every café that graced small, Canadian prairie towns. I imagine customers sitting at the counters of these cafés, savouring a slice with a good cup of coffee, talking about the weather, with little bits and bobs of gossip thrown in for good measure. Flapper pie is also known as the forgotten prairie pie. Already popular before the Depression, it became particularly popular during those hard years when a few, simple, precious ingredients found in most kitchens could be turned into something delicious. This pie has a loyal following among those who have tried it and loved it. One of my mom's favourites, she made this often when we were kids, but I was a weirdo who didn't like meringue and would scoop it off just to get to the custard and crust. I've matured (a little) since then, and now find the whole thing perfectly dreamy. This pie is economical, fairly simple to prepare, and with a shot of whiskey in the filling, I think those who loved it so long ago would love it even more now.

SERVES 6–8

CRUST
2 cups graham cracker crumbs
¼ cup + 2 Tbsp melted unsalted butter
3 Tbsp granulated sugar
Pinch of cinnamon (optional)

MERINGUE
1 Tbsp cornstarch
½ cup + 2 Tbsp granulated sugar
¾ tsp cream of tartar
5 large egg whites, at room temperature
1 tsp vanilla bean paste or pure vanilla extract
Pinch of salt

VANILLA CUSTARD
½ cup + 2 Tbsp granulated sugar
¼ cup cornstarch
¼ tsp salt
5 large egg yolks, at room temperature
2½ cups whole milk
¼ cup whipping cream
2 Tbsp unsalted butter, softened
1 Tbsp rye whiskey, bourbon, brandy or rum
1 tsp vanilla bean paste or pure vanilla extract

❊ Preheat the oven to 325°F. Place the rack in the centre of the oven.

❊ To make the crust, stir together the graham cracker crumbs, melted butter and sugar in a medium bowl. Add some cinnamon too, if you like. The mixture should hold its shape when you squeeze it in your hand. If it doesn't, add a little bit of water, 1 tsp at a time, until it does. Press the crumbs into the bottom and up the sides of a 9-inch pie plate, reserving 1 Tbsp of crumbs for garnishing the pie. Bake for 15 minutes, until the crust is lightly browned and smells nutty. Remove it from the oven and let it cool on a wire rack.

❊ While the crust is baking, make the meringue. Whisk the cornstarch with ⅓ cup water in a small saucepan over medium heat. Bring it to a simmer, whisking constantly. When it's thick and translucent, remove the pan from the heat. Stir together all the sugar and cream of tartar in a small bowl. In a stand mixer fitted with a whisk attachment, beat the egg whites, vanilla and salt on medium speed until the whites are frothy. Increase the speed to medium-high and gradually beat in the sugar mixture 1 Tbsp at a time until soft peaks form. With the mixer still running on medium-high speed, add the cornstarch slurry 1 Tbsp at a time until stiff, shiny peaks form. Stop the mixer,

scrape down the sides and stick a finger into the meringue. If you don't feel any sugar crystals when you rub your fingers together, the meringue is finished. Set it aside at room temperature while you make your filling.

❄ To make the vanilla custard, whisk the sugar, cornstarch and salt together in a medium saucepan. The pan is still off the heat at this point. Whisk in the yolks, then gradually whisk in the milk and cream. You may need to use a plastic spatula to scrape the edges of the pan so that everything gets fully whisked. Place the saucepan over medium heat and cook for 8-10 minutes, whisking constantly, until it's thick. Be sure the custard simmers for at least 2 minutes—this will cook the cornstarch out. If cornstarch isn't cooked long enough in a custard, the custard will have a starchy taste. Remove the pan from the heat and stir in the butter, whiskey and vanilla. Pour the hot filling into the cooled crust.

❄ Immediately spread the meringue on top of the filling, being sure to push it right up against the edge of the crust so it is attached and won't shrink away while it bakes. Use the back of a soup spoon to create lovely peaks and swoops. Sprinkle the reserved 1 Tbsp of graham crumbs on top. Bake the pie until the meringue is golden brown, 18-20 minutes. Remove the pie from the oven and let it cool on a wire rack until it's at room temperature. Refrigerate, uncovered, for 4 hours before serving. This will set the custard. Slice and serve.

❄ Flapper pie is best eaten the day it's made, but if there are leftovers, cover the pie with plastic and store it in the refrigerator for up to 1 day.

NOTES

There's no need to beat the meringue a second time before you spread it on the filling.

The vanilla custard is great on its own as a pudding, or piped into éclairs (page 218). Store the custard in an airtight container in the refrigerator for up to 4 days.

Goodbye. Goodbye. Take care of yourself. You too. I'll miss you. I'll miss you. I'll write you. You better. Okay. Okay. Bye. Bye.

GILBERT AND THE PEAR

The first summer I worked in Yukon, the chef for the guests was named Gilbert. He was French-from-France, which automatically made him charming, handsome and incredibly talented. I fell in love with him immediately. We worked side by side for almost four months, developing a friendship and nothing more. (Unrequited love is, unfortunately, a general theme in my life.) I loved hearing his stories of growing up in southern France, and he enjoyed my tales of my prairie upbringing. He was an amazingly talented chef, and I still have a little notebook full of tips he passed on to me. As a young cook, this was my first foray into working with someone of his calibre.

We had a great time in that kitchen, playing music and telling jokes and not quite believing our luck that we were doing what we loved in such a spectacular part of the world. We were quite lucky in that the owners of the lodge wanted both staff and guests to eat very well over the summer, so we had lots of great ingredients to work with. Fruit, though, mainly consisted of apples and oranges, and it wasn't too often that anything more exotic came in with our grocery order. You've probably noticed by now how much I adore fresh fruit, so this whole living on apples and oranges wasn't quite my jam, as it were. Then, one day, as I came back into the kitchen after having a break, I saw it resting on my cutting board. A perfect, ripe pear. The groceries had come in while I'd been napping and Gilbert had left that piece of fruit for me, as he knew how much I was craving something different. It was the best pear I've ever eaten.

As the season wound down, we knew we were going to have to say goodbye. That final day, Gilbert and I, and a few others, ended up taking a bumpy, seemingly endless cargo van ride back to Whitehorse, where we ate too many chicken wings and drank too much beer. Being back in civilization after four months of isolation makes you go a little nuts. You want to eat all the things and drink all the things, and talk to strangers, and well, it was a great party. The next day, Gilbert and I said goodbye to our friends and flew to Vancouver for that dreaded moment at the airport when you have to say goodbye to someone you know you're never going to see again, and yet care for so very much. You memorize the scar they have over their left eyebrow, and how the light catches the flecks of gold in their eyes. You stare at each other, just to memorize how they look because you don't want to forget it. Ever. Going in for that last hug, you inhale the smell of their neck and silently say all the things you wish you were brave enough to say out loud. Then it's over. Goodbye. Goodbye. Take care of yourself. You too. I'll miss you. I'll miss you. I'll write you. You better. Okay. Okay. Bye. Bye.

I never saw Gilbert again. We exchanged a few letters after that summer, but he never went back to Yukon while I worked there. But I could still feel his presence in that kitchen. And whenever a case of pears came in with the groceries, I would think of him, wishing we'd had more time together. And that is why whenever I eat a pear, I think of Gilbert.

Pear Custard Pie with Star Anise

This is an old-fashioned pie that satisfies my old-soul self. I first tasted pear pie when Great-Aunt Rose (Aunt Helen's sister) brought one to dinner when I was living in Edmonton. "What sweet genius is this?" I asked her. "It's pear pie!" she said. Fair enough. Years later in Yukon, I would replicate that pie, and my boss Anita told me one day after dinner that it was her favourite dessert of mine that she's ever tasted. "What sweet genius is this?" she asked me. "It's pear pie!" I told her. Pears whisper their flavour, rather than shout it from the rooftops. They are the underdogs of the fruit world, and I kind of love them for that. When they're turned into a pie, with a simple custard filling, you too will wonder what sweet genius this is. I love how the bit of star anise in the centre shoots its wonderful flavour out towards the rest of the pie. It's a subtle touch, but one that would be missed if it was omitted.

SERVES 6

1 disc of Large Batch Pastry dough (page 158)
4 large, ripe pears (I like Bartlett for this)
¾ cup granulated sugar
¼ cup all-purpose flour
2 large eggs, at room temperature
¼ cup melted unsalted butter
1 tsp pure vanilla extract
Pinch of salt
1 piece whole star anise

❋ Preheat the oven to 375°F. Place the rack in the lower third of the oven.

❋ Roll the pastry out on a lightly floured surface until it's about 12 inches in diameter. Place it in the bottom of a 9-inch pie plate. Trim and flute the edges. Peel and core the pears. Slice them into quarters, then slice each quarter into thirds. Arrange the pear slices in a circle, in 2 layers. Both layers of pears should go in the same direction. Whisk together the sugar, flour, eggs, melted butter, vanilla and salt in a medium bowl. Pour this evenly over the pears. Nestle the piece of star anise in the centre. Bake for 20 minutes, then turn down the heat to 350°F and bake for another 20-25 minutes, until the pie is golden and set in the middle. Remove the pie from the oven and place it on a wire rack to cool for at least 1 hour before serving.

❋ Serve the pie with whipped cream. Any leftovers can be wrapped in plastic and kept refrigerated for up to 4 days.

Key Lime Pie with Chocolate Cookie Crust

I love it when citrus season rolls around in late winter. Blood oranges, Meyer lemons and key limes always find their way into my shopping basket. While I eat the oranges for breakfast and turn the lemons into curd, it seems that key limes are destined only for pie in my world. Smaller, with a stronger, punchier flavour than its cousin the Persian lime, which we commonly see in grocery stores, the key lime has an herbal assertiveness that loves to be tamed by cream and sugar. The main ingredient in the filling is sweetened condensed milk, which I'm certain is the nectar of the gods. The cream cheese and sour cream provide a bit of body, the whipping cream adds richness and the key lime juice adds the famous tartness it is known for. This is not a complicated pie—the only thing baked is the crust, and then for just eight minutes. The most difficult part of the process is waiting at least six hours to serve it. I did not slather the pie with whipped cream as some folks do. I know, someone check my forehead for a fever. I just figure it's creamy enough, and I like how the sharpness of the citrus battles with the chocolate in the crust.

SERVES 8

CHOCOLATE COOKIE CRUST
2 cups chocolate cookie crumbs
¼ cup + 2 Tbsp unsalted butter, melted and
   cooled to room temperature
3 Tbsp granulated sugar

KEY LIME FILLING
¾ cup full-fat cream cheese, softened
2 Tbsp granulated sugar
1 (10 oz) can sweetened condensed milk
½ cup whipping cream
½ cup fresh key lime juice (about 15 key limes)
⅓ cup full-fat sour cream
1 Tbsp grated lime zest
Lime slices, for garnish

❋ Preheat the oven to 375°F. Place the rack in the lower third of the oven.

❋ To make the chocolate cookie crust, stir together the cookie crumbs, melted butter and sugar in a medium bowl. They should hold together in a clump when you press them in your fist. If they don't, add about 1 Tbsp of water at a time until they do. Press the crumbs into the bottom and up the sides of a 9-inch pie plate. Bake for 8–10 minutes, until the crust is dry and fragrant. Remove the crust from the oven and let it cool completely on a wire rack.

❋ To make the filling, in a stand mixer fitted with a paddle attachment, beat together the cream cheese and sugar until smooth, about 1 minute, scraping down the bottom and sides of the bowl. Add the condensed milk, whipping cream, lime juice, sour cream and zest. Beat on medium-high speed for about 3 minutes, scraping down the bottom and sides of the bowl. The mixture will be smooth and creamy. Pour it into the prepared cookie crust, smoothing the top. Refrigerate, uncovered, for at least 6 hours before serving. Garnish with lime slices.

❋ Key lime pie is best eaten the day it's made, but leftovers will keep well in the refrigerator for up to 1 day if covered with plastic.

NOTES

Feel free to substitute graham cracker crumbs or crushed ginger cookies for the chocolate cookie crumbs, though the flavour will obviously be different.

If you're unable to find key limes, Persian limes will also work well. Seeing as Persian limes are larger, you'll require fewer of them to yield ½ cup of juice for this pie.

CIRCLE OF FRIENDS

God love them, they couldn't handle me being so sad and had decided to do something about it. Oh, to be so lucky to have friends like this in your life.

On a late fall evening in 1994, I climbed up the stairs to my apartment after a long day of art classes and a 6:00 p.m. tai chi class I had talked myself into going to, even though it was terribly tempting to skip it. That fall I didn't really feel like doing anything. My first real heartbreak in early September had left me gutted and sad, and frankly not very inspired to do very much. A late bloomer to this whole love business, I now had to figure out how to deal with the empty space once occupied by a friend and a lover. My go-to karaoke song became "Nothing Compares 2 U" (now there's a visual) and I self-soothed by slinking down in dark theatres, watching foreign language films and nibbling on chocolate croissants that I'd sneaked in. I was in Montreal, remember. The land of the best carbs ever. I read a lot of E.E. Cummings and a lot of Carol Shields and eventually turned this pain into some pretty good art projects.

But on that late October night, all I wanted to do after I climbed those stairs was have a hot bath and go to bed, likely after a good cry. My friends, those sneaky, beautiful creatures, had other plans for me, though. I walked into the kitchen, turned on the light and there were five of my closest friends yelling "Surprise!" at me. Being the sensitive sort, I broke down into an ugly cry as they brought me into a group hug. God love them,

they couldn't handle me being so sad and had decided to do something about it. Oh, to be so lucky to have friends like this in your life. Friends who will say, "Cheer up, kid. There's a better man out there for you." And they were right. After we wiped away tears, there was tea and chocolate marshmallow pie, which my roommate and dear friend Josée had baked up for the occasion. We tucked into thick slices of rich and creamy chocolate love, and they made me laugh with their stories and jokes. I was blessed to be surrounded by such kindness. I also learned some valuable lessons that night: 1) Having good friends willing to hide in the dark so they can jump out and shower you with love is one of the best things. Ever. 2) Never underestimate the power of pie as a cure for heartache. 3) Sometimes you just have to get on with letting go.

Stephen King once wrote, "Writers remember everything . . . especially the hurts. Strip a writer to the buff, point to the scars, and he'll tell you the story of each small one." Dang, ain't that the truth. While those hurts occupy a corner of my memory, almost like it was yesterday, so do the kind hearts who lifted me up when I was down, stroked my back and said, "Renée, everything is going to be okay."

Chocolate Marshmallow Pie

Where to begin when describing this pie? For obvious, sentimental reasons (see previous page), it's one of my favourite recipes in this cookbook. Like all good chocolate cream pies, it is lusciously creamy and full of rich chocolate flavour. The best part is that it tastes like you put way more effort into it than you actually did. If you want to impress a loved one with your mad baking skills, or if you need a quick dinner party dessert, this is your recipe. The most difficult thing you have to do is blind-bake a pie crust and melt some marshmallows. Oh, and whip some cream. If you want to use a frozen premade pie crust, I won't judge. I'm just glad you're making pie! The filling has a wonderful texture that reminds me of chocolate mousse, but the marshmallows give it a bit of structure and depth, allowing it to hold its shape even the day after you make it. Thank you to Josée and her mom, Leonore, for sharing this recipe with me. I've carried it in my heart for all of these years and there's nothing quite like seeing it in print now.

SERVES 6

1 disc of Large Batch Pastry dough (page 158)
½ cup chopped (½-inch chunks) dark chocolate
2 Tbsp granulated sugar
¼ tsp salt
½ cup whole milk
20 large marshmallows (use a good brand)
1¾ cups whipping cream

❋ Preheat the oven to 425°F. Place the rack in the lower third of the oven.

❋ On a lightly floured surface, roll out the pastry into a 12-inch circle and place it in a 9-inch pie plate. Trim and flute the edges. Line the pie crust with aluminum foil or parchment paper, making sure it's snug against the edges but not overlapping the top of the pie, and fill it with pie weights or dry beans, being sure to push the beans up the sides. This prevents the sides from sagging and the bottom from puffing up as it bakes. Place the pie crust on a baking sheet and bake for 12–15 minutes, until the fluted edges of the crust are beginning to turn golden. Remove the pie crust from the oven. Remove the foil and weights. Return the pie crust to the oven (it's still on the baking sheet) and bake for another 8–9 minutes, until the bottom looks lightly golden and dry. Remove the pie crust from oven and take it off the baking sheet. Let it cool completely on a wire rack before filling.

❋ To make the filling, melt the chocolate, sugar and salt in a large saucepan or Dutch oven over medium-low heat until smooth, stirring constantly. Stir in the milk and marshmallows, and increase the heat to medium. Stir the mixture constantly, until the marshmallows have completely melted. This does take some time, about 10 minutes, so be patient. Remove the pan from the heat and let the mixture cool to room temperature. In a stand mixer fitted with a whisk attachment, beat the whipping cream until stiff peaks form. Gently fold the cream into the cooled marshmallow mixture until no white streaks remain. Scrape the chocolate marshmallow filling into the prepared pie crust. The back of a spoon is great for making it look all swoopy and pretty. Refrigerate the pie, uncovered, for 1 hour before serving.

❋ This pie is best eaten the day you make it, but it can be covered with plastic wrap and refrigerated for up to 1 day.

RECIPES

CUSTARDS
AND
PUDDINGS

Sticky Toffee Pudding with Molasses Sauce

Sticky toffee pudding is really just a moist date cake with an incredible toffee sauce. Using molasses creates an exquisite, earthy, creamy sauce I want to pretty much pour over everything, or even to take a spoon to while the refrigerator door hangs open. If you don't like dates, don't give up on this recipe. You won't even really notice them. Promise. You'll be too busy drooling over the sauce. This is my version of one of my favourite recipes from Cinda Chavich's most wonderful cookbook *High Plains*.

SERVES 8

PUDDING
2 cups finely chopped pitted Medjool dates
1¼ cups boiling water
¼ cup molasses
½ cup salted butter, softened, plus more for greasing the ramekins
1 cup packed brown sugar
1 large egg, at room temperature
1 tsp pure vanilla extract
1 cup all-purpose flour

1 tsp baking soda
1 tsp baking powder

MOLASSES SAUCE
1 cup packed brown sugar
¼ cup molasses
½ cup cold salted butter, cubed
2 cups whipping cream
Sweetened whipped cream, for garnish

✳ Preheat the oven to 350°F. Place the rack in the centre of the oven. Butter 8 ovenproof 1-cup (8 oz) ramekins or a 9-inch round ceramic baking dish.

✳ To make the puddings, place the chopped dates in a medium bowl and pour the boiling water over them. Stir in the molasses. Let the dates cool to lukewarm.

✳ In a stand mixer fitted with a paddle attachment, cream the butter until it's fluffy. Add the brown sugar and beat until well combined. In a small bowl, whisk together the egg and vanilla. In another bowl, mix the flour with the baking soda and baking powder. Add the flour mixture and the egg mixture alternately to the butter mixture, beginning and ending with the flour, and beating well after each addition. Stir the cool dates into the batter. Scrape the sides of the bowl well and then divide the batter evenly between the ramekins—they should be about two-thirds full—or pour it into the baking dish.

✳ Place the ramekins or baking dish on a baking sheet and bake for 20 minutes. Turn down the heat to 300°F and bake for another 30 minutes if using ramekins, or 45–50 minutes, or until a toothpick inserted in the centre comes out clean, if using a single baking dish. If the pudding is getting too dark around the edges, you can cover it with aluminum foil for the last 15 minutes.

✳ While the puddings bake, you can make the sauce. Place the brown sugar and molasses in a saucepan and bring to a boil over medium-high heat, stirring constantly. Boil for 1 minute, then whisk in the butter, a few cubes a time. Add the cream and boil over medium-high heat until the sauce is reduced, slightly thickened and deep in colour, 8–10 minutes. The sauce will thicken as it cools. You should have 2 cups of sauce.

✳ Remove the puddings from the oven and carefully remove them from the baking sheet. Let them cool slightly on a wire rack. Run a sharp knife around the edge of each ramekin to loosen the puddings and invert them onto plates.

✳ Serve warm, garnished with the toffee sauce and sweetened whipped cream. Wrap the puddings well in plastic and keep them in the refrigerator for up to 5 days. The sauce keeps well in an airtight container for up to 2 weeks.

CRANBERRY CURD

Curd. Such an unfortunate word for such a glorious product. You're likely aware of lemon or lime curd, perhaps even blood orange curd, but cranberry curd is just as fantastic—maybe even more so because it is thicker, thanks to the high amount of pectin in cranberries, and has a lovely pink colour that the girly girl in me loves. And it tastes Amazing with a capital A.

Cranberries aren't just for Christmas. I like to buy bags of them when they're cheap around the holidays and keep them in my freezer for whenever my baking needs a little tartness. Making curd requires a few steps, so don't be intimidated by the straining and stirring. Once you stick a spoon in the jar, you'll be hooked, I swear. I love layering cranberry curd in cakes (page 150) and trifles (page 214) and spreading it on scones (page 40), toast, waffles and pancakes. It's carb-friendly! Once you've made cranberry curd, you'll no doubt find ways to eat it—even if it's just straight out of the jar.

MAKES ABOUT 4 CUPS

3 cups fresh or frozen cranberries
¾ cup + 2 Tbsp granulated sugar
4 large eggs, at room temperature
4 large egg yolks, at room temperature
2 Tbsp fresh lemon juice
¼ tsp salt
½ cup unsalted butter, softened and cubed

※ Place the cranberries in a medium saucepan with ½ cup water over medium heat. Stir until they're popped and mushy, about 5 minutes. Press this mixture through a fine mesh sieve over a medium bowl. Using the back of a spatula works well for pressing down on them. Cool the cranberry purée to room temperature. Discard all of the pulpy bits. Add the sugar, eggs, yolks, lemon juice and salt to the bowl with the cranberry purée. Stir until smooth and even. Pour this mixture back into a clean medium saucepan over medium heat. Stir continuously until it thickens and coats the back of a spoon. When you run your finger across the spoon, the curd should not fall past the line—that's how you know it's thick enough. This takes 10-12 minutes.

※ Remove the saucepan from the heat and add the butter all at once, stirring well until it's smooth and all of the butter is melted. Pour the cranberry curd through a clean fine mesh sieve and into a clean bowl. This will remove any eggy bits. Let the cranberry curd come to room temperature before covering the top of the bowl with plastic wrap and chilling for at least 3 hours before using.

※ The cranberry curd keeps well for up to 1 week in an airtight container in the refrigerator, or can be frozen for up to 1 month.

DARK CHOCOLATE POTS DE CRÈME WITH ORANGE AND BRANDY

I like to whip these up on Valentine's Day. Whether you are in (or out) of love on VDay, you deserve chocolate. The fat content is out of this world, but this is the one day to indulge. And if you're single, calories don't count. True! These chocolate pots de crème were on regular dessert rotation when I was chef at Rutherford House in Edmonton years ago. They were a hit with staff (hi, Sonia!) and customers alike, and I had a hard time keeping them in stock. Good thing they only need about 20 minutes to prep and a day to chill, so whipping them up is no big deal. If you aren't a fan of the chocolate/orange combo (although the orange flavour is quietly pleasant, not all up in your face), then leave the zest out completely. I won't be offended. Chocolate pots de crème are luscious and oh-so-rich—thick and creamy with serious chocolate taste. The longer they chill the better the flavour, so prepare them a day or two before you want to serve them. It might sound crazy, but you do need the pillow of whipped cream on top to balance out the chocolate indulgence. If you let them sit at room temperature for 30 minutes before serving, they'll be softer and creamier. Don't feel bad if you can't eat all of one pot de crème in a sitting—it's seriously taken me three days to finish one. As with everything else in life, I'm just pacing myself.

MAKES 6–8 POTS DE CRÈME

1²/₃ cups whipping cream
1½ cups chopped (½-inch pieces) dark chocolate
3 large egg yolks, at room temperature
2 Tbsp brandy
1 Tbsp grated orange zest
3 Tbsp salted butter, softened
Sweetened whipped cream and orange peel,
    for garnish

✳ Heat the whipping cream in medium saucepan over medium-high heat until bubbles form along the edge of the pan. Don't stir while the cream is heating. Remove the pan from the heat and add the chocolate. Whisk until the chocolate is melted and smooth. Whisk in the egg yolks, brandy and orange zest. Stir in the butter, 1 Tbsp at a time, stirring well after each addition. Divide the mixture among 6 or 8 small ramekins or teacups. Cover and chill the ramekins for at least 8 hours or overnight.

✳ Before serving, let the pots de crème rest at room temperature for 30 minutes. Garnish with a dollop of whipped cream and a sliver or two of orange peel. Cover the tops of the pots de crème with plastic and they will keep well in the refrigerator for up to 5 days.

NOTE

If you don't want to add the brandy, add 1 tsp of pure vanilla extract instead.

Vanilla Panna Cotta with Strawberry-Lavender Compote

Panna cotta is literally *cooked cream* in Italian, and that's pretty much what we do to make this magical dessert, with gelatin powder being the secret ingredient. If you don't have any vanilla beans in your pantry, a drop or two of pure vanilla extract will be fine—you just won't get those pretty black dots in your pudding. The extra beauty of this dessert is that you can prepare it way in advance. Hello, perfect party dessert.

Let's talk about the compote for a moment: I adore baking with lavender because it adds such a lovely floral dimension to desserts. One spoonful of this compote and you'll know what all the fuss is about. It's a little tangy, a little sweet, with bursting strawberry flavour and just a whisper of lavender. This is lovely to serve in spring and summer, when strawberries are at their finest and it's too hot to turn the oven on.

PANNA COTTA
2½ tsp unflavoured powdered gelatin (1 pkg)
1¼ cups whipping cream
⅓ cup + 1 Tbsp granulated sugar
¼ tsp salt
1 vanilla bean, halved lengthwise
1¼ cups buttermilk
1 cup full-fat sour cream

STRAWBERRY-LAVENDER COMPOTE
2 cups sliced fresh strawberries, divided
½ cup granulated sugar
1 Tbsp fresh lemon juice
1 tsp dried culinary lavender
Pinch of salt

❈ To make the panna cotta, place ¼ cup cold water in a small bowl and sprinkle the gelatin overtop. Let it stand for 10 minutes. Meanwhile, heat the cream, sugar and salt in a medium saucepan over medium-high heat. Scrape in the vanilla bean seeds and then throw the whole pod in too. Bring the cream mixture just to a simmer, whisking occasionally. Add the gelatin and stir until it dissolves. Remove the pan from the heat and let it cool for 5 minutes. Remove the vanilla pod and whisk in the buttermilk and sour cream. Divide the cream mixture between 6-8 small serving dishes or jars and chill, uncovered, in the refrigerator until set, at least 4 hours.

❈ To make the compote, place 1 cup of the strawberries in a medium saucepan with the sugar, lemon juice, lavender and salt. Cook over medium-high heat until the berries start to break down, about 10 minutes, being sure to stir often. Turn down the heat to medium-low and continue cooking until the sauce coats the back of a spoon, 15-20 minutes, stirring occasionally. Take the back of your spoon and smoosh the berries, breaking them up even further. Add the remaining 1 cup of berries and cook for 5 minutes longer, stirring occasionally. Remove the pan from the heat and let cool completely.

❈ The compote will keep well in an airtight container in the refrigerator for up to 1 week.

❈ Once the panna cotta has set, top with the compote.

❈ The panna cotta can be made up to 5 days ahead. Cover it tightly with plastic wrap and refrigerate until needed.

The compote works well as a filling for Classic Vanilla Cake (page 150), spread on Buttermilk Scones (page 40) or scooped on top of Honey Bourbon Vanilla Ice Cream (page 296).

You can find culinary lavender in specialty ingredient shops. But if you omit it, the dessert will still be delicious–just not lavender-flavoured.

Butterscotch Pudding Parfaits with Maple Pumpkin Seed Brittle

Pudding is a big bowl of comfort. Just give me a spoon and I'm happy. Whenever I whip up a batch of pudding, I always ask myself why I don't do it more often. You guys. It's so easy! Sure, you could crack open a box of the stuff you find on store shelves, but this tastes so much better—and you know what goes in it. Super creamy and full of brown sugar whiskey goodness, you could easily be quite content eating the pudding as is, but layered with crunchy pieces of maple pumpkin seed brittle and sweetened whipped cream, it's even more delicious. Spoon the layers into your favourite glass dishes so everyone can marvel at just how pretty it is.

SERVES 6

BUTTERSCOTCH PUDDING
¼ cup unsalted butter
1 cup packed dark brown sugar
¾ tsp flaky or coarse salt
3 Tbsp cornstarch
2 cups whole milk, divided
4 large egg yolks, at room temperature
½ cup whipping cream
1 Tbsp whiskey (optional)
1 tsp pure vanilla extract

TO ASSEMBLE
1 cup whipping cream
2 Tbsp icing sugar
1 tsp pure vanilla extract
1 cup crumbled Maple Pumpkin Seed Brittle
(page 278)

❋ Melt the butter in a medium saucepan over medium heat. Add the brown sugar and salt, stirring until the sugar is well moistened and bubbles form around the edge of the pan. Remove the pan from the heat. In a small bowl, whisk together the cornstarch and ¼ cup of the milk until smooth, and then whisk in the egg yolks. Gradually pour the remaining milk and the cream into the melted brown sugar, whisking constantly, then whisk in the cornstarch mixture. Don't worry if some of the brown sugar hardens. It will melt as you continue whisking and the mixture warms up.

❋ Put the pan over medium-high heat and bring the mixture to a boil, whisking frequently. As soon as it begins to bubble, turn down the heat to low and cook for 2 minutes. Do not stop whisking! You want the consistency to be fairly thick, like hot fudge sauce. Remove the pan from the heat, stir in the whiskey (if using) and the vanilla. Pour the pudding into a serving dish. Let it cool for 5 minutes then place plastic wrap directly on top of the pudding. This will help prevent a '"skin" from forming on top of the pudding. Refrigerate for 4 hours.

❋ The butterscotch pudding can be served on its own. Covered with plastic wrap, it will keep refrigerated for up to 4 days.

❋ To transform the pudding into parfaits, beat the cream, icing sugar and vanilla together in a stand mixer fitted with a whisk attachment until stiff peaks form. In 4–6 serving dishes or glasses, layer butterscotch pudding, whipped cream and crumbled brittle, in that order. Repeat with a second layer, finishing with the brittle.

❋ The parfaits will keep for 1 day, covered with plastic wrap, in the refrigerator.

NOTES

If you're feeding little ones, omit the whiskey and just use 1 tsp of pure vanilla extract.

For a fantastic pie, pour hot butterscotch pudding into a baked pie shell (see Chocolate Marshmallow Pie, page 184) and let it set for 4 hours. Top with whipped cream and chocolate shavings.

Rhubarb Fool with Cardamom Cream

A fool is a classic British dessert consisting of pretty poached fruit and cream layers. For whatever reason, it always makes me think of Nigel Slater and Agatha Christie—two of my favourite Brits ever. All sorts of combinations and permutations of fool abound (look at me busting out the math lingo!) but it's best to use whatever fruit is in season. My rhubarb plant is terribly generous, so I like to simmer chunks of it with a little white wine and a vanilla bean. It's a grand way to usher in warmer weather. I could have used straight sweetened whipped cream, but I fancied it up by adding a little ground cardamom. With its good looks and stunning taste, this is a great recipe to have in your back pocket for summer entertaining.

SERVES 4–5

RHUBARB FOOL
3½ cups chopped (¾-inch pieces) fresh rhubarb
½ cup granulated sugar
½ cup white wine
1 vanilla bean, split lengthwise

CARDAMOM CREAM
¼ cup granulated sugar
1 tsp ground cardamom
1½ cups whipping cream
¼ cup full-fat sour cream
⅓ cup shelled and finely chopped pistachios, for garnish

※ To make the fool, place the rhubarb in a medium saucepan with the sugar and wine. Scrape in the seeds from the vanilla bean and then throw the pod in too. Bring to a boil over medium-high heat, then turn down the heat to low, simmering away for about 15 minutes, stirring occasionally, until the fruit is soft, but still holds it shape. Remove from the heat and let cool completely. Remove the vanilla bean pod and discard it.

※ To make the cream, in a stand mixer fitted with a whisk attachment, mix together the sugar and ground cardamom on low speed. Pour in the whipping cream. Beat on high speed until stiff peaks form. With the mixer running on low speed, slowly beat in the sour cream.

※ Layer the cooled fruit and cream in pretty glass cups/jars—you want to see the gorgeous layers. Spoon some fruit in first, then some cream, then more fruit and end with a layer of cream. Cover the fools with plastic wrap and let them chill at least 1 hour before serving. Garnish with chopped pistachios just before serving.

※ These will keep, covered with either plastic wrap or their lids if you are using jars, in the refrigerator for up to 5 days.

NOTES

This would make a lovely trifle, when layered with chunks of Classic Vanilla Cake (page 150).

Use the same volume of sliced strawberries, blueberries, raspberries, blackberries, cherries, peaches, nectarines, apricots or plums instead of the rhubarb in the compote. Reduce the amount of sugar to ¼ cup if you do so. Softer fruits will take less time to cook, so check those frequently after the first 5 minutes.

WILD RICE PUDDING WITH BROWN SUGAR BRÛLÉE

If you ever think rice pudding is boring, I'm here to tell you otherwise. This is grown-up, fancy-pants rice pudding. Nothing like the stuff served in hospitals or church basements. It uses short-grain arborio rice and wild rice, which provides a lovely chewiness not often found in rice puddings, and is baked in the oven with cream, milk, sugar, orange peel and cinnamon sticks. Whipping cream makes this pudding quite luxurious, and if that wasn't enough, the caramelized brown sugar crust really is the perfect finishing touch. Scented with citrus and spice, this is a dinner-party-worthy dessert. It is best served warm and goes ever so well with a cup of your favourite tea.

SERVES 6–8

2 cups half-and-half cream
2 cups whole milk
1 cup arborio rice
½ cup granulated sugar
1 Tbsp grated orange peel
2 tsp pure vanilla extract

½ tsp freshly grated or ground nutmeg
2 cinnamon sticks
⅓ cup wild rice
⅔ cup whipping cream
½ cup packed brown sugar

❋ Preheat the oven to 325°F. Place the rack in the centre of the oven. Butter a 10-inch square ceramic baking dish.

❋ Stir together the half-and-half, milk, arborio rice, sugar, orange peel, vanilla and nutmeg in a large bowl. Scrape this into the prepared baking dish. Nestle the 2 cinnamon sticks in the rice. Cover tightly with aluminum foil and bake for 1 hour.

❋ Meanwhile, place the wild rice in a small saucepan and cover with 2 cups of cold water. Cover, bring to a boil over high heat then turn down the heat to low and simmer for 45 minutes, until the rice is tender. Drain and set aside.

❋ Stir the wild rice into the rice pudding at the 1-hour mark and discard the foil. Bake, uncovered, for 15 minutes. Remove the baking dish from the oven and discard the cinnamon sticks. Stir in the whipping cream and return the dish to the oven for another 5 minutes, or until most of the liquid has reduced. You want the pudding to be creamy. Remove the dish from the oven and turn on the broiler.

❋ Sprinkle the brown sugar on top of the pudding and place the dish in the centre of the oven under the broiler until the sugar has almost completely melted. Turn off the heat and leave the pudding inside until the sugar is fully melted and darkened slightly, but be sure the sugar doesn't burn. Remove the dish from the oven and let the pudding cool on a wire rack.

❋ Serve warm. The pudding will keep well if covered with plastic and refrigerated for up to 2 days, but the brown sugar will likely melt. That's okay, though, it still tastes great.

NOTE

If you would like to make the rice pudding without the wild rice, increase the arborio rice to 1⅓ cups in total.

Baklava Parfaits

Baklava holds a special place in my heart. It reminds me of living in Montreal and stepping into the Greek bakeries on the Plateau. They smelled like honey and oregano and there was always a pastry case full of fragile phyllo delicacies. Plus, the Greek grandmas liked talking to me. They were impressed I was so tall and so far away from home. For a buck, I could get baklava oozing with honey and full of roasted nuts, which was pretty ideal for a kid with a huge sweet tooth on a budget. I'd get pieces for my roommates as well, and we'd tuck into them after dinner while we talked about our day. I've never made baklava like those Greek grandmas make, but this dessert combines the flavour of baklava with a rich mascarpone filling sweetened with honey. This is a great time to use glassware for dessert—it shows off the layers perfectly.

PHYLLO CRUMBLE
3 Tbsp unsalted butter, melted
1½ Tbsp liquid honey
½ tsp ground ginger
½ tsp ground cardamom
¼ tsp salt
4 sheets phyllo pastry, thawed

MASCARPONE FILLING
1 cup whipping cream
1 cup mascarpone cheese, softened
  (see my recipe on page 28)
1 cup plain Greek yogurt
¼ cup liquid honey, plus more for garnish
2 tsp grated orange zest
½ tsp ground cardamom
Pinch of salt
½ cup sliced almonds, toasted

✻ Preheat the oven to 325°F. Place the rack in the centre of the oven. Line a baking sheet with parchment paper.

✻ To make the crumble, whisk together the melted butter, honey, spices and salt. Place 4 sheets of phyllo pastry on the counter. Take one and place it on the prepared baking sheet. Brush it with the honey mixture. Place another phyllo sheet on top and brush it with the honey mixture. Repeat using the rest of the phyllo and the honey mixture. Bake for 9–12 minutes, until the pastry is golden and fragrant, rotating the baking sheet 180 degrees after 5 minutes. Remove the baking sheet from the oven and let it cool completely on a wire rack.

✻ Break the phyllo into small pieces. You might not use it all in this recipe, but it keeps well in an airtight container on the counter for up to 1 week.

✻ To make the filling, in a stand mixer fitted with a whisk attachment, beat the cream until stiff peaks form. In a medium bowl, stir together the mascarpone cheese, yogurt, honey, orange zest, cardamom and salt. Fold in the whipped cream. Scoop some of the cream mixture into the bottom of the serving dishes and top with a generous sprinkling of phyllo crumble and toasted almonds. Add another layer of cream and garnish each serving with phyllo crumble, toasted almonds and a good drizzle of honey.

✻ These parfaits are best enjoyed the day they are made, but any leftovers will keep for up to 1 day in the refrigerator—just be sure to cover them with plastic wrap.

NOTE

Substitute finely chopped pistachios or toasted walnuts for the sliced almonds.

Eton Mess with Chocolate Meringue and Red Wine Strawberry Sauce

Eton Mess is a traditional British dessert served at Eton College's annual cricket game against Harrow School. That being said, you don't need to be a preppy school boy or cricket champ to enjoy this delicious amalgamation of meringue, cream and strawberry sauce. This is one of those desserts that tastes fantastic and, because you'll be breaking the meringue into pieces, there's no pressure for it to be pretty and perfect. If cracks and imperfections appear while it bakes, no one will notice when it's in a pool of divine strawberry sauce and whipped cream. This is a great dessert for everyone to build their own at the dining table. Just place all of the components in separate bowls and get everyone to help themselves. If your family is like my family, you may want to double the whipped cream.

SERVES 6–8

CHOCOLATE MERINGUE
4 large egg whites, at room temperature
½ tsp cream of tartar
1 cup granulated sugar
1 Tbsp cornstarch
2 Tbsp unsweetened cocoa powder
1 tsp balsamic vinegar

RED WINE STRAWBERRY SAUCE
3 cups sliced, fresh strawberries
1 cup red wine
½ cup granulated sugar
Ground black pepper
1 cup whipping cream
1 Tbsp granulated sugar
1 tsp pure vanilla extract

❋ Preheat the oven to 325°F. Place the rack in the centre of the oven. Line a baking sheet with parchment paper.

❋ To make the meringue, in a stand mixer fitted with a whisk attachment, beat the egg whites on high speed until soft peaks form. Sprinkle in the cream of tartar and beat for 1 minute. Stir together the sugar and cornstarch in a small bowl. With the mixer running on medium speed, gradually add the sugar mixture, 1 Tbsp at a time. Increase the speed to high and beat until stiff and shiny peaks form, 4–5 minutes. Sift the cocoa over the whites and gently fold it in along with the balsamic vinegar.

❋ When the meringue is uniform, spread it into a 9-inch circle on the prepared baking sheet. Place it in the oven and then turn down the heat to 300°F. Bake for 50–60 minutes, until the edges are faintly golden and the top is set but has some spring to it. Turn the oven off and prop the door open with a wooden spoon. Let meringue stay inside until it's completely cool, 1–2 hours. Remove the meringue from the oven and break it into pieces.

❋ The meringue will keep in an airtight container at room temperature for up to 1 week.

❋ To make the sauce, combine the strawberries, red wine, sugar and a generous grinding of black pepper in a medium saucepan over medium-high heat. Bring to a boil, turn down the heat and simmer for 30–35 minutes, stirring occasionally, until the sauce is reduced and slightly thickened. Cool to room temperature before using.

❋ The sauce will keep in an airtight container in the refrigerator for up to 1 week.

❋ In a stand mixer fitted with a whisk attachment, beat the whipping cream, sugar and vanilla on high speed until stiff peaks form.

❋ To assemble the Eton Mess, layer pieces of chocolate meringue, spoonfuls of red wine strawberry sauce and whipped cream in individual dessert dishes.

LEAVING THE NEST

In the late spring of 1993, I received my acceptance letter from Concordia University in the mail. I remember opening it with trembling hands and feeling a lump in my throat. I told myself that I would be all right either way. This, of course, was a lie. I wanted this letter to be good news. Congratulations, it said. *I've done it*, I thought. *Holy crap* also came to mind. After squeals of joy, my sister and I jumped into my shiny red Ford Festiva (with a zipper on the side, no less) and drove over to where my mom was working. I had to tell her the good news in person, and the end of her work day seemed way too far away. Of course, she was happy for me, but once the joy had runneth over, reality soon set in. I was going to be moving across the country. Alone.

In the last few weeks leading up to my departure from Saskatoon, I starting writing in a small coil-bound notebook all of the recipes I would need to bring with me to Montreal. The very first recipe was Cheesecake Swirled Brownies, with not one but two happy faces scrawled beside it. Clearly, I had my priorities straight when it came to this moving away from home stuff. There were recipes for chocolate cake, chocolate sauce, peanut butter bars, coffee cake, chocolate chip cookies and more peanut butter bars (like I said, priorities). When the last week of August rolled around, this notebook was tucked away into my giant suitcase, along with a few other treasured belongings. I think I cried the whole way to the airport, then the whole time in the airport. I think I probably stopped crying somewhere over Brandon, Manitoba. For such a mama's girl, this giant leap into the rest of my life was incredibly difficult to make, and I don't know if I could have done it without the love and support of my dear mom. She let her little girl go, and for that I'll be forever grateful.

I was living with my dear friend Josée in Montreal, and soon our large, drafty third-floor apartment on the Plateau became home. Walls were painted blue and purple and second-hand furniture was brought up two flights of narrow, winding stairs. Dinner was made in our kitchen while Talking Heads and Ani DiFranco played on the CD player. We'd sit outside on our balcony, drinking wine bought from the dépanneur on the corner. This living away from home business was pretty good, but I still missed my mom like crazy. Every couple of months she would assemble a care package for me, filled with things like socks and tea, always a bit of baking and recipes for whatever had caught her eye lately—things like brownies, peanut butter pie and black-bottom banana bars (we share priorities), but also her recipes for white bread, baked spaghetti and hamburger soup. Comforting food, from afar. I would tape these recipes into that same coil-bound notebook, which was gradually filling up with my own recipe clippings from magazines and newspapers. But it was her letters I most looked forward to, written in the careful cursive that only moms seem to possess. Once she had dished the latest news of family and weather, of Dusty the dog's latest chewing destructions and what she was making for dinner, she would sign off with her usual *Love you, Mom* and a few hearts. I would then wipe away my tears and head to the kitchen to bake. It seemed like the right thing to do—the thing that would bring a little bit of my mom into my Montreal kitchen. Soon the smell of chocolate would waft around the apartment, and my roommates would put down their books and come out for tea and a bit of cake. Chocolate is the official cure for homesickness. I'm sure of it.

One time during these baking sessions, a fellow art student and new friend was over for tea and cake. She leafed through my notebook, which by now getting quite full of recipes, but also pages of doodles and drawings—things that would come about as I talked to my mom on the phone. She suggested that I should somehow turn these pages into an art project—something that would speak of food, family, friendships, love and home. I never followed through with that idea during my time at Concordia, but all these years later, I think I've finally done it.

Chocolate and Chili Hot Fudge Pudding Cake

I still have that coil-bound notebook (see previous page), and almost 25 years later, it's finally beginning to fall apart. Chocolate and butter-stained pages, which can be traced back to the beginning of my adulthood, are as much about the memories as the recipes. This pudding cake is one of the recipes my mom sent to me, but I've made a few changes to the original version. I reduced the sugar and swapped melted butter for oil, added a bit more salt and spiced things up with chili powder. That's right, chili powder. Just the little kick of heat at the end makes you think, *hmmmmm, something is happening here and I like it.* The assembly is quick and simple, making it something to throw together at the last minute if you need to. The real magic is in the hot water being poured overtop. It creates a rich and creamy pudding on the bottom, while a tender cake bakes above it. This is a comforting dessert that will always taste of home to me.

SERVES 6

1 cup all-purpose flour
½ cup granulated sugar
¼ cup + 2 Tbsp unsweetened cocoa powder
2 tsp baking powder
½ tsp salt
¼ tsp ground chipotle powder or hot chili powder

½ cup whole milk
2 Tbsp melted unsalted butter
1 tsp pure vanilla extract
¾ cup packed brown sugar
1¾ cups just-boiled water

❈ Preheat the oven to 350°F. Place the rack in the centre of the oven.

❈ Whisk together the flour, sugar, the 2 Tbsp cocoa powder, baking powder, salt and chili powder in a medium bowl. Stir in the milk, melted butter and vanilla until smooth. Scrape the batter into an ungreased 9-inch round ceramic baking dish. Stir together the brown sugar and the ¼ cup cocoa powder in a small bowl. Sprinkle this over the batter. Pour the hot water over it all. Do not stir. Bake for 35–40 minutes, until the top springs back when lightly touched and a toothpick inserted into the cake comes out clean.

❈ Serve warm, with whipped cream or vanilla ice cream. This keeps well in the refrigerator for up to 3 days when covered with plastic wrap.

BURNT CARAMEL AND EARL GREY CUSTARDS

This is a really, really good recipe for custard. And not just any custard. The custard of your dreams, or at least my dreams. "Luxurious" comes to mind. "Caloric" (but *carpe diem*) does too. Rich and supple, with a velvet finish, the infusion of Earl Grey tea and vanilla elevates the flavour.

This is a great make-ahead dish if you are throwing a party and want a dessert to impress your friends. You have to boil sugar and bake these with scalding hot water, though, so be careful, okay? Sugar and steam burns aren't fun. I know—I've had both. But really the hardest part about this recipe is letting it chill until you can take a spoon and slowly tuck into your little dish. I guarantee your eyes will roll back into your head.

SERVES 6–8

CUSTARD
4 cups whipping cream
1 Earl Grey tea bag
1 tsp vanilla bean paste or pure vanilla extract, or seeds and pod of a vanilla bean
1 cup granulated sugar, divided

CARAMEL
6 large egg yolks, at room temperature
½ tsp flaky salt, such as Maldon
Sweetened whipped cream, for garnish (optional)
Flaky salt, for garnish (optional)

❋ Preheat the oven to 300°F. Place the rack in the centre of the oven.

❋ Pour the whipping cream into a medium saucepan. Bring it to a boil over medium heat, then remove the pan from the heat. Stir in the Earl Grey tea bag and vanilla. Let the mixture steep for 7 minutes, then remove the tea bag, squeezing out the tea into the cream. Stir well. Don't start making the caramel until you've done this bit.

❋ Bring ¾ cup plus 2 Tbsp of the sugar and 2 Tbsp of water to a boil in a medium saucepan over medium-high heat, swirling to dissolve the sugar. Boil, occasionally swirling the pan, but not stirring, and brushing down the sides with a wet pastry brush, until the mixture is deep amber, 5–7 minutes. If the sugar seems to be dry on top and not melting, your heat isn't high enough. Increase the heat and use a spoon to stir the sugar around until it melts and caramelizes. Be sure to watch it carefully—you don't want to really burn it! Once the sugar is a deep amber colour, remove the pan from the heat. Slowly add the steeped cream to the hot caramel—it's going to bubble like crazy, so go gently. Put it back on medium heat and cook, stirring occasionally, until smooth, about 2 minutes. Whisk the egg yolks with the salt and the remaining 2 Tbsp sugar in a large bowl. Slowly pour in the caramel cream, whisking constantly. Start with just a few drops of the hot cream at a time, then gradually increase the amount.

❋ Divide the custard among eight 6 oz (¾ cup) (or thereabouts) ovenproof ramekins or cups. Place the ramekins in a large, shallow roasting dish and pour in cold water until it reaches halfway up the sides of the ramekins. Bake until the custards are set, but still slightly jiggly in the middle. This can take anywhere from 60 to 80 minutes, depending on the size of ramekin. It's taken 80 minutes when I used 8 oz (1 cup) ramekins and 60 minutes when I used 6 oz (¾ cup) ramekins. Use tongs to carefully remove the ramekins from the hot water and set them on a wire rack to cool. Once they're at room temperature, cover the custards with plastic wrap and chill them for at least 3 hours before serving.

❋ Garnish with whipped cream and flaky salt, if you wish. Keep the custards covered with plastic wrap in the refrigerator for up to 5 days.

Lemon Posset with Cinnamon and Bay Leaf

Posset. What a lovely word for a chilled dessert thickened with cream. Up until relatively recently, the term meant a warming drink rather than a chilled pudding—a medieval cup of cocoa, if you will. Lately, there's been a revival of sorts, and possets are now finding their place on more and more dessert menus. After testing this recipe, I can totally see why. In its essence, the posset is quite simple to prepare and holds up well in the refrigerator for up to five days—for those who love to plan ahead for parties, I was thinking about you. The dessert is quite lemony—there may have been a slight puckering of lips—but the background notes of ginger, bay leaf, cinnamon and clove add a touch of sophistication as well as flavour. Garnish the small dishes with some fresh berries and perhaps a crispy cookie on the side. Thanks to my dear friend Dan Clapson for sharing his recipe with me (and you!). He was the first person to show me the way to lemon posset land, and for that I am ever grateful.

SERVES 4–6

¾ cup granulated sugar
¾ cup lemon juice (about 3-4 lemons)
1 Tbsp grated lemon zest
1-inch piece fresh ginger, peeled
1 bay leaf

1 cinnamon stick
2 whole cloves
2¼ cups whipping cream
1 cup assorted fresh berries, for garnish

❊ In a medium saucepan, stir together the sugar, lemon juice, lemon zest, ginger, bay leaf, cinnamon stick and cloves. Bring the mixture to a simmer over medium-high heat. Once the sugar has dissolved, turn down the heat to low and let the mixture steep for 10 minutes. This will infuse the aromatics. Remove this lemon syrup from the heat and pour it through a fine mesh strainer into a large bowl. Discard the bay leaf, cinnamon stick and cloves.

❊ Place the whipping cream in a medium saucepan over medium-high heat and bring it just to a simmer. Turn down the heat to low and let it cook for 5 minutes, stirring regularly so it doesn't scald. Remove the cream from the heat and use a spoon to stir it into the lemon syrup until a custard-like consistency is achieved. Pour the custard into ramekins or cups (choose the size that works best for your guests), let them sit for 30 minutes at room temperature and then cover them with plastic wrap and refrigerate for at least 4 hours before serving. Garnish with fresh berries.

❊ The lemon possets can be covered with plastic wrap and refrigerated for up to 5 days.

A WORD ABOUT TRIFLES

Trifles are great for when things go awry in the kitchen.

I'll let you in on a little pastry chef secret. Trifles are great for when things go awry in the kitchen. Say you dropped a cake as you were carrying it from the oven to the counter, or maybe you forgot to set your timer and the edges of the cake got too dark. You know what? It happens to the very best of bakers. Instead of crying over the not-so-perfect-cake, cut off those burnt bits and, as long as the middle doesn't taste burnt, you have yourself some perfect trifle material. And don't ever throw away broken cake (unless it landed directly on the floor, ewwww)—it's perfect for trifle! Once it's layered in pretty glass jars with cream, pudding and fruit (and booze), no one will ever know.

But say there wasn't a kitchen mishap and you just want to serve trifle to your guests? Heck to the yes! Just layer bits of cake with spoonfuls of compote and cream, and store (covered) in the refrigerator for up to I day. I'm going to share with you some of my favourite trifle combinations here.

Pictured here is the Classic Vanilla Cake (page 150) with Sour Cherry Compote (page 42), Cranberry Curd (page 190), crumbled Classic Vanilla Cake and unsweetened whipped cream. If you like your trifles a little (or a lot) boozy, drizzle in some rum, brandy or your preferred libation on top of the cake layers to make things a little more indulgent.

OTHER POSSIBILITIES ARE:
* Classic Vanilla Cake (page 150) + Blueberry Ginger Compote (page 32) + Farmstand Cream (page 42)
* Classic Vanilla Cake (page 150) + Red Wine Strawberry Sauce (page 204) + Cranberry Curd (page 190) + unsweetened whipped cream
* Angel Food Cake (page 126) + Roasted Stone Fruit (page 30) + unsweetened whipped cream
* Angel Food Cake (page 126) + Strawberry Rhubarb Compote (page 26) + unsweetened whipped cream
* Chocolate Cake (page 144) + Sour Cherry Compote (page 42) + unsweetened whipped cream
* Chocolate Cake (page 144) + Butterscotch Pudding (page 196) + Maple Pumpkin Seed Brittle (page 278) + unsweetened whipped cream

Recipes

PASTRIES

Raspberry- and Cream-Filled Éclairs with Chocolate Glaze

This recipe is for my young friend Bram, who also happens to be the firstborn of my oldest friend, Josée. I visited them in Toronto one summer, when Bram was eight or nine. A food lover in his own right, I was impressed with his passion for and knowledge of all things food-related. He's my kind of kid. As you do when you're on summer vacation, Bram and I made fancy French pastries together. I stirred the choux paste and he whipped the cream. Assembly was a team effort, and when the rest of the family came home, we fed them éclairs and they told us we were awesome.

There is definitely technique involved when working with choux paste, but the end result is so worth it and it's easier than you might think. If you look carefully, you'll see that three recipes in this chapter use it, so just in case you were wondering, yes, choux paste is one of my most favourite things.

MAKES 18–20 ÉCLAIRS

ÉCLAIRS	CREAM FILLING	CHOCOLATE GLAZE
½ cup whole milk	2 cups whipping cream	⅔ cup finely chopped
½ cup water	1 Tbsp granulated sugar	(chocolate chip-sized pieces)
¼ cup + 2 Tbsp unsalted butter	1 tsp vanilla bean paste or pure	dark chocolate
1 Tbsp granulated sugar	vanilla extract	1 Tbsp light corn syrup
⅛ tsp salt	2 cups fresh raspberries	½ cup whipping cream
1 cup all-purpose flour		
4-5 large eggs, at room		
temperature		

❋ Preheat the oven to 450°F. Place racks in the upper and lower thirds of the oven. Line 2 baking sheets with parchment paper.

❋ To make the éclairs, combine the milk, water, butter, sugar and salt in a medium saucepan and bring to a simmer over medium heat, stirring once or twice. Once the butter melts and the mixture is bubbling, turn down the heat to low and add the flour all at once. Stir immediately with a wooden spoon or heatproof spatula. Keep stirring until the mixture is thick and pulls away from the sides of the saucepan, about 5 minutes. This allows the moisture to evaporate and allows more fat to be absorbed when the eggs are added. When the dough steams a little and smells kinda nutty, you know you're doing great!

❋ Immediately transfer the dough to a stand mixer fitted with a paddle attachment. Beat on medium speed for about 1 minute to cool the dough. Add 4 eggs, one at a time and beating each one until it's thoroughly incorporated. Be sure to stop the mixer and scrape down the bowl after each addition. After you've beaten in the last egg, the mixture should be glossy and thick, but still pourable. When scooped into a spoon, the dough should slowly pour off the spoon. If it doesn't fall off, or it comes off in one big lump, beat in the fifth egg. Congratulations! You've just made choux paste!

❋ Scoop the dough into a piping bag with a large, round tip, or use a resealable plastic bag and cut a corner off. Pipe the éclairs onto the prepared baking sheets so they are approximately finger length and width. I have huge hands, so my éclairs are about 4 inches long and 1 inch wide. Bake the éclairs for 12 minutes, then rotate the pans from bottom shelf to top and turn down the heat to 350°F. Bake for another 15-20 minutes, until they're a medium golden brown and dry to the touch. Remove the pans from the oven and place them on wire racks to cool. Immediately poke a few holes on top of the éclairs using a toothpick. This lets the steam out so they don't go soggy inside. Let the éclairs cool completely before filling with cream.

❋ To make the filling, in a stand mixer fitted with a whisk attachment, beat the whipping cream, sugar and vanilla on high speed until medium peaks form.

❋ To make the glaze, place the chocolate and corn syrup in a medium bowl. Heat the cream in a small saucepan over medium-high heat, until it just starts to bubble. Remove the cream from the heat and pour it over the chocolate mixture. Let it sit for 2 minutes, then stir until it's completely smooth. Pour the glaze into a long, shallow bowl.

❋ To assemble the éclairs, cut each éclair in half using a serrated knife. Fit a piping bag with a star tip and fill it with the whipped cream filling. Pipe the cream over the bottom of each éclair. Arrange 5 raspberries on top of the cream. Dip the top of each éclair into the chocolate glaze and gently set it on top of the raspberries. Repeat until all of the éclairs are assembled. Garnish with fresh, edible flowers, if you like.

❋ Éclairs are best eaten the day they are made, but you can freeze them after they've been baked and before they've been filled or glazed for up to 1 month. Just thaw completely and proceed with the recipe as above.

NOTE

Some types of edible flowers include violas, nasturtiums, strawberry blossoms, stock flowers, borage, mini dianthus, cilantro blossoms, pea flowers, pansies (my favourite) and chamomile flowers. But a few words of caution:

❋ *Never eat flowers that have been treated with pesticides or other toxins.*

❋ *Don't eat flowers that you've picked from the side of the road.*

❋ *If you're in any doubt about the edibility of a flower, ask an expert or check a reliable source online.*

*We tossed them in sugar and ate them
with our afternoon tea and for a few small
hours on a winter's day, my heart began
to think about mending.*

THE HEALING POWER OF A DOUGHNUT

If there is one blog post out of the more than three hundred I've written that stands out the most, it's the one about sugar-coated cake doughnuts. It was also the most difficult to write. Tears were running down my face for the majority of it, and I had to take breaks to blow my nose and cuddle the cats. You see, the man I had been dating for the majority of 2012 had broken up with me. That wasn't the worst part. It was New Year's Day. And he did it by text message. There was no face-to-face dumping, like I was all too used to. There was no explanation, and he certainly wasn't returning my phone calls. I was ghosted. I was gutted. We had talked about marriage and babies and the whole bit. I'd been banking on a future with this dude, but instead my small world came to a screeching halt and for two weeks I could barely leave the house without crying.

I found myself deliberating on whether or not I should get so personal on my blog. I'd always been so genuine and straight-up with my readers, I didn't want to pretend that everything was all right when it wasn't. I could have thrown a detox salad their way and kept quiet. But I told them the truth and I'm glad I did. Heartbreak, unfortunately, is universal. Maybe you've done the ugly cry in the farmers' market too, or you've driven by the place where you had your first date and wanted to scratch your eyes out. After I wrote the blog post, the outpouring of support and kind words from people I had never met astounded me. Those words of encouragement lifted me up for months afterwards, and all these years later they still warm my heart.

After I got through telling my tale of heartbroken woe, I wrote about how my mom lured me out of the house with the promise of making cake doughnuts. I know it was hard for her to see me in such a state, and nothing she could say or do was going to stop my heart breaking. But she made me doughnuts, and I photographed the entire process, from the rolling of the dough to the cutting of the doughnuts, to my mom standing over the roasting pan of oil, wearing her green Christmas apron, frying them until they were golden. We tossed them in sugar and ate them with our afternoon tea and for a few small hours on a winter's day, my heart began to think about mending.

Sugar-Coated Cake Doughnuts

This recipe is my mom's version of a recipe from *The Heritage Collection of Home Tested Recipes*, published by *Chatelaine* in 1968. For as long as I can remember, my mom has had this recipe booklet in among her collection of cookbooks and handwritten recipes. I always knew we were in for a treat when Mom began heating oil in the giant roasting pan! The recipe is straightforward and fast. In no time at all, you can have fresh, warm, sugar-coated doughnuts, with a sweet, crispy outside and a tender, cakey middle.

MAKES ABOUT 2 DOZEN DOUGHNUTS

2 large eggs, at room temperature
1 cup granulated sugar
2/3 cup whole milk, at room temperature
1/3 cup whipping cream, at room temperature
1 tsp pure vanilla extract
3–3½ cups all-purpose flour (approx.), divided

1 Tbsp baking powder
1 tsp salt
½ tsp freshly grated or ground nutmeg
8 cups canola or vegetable oil for deep-frying
1½ cups granulated sugar, for coating

❉ Line 2 baking sheets with a few layers of paper towel.

❉ In a large bowl, beat the eggs lightly and mix in the sugar. Beat in the milk, cream and vanilla. In a separate bowl, stir together 1 cup of the flour, the baking powder, salt and nutmeg. Add the flour mixture to the egg mixture and stir together. Add enough additional flour, 1 cup at a time, to make a soft dough. Divide the dough into 3. Pat each piece gently onto a lightly floured work surface and roll to about ¼ inch thick. Use a doughnut cutter to cut the dough into doughnut shapes. Repeat with the remaining dough.

❉ In a large roasting pan with high sides, pour in the oil and heat over medium-high heat on the stovetop until the temperature reaches 370°F, or until a piece of dough is dropped in and it turns golden. Fry the doughnuts 5 at a time until they are golden on both sides, about 2½ minutes in total. Using tongs, turn them frequently in the oil to ensure both sides are browned evenly. Carefully remove the doughnuts from the oil and place them on the prepared baking sheets. Place the granulated sugar in a shallow bowl. While all of the doughnuts are still warm, toss the ones you want to eat in granulated sugar.

❉ If you're freezing any, skip the sugar coating for now. They freeze really well in an airtight container for 1 month–just thaw, warm slightly and toss in sugar. The doughnuts tossed in sugar keep well for 1 day in an airtight container.

NOTES

Don't forget those little doughnut holes! My mom always fries them first, then tosses them in sugar. They only take a minute to cook and are a treat for the little (and big) people awaiting the real thing. Any irregular pieces of dough left over from cutting can also be fried until they are golden brown.

Yes, you can use your roasting pan that would normally contain a turkey! If not, a Dutch oven will do, though you won't be able to fry as many doughnuts at one time.

If you don't have a doughnut cutter, use 2 different sizes of round cookie cutters (approximately 3 inches in diameter and 1 inch in diameter, respectively) to cut the doughnuts and the holes.

Pumpkin Cinnamon Buns with Maple Chai Glaze

Making anything with yeast can intimidate some people. I'm one of them. I'm always a little scaredy-cat when I have to open a packet of yeast and bake bread and what have you, but like anything good in life, you just have to get over the fear and do it already. Pep talk! The dough is quite easy to throw together—your stand mixer does most of the work—and is soft and really quite lovely to work with. There are a couple of rises involved, but devoting a Sunday afternoon to baking cinnamon buns is never a bad thing. One bite and you'll know the time involved was worth it. Gooey in their glorious glaze, these are best for sharing with those you love (just maybe not your cats).

MAKES 10 CINNAMON BUNS

PUMPKIN DOUGH
3½ cups all-purpose flour
¼ cup granulated sugar
¼ cup packed dark brown sugar
1 package instant (rapid rise) dry yeast (about 2½ tsp)
1 tsp salt
½ tsp ground cinnamon
¼ tsp ground ginger
¼ tsp ground nutmeg
⅓ cup unsalted butter, softened and cubed, plus more for greasing the pan
⅓ cup whole milk, at room temperature
⅓ cup half-and-half cream, at room temperature
1 large egg, at room temperature
⅔ cup canned pumpkin purée

CINNAMON FILLING
¾ cup packed dark brown sugar
¼ cup granulated sugar
1 tsp ground cinnamon
½ tsp ground cloves
½ tsp ground nutmeg
½ tsp coarse salt
¼ cup + 2 Tbsp unsalted butter, melted and divided

MAPLE CHAI GLAZE
¼ cup unsalted butter, softened
½ cup buttermilk
2 chai tea bags
¾ cup granulated sugar
1 Tbsp pure maple syrup
1 tsp baking soda
½ tsp pure vanilla extract

❋ Butter a 10-inch round (or square!) baking dish. Lightly grease a large bowl with canola oil or your preferred cooking oil.

❋ To make the dough, in a stand mixer fitted with a paddle attachment, mix the flour, sugars, yeast, salt and spices on low speed. Add the butter and mix on medium speed until incorporated. Add the milk, half-and-half and egg and mix on low speed until incorporated. Add the pumpkin purée and mix on medium speed for 3 minutes. The dough will be light orange and feel soft and sticky. Remove the dough from the bowl and form it into a ball, placing it in the lightly greased large bowl. Cover with plastic wrap and let it rise for 1 hour in a warm, draft-free place.

❋ To make the filling, stir together the sugars, spices and salt in a small bowl, then stir in ¼ cup of the melted butter.

❋ Once the dough has risen for 1 hour, roll it out on a lightly floured work surface into a large rectangle, approximately 20 inches by 10 inches. Brush the dough with the remaining 2 Tbsp of melted butter, then sprinkle the filling mixture overtop, leaving a ¼-inch border around the edges. Use the palms of your hands to lightly press the filling into the dough. Starting with a long end, roll the dough up tightly and place it seam side down on the counter. Cut it into ten 2-inch pieces and place them on the greased baking dish. Cover with plastic wrap and let them rise for 1 hour.

❋ Preheat the oven to 375°F. Place the rack in the centre of the oven.

❋ Bake the cinnamon buns for 25–30 minutes, or until the tops are golden brown.

❄ While the buns are baking, make the glaze. Melt the butter in the buttermilk in a medium saucepan on low heat. Turn off the heat and steep the chai tea bags for 15 minutes. Remove the bags and squeeze out the tea into the buttermilk. Add the sugar, maple syrup and baking soda, stirring well, and bring to a boil over medium-high heat. Let the mixture boil for 5 minutes, stirring often. It will be quite foamy—that's normal. When it's a dark amber colour, after about 5 minutes, turn off the heat and stir in the vanilla. Set it aside and let it cool.

❄ When the buns have finished baking, remove the dish from the oven and immediately invert them onto a serving platter and pour the warm glaze over them. If you're not comfortable inverting the cinnamon buns, simply pour the glaze over the cinnamon buns while they are hot and still in the baking dish.

❄ The cinnamon buns are best when served warm and eaten that day. You can store them in an airtight container for up to 1 day, or freeze them (with or without their glaze) for up to 1 month.

NOTES

I used canned pumpkin purée. If you're using homemade purée, be sure it's been strained of its liquid—you don't want it too runny.

The dough is quite soft and sticky, so be sure to flour your hands when you roll it out and work with it.

Rapid rise yeast or instant yeast does not need to be activated by warm liquid like traditional or active yeast does. Simply add the rapid rise yeast to the dry ingredients.

CREAM CHEESE PISTACHIO TWISTS

Over the years, I've worked with some supremely talented chefs, cooks, and pastry chefs. This recipe comes from a friend and former co-worker who was a wizard in the bakeshop. She was mainly self-trained—she had only taken a few classes at a cake supply store—but she was masterful when it came to decorating cakes, and her wedding cakes were extraordinary. I loved popping my head into her little corner of a work space to see her latest creations. She was an inspiration and a joker, and often my mood was elevated from our little visits. Her recipe for these not-too-sweet-yet-indulgent twists is one of my favourites.

MAKES ABOUT 4 DOZEN TWISTS

TWISTS
1 cup unsalted butter, softened
1 cup full-fat cream cheese, softened
1 Tbsp granulated sugar, plus extra for sprinkling
2 cups all-purpose flour
½ tsp baking powder
½ tsp salt
1 large egg white beaten with 1 Tbsp water,
   for glazing

PISTACHIO FILLING
1¼ cups shelled pistachios
½ cup packed brown sugar
2 tsp ground cinnamon

❊ To make the twists, in a stand mixer fitted with a paddle attachment, beat the butter, cream cheese and sugar on high speed until soft. Turn the mixer off and add the flour, baking powder and salt. Mix on medium-low speed until everything is combined and a soft dough forms. This could take some time, but in the end you should have a soft, smooth dough. Gather the dough into a ball, place it on a lightly floured surface and cut it into 3 evenly sized pieces. Flatten each piece into a disc. Wrap each disc in plastic and refrigerate for 30 minutes.

❊ While the dough is chilling, finely chop the pistachios so they are practically ground (you need 1 cup). (You could use a food processor to do this, but it's not really necessary and it adds to the cleanup.) Put them in a bowl along with the brown sugar and cinnamon. Give it a stir.

❊ Preheat the oven to 350°F. Place the rack in the centre of the oven. Line 3 baking sheets with parchment paper.

❊ On a lightly floured surface, roll each piece of dough out into a circle so it's fairly thin, about ⅛ inch thick and 11 inches in diameter. Place a 10½-inch dinner plate over the circle and trim off the excess. Brush with the egg white/water and sprinkle with one-third of the pistachio filling. Cut the circle into 4 sections, and then cut each section into 4 so you have 16 triangles. Roll each triangle up, from the widest part to the point. Place on the prepared baking sheet, about 2 inches apart. Brush with the egg white/water mix again and sprinkle with granulated sugar. Bake for 17–19 minutes, until golden. Cool on the pan on a wire rack. Repeat this process with the other 2 pieces of dough.

❊ The cream cheese pistachio twists keep well in an airtight container for 2 days, or can be frozen in an airtight container for up to 1 month.

NOTE

If you don't have a 10½-inch dinner plate, use a tape measure or a ruler as a guide.

Petits Pains au Chocolat

I've never been to France. Heck, I've never even been to Europe, which is a travesty in itself. When I get there, and I know I'll get there before I leave this planet, I suspect there will be a great deal of pastry and coffee consumption. Two of my favourite things, right there. But if, like me, you don't have the means to hop on a plane to Paris right this very second, these irresistible pastries can be made in your very own home in under an hour. Not bad, that. All you need is puff pastry and good chocolate. I emphasize *good* here, because chocolate is essentially the star of the show, and so you want it to taste amazing. These are lovely on a brunch table, still warm from the oven so the chocolate is melty and gorgeous. This recipe makes enough for a crowd, but it can easily be cut in half. You can prep these the night before and then simply pop them into the oven in the morning. They're ready just as the coffee finishes brewing—perfect timing for an absolutely scrumptious start to the day.

MAKES 18 PASTRIES

1 lb (1 pkg) frozen all-butter puff pastry, thawed
    in the refrigerator
1 large egg, beaten with 1 Tbsp of water
12 oz good-quality dark chocolate bars (about
    3 bars)
Granulated or coarse sugar

※ Preheat the oven to 400°F. Place racks in the upper and lower thirds of the oven. Line 2 baking sheets with parchment paper.

※ A package of rolled puff pastry contains 2 sheets measuring 9×9 inches each. Cut each sheet into nine 3-inch squares. Alternatively, if you are buying puff pastry in a block rather than already rolled out, roll out the puff pastry so it is 1/8 inch thick and 9 inches square. Chop the chocolate into eighteen 2×1-inch pieces. Brush each puff pastry square with the egg wash. Place 1 chocolate piece in the centre of each pastry square. Fold the dough tightly around the chocolate, making sure it is completely enclosed. Place the pastry bundles seam side down on the baking sheets, about 2 inches apart. Cover them with plastic wrap and refrigerate until needed. You can do this a day ahead.

※ Brush the tops of the pastry bundles with the egg wash and sprinkle with granulated or coarse sugar. Bake until the pastries are golden brown, 18-20 minutes, rotating the pans' shelf positions halfway through.

※ Serve the petits pains au chocolat warm or at room temperature. These are best enjoyed the day they are baked, but can be stored in an airtight container at room temperature, dusted with icing sugar, if you like, for up to 1 day and gently reheated in a low oven (250°F) for 3 minutes.

NOTE

Look for brands that use all butter for the puff pastry. Some brands will use oil or hydrogenated fats and this will affect the taste.

Brown Butter Lemon Poppy Seed Madeleines

When you're eating a madeleine, the brain processes all sorts of happy thoughts such as 1) it tastes like a rich, buttery cake, but 2) it's in the shape of a cookie, and 3) would it be very wrong to eat another and another? These tiny French butter cakes, which require their very own special baking pan, are worthy of all the accolades that regularly come their way. Browned and crispy on the outside, soft and spongy in the middle, they're a bit of a process to make, but oh so terribly worth it.

I've browned the butter in this version, which adds lovely nutty, toffee notes to the cake, and unlike other cakes, it's stirred in at the very end. Lemon and poppy seed are a classic combo, and if you feel like drizzling a little glaze of icing sugar and lemon juice on top, please do. These are wonderful to bake and package up for near and dear ones around the holidays. You may think that when you purchase your madeleine pan you won't use it very much, but I assure you, such thoughts are nonsense.

MAKES 1 DOZEN MADELEINES

½ cup + 1 Tbsp unsalted butter
¾ cup + 1 tsp all-purpose flour, divided
1 Tbsp poppy seeds
½ tsp baking powder
½ tsp flaky salt, such as Maldon
2 large eggs, at room temperature
½ cup granulated sugar

1 Tbsp fresh lemon juice
1 Tbsp grated lemon zest
1 tsp pure vanilla extract

❋ Melt the butter in a small saucepan over medium-high heat. The butter will froth and bubble and then turn golden. (It's okay to give it a bit of a stir.) When it starts to brown and smell nutty, remove the pan from the heat. Remove 1 Tbsp of the brown butter to a small bowl. Let the remaining brown butter cool in the pan.

❋ Combine ¾ cup of the flour, the poppy seeds, baking powder and salt in a medium bowl. In a stand mixer fitted with a paddle attachment, beat together the eggs, sugar, lemon juice, lemon zest and vanilla until creamy, about 5 minutes. Fold the flour mixture into the egg mixture, then fold in the ½ cup of cooled brown butter ever so gently. Be careful not to overmix. Refrigerate the batter, uncovered, for at least 1 hour, but no more than 3 hours.

❋ Meanwhile, stir together the reserved 1 Tbsp of brown butter with the 1 tsp of all-purpose flour and use a pastry brush to grease the wells of the madeleine pan. Place the pan in the freezer for at least 1 hour.

❋ Preheat the oven to 375°F. Place the rack in the centre of the oven.

❋ Use a heaping soup spoon to fill each well in the madeleine pan, but don't fill them right to the top or they'll spill over as they bake. I use my fingers to spread the batter out evenly. Place the pan on a baking sheet and bake for 13–14 minutes. The edges will be light golden brown and the tops will spring back when gently touched when they're ready. Remove the pan from the oven and the baking sheet and let it cool for 2 minutes on a wire rack. Use a fork or a knife to gently remove the madeleines from the pan and place them on a wire rack or tea towel to cool completely before dusting with icing sugar.

❋ These are best enjoyed the day they are made, but can be kept in an airtight container at room temperature for up to 1 day.

J.D. Salinger wrote that "certain things should stay the way they are. You ought to be able to stick them in one of those big glass cases and leave them alone. I know it's impossible, but it's too bad anyway."

SMALL-TOWN SATURDAY NIGHTS

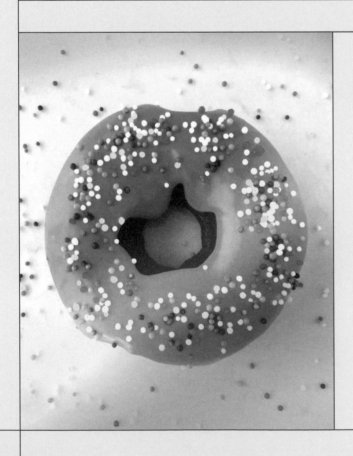

J.D. Salinger wrote that "certain things should stay the way they are. You ought to be able to stick them in one of those big glass cases and leave them alone. I know it's impossible, but it's too bad anyway."

I've been blessed to have felt this way a good many times in my life, and perhaps never more so than in my late teenage years, growing up in a small town that bordered Alberta and Saskatchewan. I had a tight group of good friends—the kind of friends you spill all your secrets to while staying up too late and eating ice cream cake. The summers of 1990 and 1991 were especially fun. We were going into Grade 12, then university. Friday and Saturday nights mainly consisted of us spraying our hair too high and dancing around to the B-52s or INXS in someone's living room. Eventually we would pile into a parent's car (or if we were lucky, our own) and drive up and down the four-lane main drag, otherwise known as the four-laner. General objectives of this activity were twofold: scout for boys (preferably not from our high school) and stop for snacks.

I won't dish too much dirt on the boys (a girl has to have some secrets), but when the cruising came to an end, we almost always stopped in at the local Tim Hortons for a doughnut. With our honey crullers and chocolate glazed, we'd sit at our table and go over the evening's events, or lack thereof. When the curfews approached, the driver would drop each of us off at our houses. More often than not we lingered in the driveway as we said goodnight to each other. Talk tends to get more serious when sitting in the dark. Topics covered usually included the looming future and what the hell are we doing with our lives. The usual teenage angst. While we were excited to be growing up and moving further out into the world, in our hearts we were scared and a little sad that what we had would eventually end.

After graduation, I was the first to move away, then a few others followed. Some stayed behind, and while you make all kinds of efforts to visit and talk, nothing is ever quite the same as it was on those high school weekend nights. A couple of those girls are still my closest friends in the whole world. Whenever we find ourselves in each other's city, talk over bowls of ramen or coffee and doughnuts tends to still be along the lines of what the hell are we doing with our lives and the looming future. The usual adult angst. I'm so happy our friendships have stood the test of time. Those pals you had when phones still had cords are the best pals you can ever ask for. We've seen marriages, births, big moves, breakups, death, great big joys and the depths of despair, dreams come to life, and dreams come to an end. I still have to bust a move whenever the B-52s come on the radio—even if means dancing in the seat of my car. I don't care if I look like an idiot. I'm 17 again, with big hair and big dreams. For a second it feels like the friends of my youth are sitting in the car with me, rocking out in spirit.

French Honey Crullers

Given the many nights of my youth spent sitting in a small-town doughnut shop, I knew that the cruller had to be in this cookbook. I'm happy to say that this, perhaps the most sophisticated doughnut of the bunch, tastes way better than those you can get at your local drive-through. After successive successful test batches, I may have fist-pumped the air. Just sayin'. These crullers involve the deep fryer and the making of choux paste, but they are easier than they look. Don't fret too much if the shapes are a bit wonky—that's what the glaze is for. It's like the under-eye concealer of the dessert world. When the crullers are puffed and golden, let them drain for a bit, then dunk them in the honey glaze. Double-dunk, if you wish. Triple-dunking is encouraged. The first bite of a homemade cruller is quite memorable. You might need to sit down. You've been warned.

MAKES 15 CRULLERS

FRENCH CRULLERS
½ cup whole milk
½ cup water
¼ cup + 2 Tbsp unsalted butter, softened
2 Tbsp icing sugar
¼ tsp salt
¼ tsp ground nutmeg
1 cup all-purpose flour
4-5 large eggs, at room temperature
8 cups canola or vegetable oil, for frying

HONEY GLAZE
1½ cups icing sugar
3 Tbsp whole milk
2 Tbsp liquid honey
2 tsp fresh lemon juice

❋ Cut fifteen 3×3-inch squares out of parchment paper and place them on a baking sheet. Lightly spray each square with cooking spray, or use a pastry brush to grease them with a little oil.

❋ To make the crullers, combine the milk, water, butter, sugar, salt and nutmeg in a medium saucepan and bring it to a simmer over medium heat, stirring once or twice. Once the butter melts and the mixture is bubbling, turn down the heat to low and add the flour all at once. Stir immediately with a wooden spoon or heatproof spatula. Keep stirring over low heat until the mixture is thick and pulls away from the sides of the saucepan, about 5 minutes. This allows the moisture to evaporate and allows more fat to be absorbed when the eggs are added. When the dough steams a little and smells kinda nutty, you know you're doing great!

❋ Immediately transfer the dough to the bowl of stand mixer fitted with a paddle attachment. Beat on medium speed for about 1 minute to cool the dough. Add 4 eggs, one at a time and beating each one until it's thoroughly incorporated. Be sure to stop the mixer and scrape down the bowl after each addition. After you've beaten in the last egg, the mixture should be glossy and thick, but still pourable. When scooped into a spoon, the dough should slowly pour off the spoon. If it doesn't fall off, or it comes off in one big lump, beat in the fifth egg.

❋ Scoop the dough into a large piping bag fitted with a large star tip. Pipe a ring onto each square, approximately ¾ inch high. If your rings seem too skinny, pipe a bit more on top. Place the baking sheet full of piped rings in the freezer for 30 minutes. This will help the crullers keep their beloved ridges.

❋ Heat the oil to 370°F in a large, deep saucepan. Line a baking sheet with paper towels and set a wire rack over it.

❋ Place 2 or 3 crullers, still on their parchment paper, in the hot oil, paper side up. You need to use your hands to do this, so just make sure you don't burn your fingertips. The paper will release when

it's ready and will float off. Use tongs to lift the paper out and to flip the crullers over occasionally, so they brown evenly. Fry them for about 3 minutes, until golden brown. Set the crullers on the wire rack while you fry the remainder.

❄ To make the glaze, sift the icing sugar into a medium bowl, then whisk in the remaining ingredients. Dip the tops of the crullers into the glaze while they're still warm. Place them back on the wire rack until the glaze sets.

❄ Crullers are best eaten the day they are made, but can be stored in an airtight container at room temperature for 1 day.

NOTE

Let the oil cool down completely before disposing of it in glass jars. Or you can save it for your next deep-frying adventure! Once the oil has cooled down completely, I pour it into a large plastic or glass container with a tight-fitting lid and use it up within a month.

Chocolate Baked Doughnuts with Raspberry Glaze

I see the fear in people's eyes when they are told they need to heat up oil on the stove to make delicious doughnuts at home. While these doughnuts are very good, with their rich chocolate flavour and dense cake-like texture, they aren't like their upscale deep-fried brothers and sisters. That's why people risk the potential mishaps with hot oil—because deep-fried action tastes really, really good.

MAKES 14–16 DOUGHNUTS

DOUGHNUTS
1 Tbsp coconut oil, for greasing the pans
½ cup unsweetened cocoa powder, plus more for dusting the pans
1½ cups all-purpose flour
½ cup granulated sugar
½ cup lightly packed brown sugar
1½ tsp baking powder
1 tsp salt
½ tsp baking soda
¼ tsp ground nutmeg

2 large eggs, at room temperature
1 cup buttermilk, at room temperature
2 tsp pure vanilla extract
¼ cup melted unsalted butter

RASPBERRY GLAZE
¼ cup raspberry juice from thawed frozen raspberries
2 Tbsp melted unsalted butter
2 Tbsp light corn syrup
2 Tbsp whipping cream
3 cups icing sugar

❊ Preheat the oven to 325°F. Place the rack in the centre of the oven. Grease two 6-well doughnut pans with the coconut oil and dust with some cocoa powder. Tap the excess cocoa into the sink.

❊ To make the doughnuts, stir together the ½ cup cocoa powder, flour, both sugars, baking powder, salt, baking soda and nutmeg in a large bowl. In a separate bowl, whisk together the eggs, buttermilk and vanilla. Add this to the dry ingredients and stir in the melted butter just until the mixture is combined.

❊ Scrape the batter into a piping bag (or use a resealable plastic bag and snip off the corner). Pipe the batter into the prepared pans, just until the wells are half-full. Bake for 10 minutes. The doughnuts should spring back when lightly touched. Let the pans cool on a wire rack for 15 minutes then remove the doughnuts from the pans. You may need to gently pry them out with a mini offset spatula. Let the doughnuts cool completely on the rack before glazing. If you only have 1 doughnut pan, be sure to grease the pan with oil and dust with cocoa between batches. Pour water into any empty wells.

❊ Line a baking sheet with parchment paper and set a wire rack over it.

❊ To make the glaze, beat together the raspberry juice, melted butter, corn syrup and whipping cream in a large bowl. Sift in the icing sugar and beat the glaze well until it's smooth. You can either dip the doughnuts into the glaze or spoon the glaze on top of the doughnuts. Some crumbs may fall into the glaze while dipping. If having crumbs in the glaze bothers you, then take a spoon and glaze the doughnuts that way. When you're glazing, set the doughnuts on the prepared rack. Refrigerate the doughnuts for about 30 minutes before serving. This helps set the glaze.

❊ The doughnuts are best the day they're made, but they will keep well in an airtight container in the refrigerator for up to 1 day, though the glaze may get goopy. Baked, but unglazed, doughnuts can be frozen in an airtight container for up to 1 month.

NOTE

A half recipe of the maple glaze from the Maple Bacon Long Johns on page 250 would be another delicious way to top these doughnuts.

Butterhorns with Vanilla Drizzle

Some of my sweetest Christmas memories are of Mom bringing out butterhorns from the freezer at Christmastime. We'd enjoy them with our breakfast and a good coffee, and I could barely wait until they had lost their chill before biting into one. Mom would send me off with a container of butterhorns when I travelled back to my apartment, and I cherished each and every one until they were gone.

What makes butterhorns so special? The sweet yeast dough is rich and soft, and yes, it's buttery and light. The vanilla drizzle complements the butterhorn ever so well, and once you eat one, you can't wait to grab another. This recipe is a two-step process, with the dough needing to be refrigerated overnight. The next morning, you're good to roll! Mom says she clipped this recipe out of *The Western Producer* years ago, and I'm so glad I'm able to pass it along to you now.

MAKES 2 DOZEN BUTTERHORNS

BUTTERHORNS
3 cups all-purpose flour, plus more for dusting
1 tsp salt
1 cup unsalted butter, softened and cubed
1 cup whole milk
2 large eggs, at room temperature
1 Tbsp granulated sugar
1 pkg active dry yeast (about 2½ tsp)

VANILLA GLAZE
2½ cups icing sugar
¼ cup whole milk
2 tsp pure vanilla extract

❄ To make the butterhorns, mix together the flour and salt in a large bowl. Cut in the butter using a pastry blender, mixing it well, but leaving some pea-sized bits of butter. Heat the milk in a medium saucepan over medium-high heat just until it begins to steam. Remove the milk from the heat and let it cool just until it's warm to the touch. Mix the eggs and sugar into the warm milk and stir in the yeast. Let this stand, uncovered, for 10 minutes. Stir the yeast mixture into the flour mixture and mix until a soft dough forms. Cover with plastic wrap and refrigerate overnight.

❄ The next day, remove the dough from the fridge and lightly dust your countertop with flour. Line 3 baking sheets with parchment paper.

❄ This dough is best rolled cold. Cut the dough into 3 evenly sized pieces and shape them into balls. Roll each ball into a disc about ⅛ inch thick and about 10 inches in diameter. Cut each disc into 8 triangles. Roll each triangle tightly, from the wide end to the point. Place seam side down, about 3 inches apart, on the prepared baking sheets. Cover them lightly with wax paper and let them rise for 2 hours in a warm, draft-free spot.

❄ Preheat the oven to 375°F. Place the rack in the lower third of the oven.

❄ Bake each sheet, one at a time, for 15–20 minutes, until the butterhorns are a nice golden brown on the top and bottom. Remove the pans from the oven and let them cool on a wire rack for about 13 minutes while you make the glaze.

❄ To make the glaze, whisk together the glaze ingredients in a medium bowl.

❄ Once the butterhorns are barely warm, drizzle the glaze over them. I find a fork works really well for this.

❄ The butterhorns will keep in an airtight container for up to 2 days at room temperature, or can be frozen after they are glazed for up to 1 month.

NOTE

Finely chopped toasted walnuts or pistachios can be sprinkled on top of the glaze for extra deliciousness.

A Trio of Cream Puffs

People tend to freak out when it comes to making cream puffs. I think it's best to save your freak-out for something more serious, which for me would be making croissant dough, or any time one of my cats goes rogue and is missing for more than 10 minutes, or if I find ants in the kitchen. That's when I freak. With cream puffs, once you get the technicalities down (set your timer!) you're golden. And at the end of it all, you get to pop a vanilla cream-, chocolate cream- or mocha cream-filled piece of heaven into your mouth—and that's when you'll know the effort was totally worth it. I used to request cream puffs instead of birthday cake, I love them so. One year, for a Mother's Day banquet at the country club where I worked, I offered to make 350 cream puffs for the dessert table. *That's* how much I love cream puffs. I couldn't feel my arms for a couple of days afterwards (they were in permanent piping position), but I still love the puffs.

MAKES ABOUT 20 CREAM PUFFS

PUFFS	TRIO OF FILLINGS
½ cup whole milk	3 cups whipping cream
½ cup water	¼ cup granulated sugar
¼ cup + 2 Tbsp unsalted butter, softened	1 tsp pure vanilla extract
1 Tbsp granulated sugar	2 Tbsp unsweetened cocoa powder
⅛ tsp salt	½ tsp espresso powder
1 cup all-purpose flour	Icing sugar, for garnish
4–5 large eggs, at room temperature	

❋ Preheat the oven to 450°F. Place racks in the upper and lower thirds of the oven. Line 2 baking sheets with parchment paper.

❋ To make the puffs, combine the milk, water, butter, sugar and salt in a medium saucepan and bring to a simmer over medium heat, stirring once or twice. Once the butter melts and the mixture is bubbling, turn down the heat to low and add the flour all at once. Stir immediately using a wooden spoon. Keep stirring over low heat until the mixture is thick and pulls away from the sides of the saucepan, about 5 minutes. This allows the moisture to evaporate and allows more fat to absorb when the eggs are added. When the dough steams a little and smells kinda nutty, you're doing great!

❋ Immediately transfer the dough to a stand mixer fitted with a paddle attachment. Beat on medium speed for about 1 minute to cool the dough. Add 4 eggs, one at a time and beating each one until it's thoroughly incorporated. Be sure to stop the mixer and scrape down the bowl after each addition. After you've beaten in the last egg, the mixture should be glossy and thick, but still pourable. When scooped into a spoon, the dough should slowly pour off the spoon. If it doesn't fall off, or it comes off in one big lump, beat in the fifth egg.

❋ Scoop the dough into a piping bag fitted with a ½-inch tip (or just use 2 tsp, or even a piping bag without a tip). Pipe or scoop out the dough into rounds (about 1½ inches across and ¾ inch high) on the prepared baking sheets. Leave at least 2 inches between the puffs. It'll be messy and you'll have to work quickly, but don't worry. Even if they turn out a little wonky, NO ONE CARES! You've just made cream puffs. Bake the puffs for 10 minutes, then rotate the pans from bottom to top in the oven and turn down the heat to 350°F. Bake for another 15–20 minutes, until they're a medium golden brown. Remove the pans from the oven and immediately make a small X on the bottom of each puff with a sharp knife. This lets the steam out so they don't go soggy inside. Let the puffs cool completely on the pan before filling them with cream.

❋ To make the fillings, in a stand mixer fitted with a whisk attachment, beat the whipping cream, sugar and vanilla until medium peaks form. Put about one-third of the cream into a piping bag fitted with a ½-inch tip. Fill about one-third of the puffs from the bottom, where you made that X. When all of that cream is gone, sift the cocoa powder into the remaining whipped cream. Beat on medium speed until incorporated. Put half of this cream into the piping bag (no need to wipe it out first) and use it to fill about half of the remaining puffs. Add the espresso powder to the remaining chocolate whipped cream, beat just to incorporate and then pop it into the piping bag (again, no need to wipe it out). Fill the remaining puffs with the espresso cream. Dust the cream puffs with icing sugar and serve immediately.

❋ These are best served the day you make them, but any leftovers will keep in an airtight container for 1 day in the refrigerator.

NOTES

To make ALL vanilla cream, omit the cocoa and espresso powder. To make ALL chocolate cream, increase the cocoa powder to 5 Tbsp and omit the espresso powder. To make ALL mocha, add 1 tsp of espresso powder to the chocolate cream. To make ALL espresso cream, add 2 tsp espresso powder to the vanilla cream and omit the cocoa completely.

These cream puffs can be made gluten-free. See below.

I cut an X in the bottom of the cream puffs and pipe the cream in that way, or you can simply cut them in half and fill them with cream, then top with the pastry lid. My unscientific research has shown that more cream can be added with the former method (upside). It just means you have to wash another piping bag (downside). Or you can use disposable piping bags and all will be right with the world!

GLUTEN-FREE CREAM PUFFS (MAKES ABOUT 20 CREAM PUFFS)

⅔ cup white rice flour
⅓ cup sweet rice flour
1 tsp baking powder
½ tsp xanthan gum
Pinch of salt
1 cup water

❋ Stir together the white rice flour, sweet rice flour, baking powder, xanthan gum and salt in a medium bowl. This is your flour. Proceed with the above directions for regular cream puffs, substituting this gluten-free flour blend for the all-purpose flour in the recipe.

Maple Bacon Long Johns

If this recipe doesn't shout "I am Canadian" loud and proud, I don't know what does. For those not in the know, long johns are rectangular doughnuts that can sometimes be filled with a custard and slathered with a glaze or icing. My mom made these for us when we were kids, but she just used her bread dough recipe, and they weren't stuffed with a custard. Hers were covered in a thick chocolate icing and were the best thing ever. She used her giant black enamel roasting pan and laid the fried long johns out on brown paper. I have vivid memories of watching the dough bubble and bob in the oil. And the next thing I knew, I was eating one. Okay, two. Fine, three. In this recipe, I've made a bit of a sweeter yeast dough than Mom did and slathered the long johns with a buttery maple icing and bits of salty bacon, and yes, I think they are the best thing ever. Perhaps the bacon on baked goods phenomena has jumped the shark, but not in my world. Bacon, at any time of day, in any way, is fine with me. Sweet, salty, carby, this long john makes me want to wear my red flannel shirt and play (really loud) Arcade Fire on the stereo.

MAKES ABOUT 2 DOZEN LONG JOHNS

LONG JOHNS
5 cups all-purpose flour (approx.), plus more
    for dusting the counter
1/3 cup + 1 Tbsp granulated sugar
1 tsp salt
1/4 tsp ground cinnamon
1/4 tsp ground nutmeg
1 1/2 cups whole milk
1/2 cup water
2 pkgs active dry yeast (4 1/2 tsp)
1/3 cup unsalted butter, melted and cooled

2 large eggs, beaten
1 tsp pure vanilla extract
8 cups canola or vegetable oil, for frying
    and greasing the bowl

MAPLE GLAZE
1/2 cup unsalted butter
3/4 cup pure maple syrup
2 cups icing sugar
10 slices of bacon, fried and finely chopped

❋ Lightly grease a large bowl with your preferred cooking oil.

❋ To make the long johns, in a large bowl, stir together the flour, the 1/3 cup sugar, salt and spices. Heat the milk and water together in a medium saucepan over medium heat so it reaches 115°F, or is quite warm to the touch. Pour this liquid into the bowl of a stand mixer and sprinkle the yeast and the 1 Tbsp of sugar overtop. Let this stand for 5 minutes. Fit a paddle attachment and, with the mixer running on low speed, slowly add the melted butter. Scrape the bowl and add the beaten eggs, vanilla and half of the flour mixture, still on low speed, just until incorporated. Increase the speed to medium and beat until well mixed. With the mixer running on low speed, add the rest of the flour mixture, 1 cup at a time. Increase the speed to medium once all the flour has been added and beat until it comes together. Switch the paddle attachment for a dough hook and beat on medium speed for 5–7 minutes, until the dough is soft and supple. If it seems too wet, add 1 Tbsp of flour at a time until it's smooth.

❋ Transfer the dough to the greased bowl, cover with plastic wrap or a clean kitchen towel and let the dough rise in a warm, draft-free spot for about 1 hour, or until the dough has doubled in size.

❋ Line 2 baking sheets with parchment paper.

❋ Turn out the dough onto a lightly floured surface and roll it out to approximately 8 inches by 20 inches. If it goes a little over, don't fret. Trim the edges so they are relatively straight (but don't get too hung up on making them perfect). Cut the dough into 20 bars, roughly 4 inches long and 2 inches wide. Carefully move the bars to the prepared baking sheets, spacing them about 3 inches

apart. Reroll the scraps and cut as many same-size bars as you can. Cover the baking sheets with clean kitchen towels and let them rise for another hour in a warm, draft-free spot.

❋ Meanwhile, make the glaze. Melt the butter in a small saucepan over medium heat then stir in the maple syrup until it's well combined. Remove the pan from the heat. Place the icing sugar in a large bowl. Pour the butter/maple mixture overtop and whisk well, until it is smooth and most of the lumps are gone (a few small lumps are fine). Let it rest until you're ready to glaze, though you will have to whisk it occasionally as it thickens.

❋ Line 2 baking sheets with paper towel.

❋ To fry the long johns, place the oil in a large Dutch oven or roasting pan with high sides. You need the oil to be about 2 inches deep. Heat it to exactly 360°F, and then carefully place 3–5 long johns into the hot oil, depending on the size of your pan. Fry for about 3 minutes in total, carefully flipping them now and again so they brown evenly. Carefully (use tongs!) remove them to the prepared baking sheets. Repeat the process until all of the long johns are fried.

❋ When the long johns are all fried and at room temperature, whisk the glaze so it is smooth and transfer it to a long, shallow dish. Either dip the long johns into the glaze, or use an offset spatula or knife to glaze them. Be generous with the glaze! While the glaze is still soft, sprinkle bits of cooked bacon on each long john.

❋ The long johns are best served the day they are made, though leftovers will keep for 1 day in an airtight container in the refrigerator (but note that the glaze might get a bit goopy).

| NOTE | *This glaze is smashing on both of the baked doughnut recipes in this cookbook (pages 242 and 254), but you're likely to only need a half recipe.* |

Baked Cake Doughnuts with Chocolate Glaze

I've included a second baked doughnut recipe just because if you're investing in a doughnut pan, you may as well have recipes that use it. This doughnut is lightly flavoured with maple syrup and has lovely crackly edges and a tender crumb—basically all of the things I love about cake dough-nuts. While you do lose out on some of the flavour that a good ol' deep-fried doughnut has, these are still pretty darn good. Plus, any time you get to bust out the sprinkles is a guaranteed good time. If you're not feeling the glaze, just dust the doughnuts with powdered sugar while they're still a little warm.

MAKES ABOUT 18 DOUGHNUTS

DOUGHNUTS
1 Tbsp coconut oil or butter, for greasing the pans
3 cups cake and pastry flour
½ cup rye flour
1 cup granulated sugar
1 tsp baking soda
½ tsp baking powder
½ tsp ground nutmeg or cinnamon
1 tsp salt
3 large eggs, at room temperature

1½ cups buttermilk, at room temperature
½ cup unsalted butter, melted and cooled
1 Tbsp pure maple syrup

CHOCOLATE GLAZE
¾ cup chopped (½-inch pieces) dark chocolate
½ cup whipping cream
2 Tbsp unsalted butter
1 Tbsp icing sugar (optional)
Sprinkles (optional)

❋ Preheat the oven to 400°F. Place the rack in the centre of the oven. Grease two 6-well doughnut pans with your preferred oil or butter.

❋ To make the doughnuts, whisk the dry ingredients together in large bowl. Whisk the eggs, buttermilk, butter and maple syrup together in another. Pour the wet mixture into the dry and stir just until combined. Scrape the mixture into a piping bag (or use a resealable plastic bag and cut off a corner). Pipe the batter into the wells, filling them half to three-quarters full. Bake for 9–10 minutes. The doughnuts are done when they have risen nicely, are golden brown and spring back when lightly touched. Let the doughnuts cool in the pan on a wire rack for 15 minutes then remove them from the pan and let them cool completely on the rack. Proceed with the rest of the batter, being sure to let the pans cool down so they are slightly warm to the touch and greasing them between batches. Let the doughnuts cool completely before glazing.

❋ To make the glaze, place the chocolate, cream and butter in a small saucepan and stir over low heat, until the glaze is melted and smooth. If you're using the icing sugar, whisk it in now. Pour the glaze into a shallow dish and dip each doughnut into the glaze. Don't forget the sprinkles!

❋ Glazed doughnuts are best eaten the day they're made, but any leftovers will keep in an airtight container at room temperature for up to 1 day. Unglazed doughnuts can be frozen in an airtight container for up to 1 month.

NOTES

The icing sugar gives a bit more sweetness to the glaze, so it's up to you if you want to include it.

If you don't have rye flour, substitute whole wheat or all-purpose.

A half recipe of the maple glaze for the Maple Bacon Long Johns (page 250) would be lovely on these doughnuts.

Recipes

TO GIVE AWAY

FARAWAY, SO CLOSE

When Georgia O'Keefe moved to rural New Mexico, after spending years in New York City, she would sign her letters to the people she loved, "from the faraway nearby." After all, sometimes physical distance is purely relative. We all know you can be a million miles away from the person sitting on the other side of the couch or deeply invested in the life of your loved one living on the opposite side of the country. Having lived in as many places as I have, I've made good friends who are now scattered all over. I really love to stay in touch with them, especially at Christmas. I'm totally that person in the line-up at the post office who has over 50 cards and an armload of packages full of baked goods that need to be sent on their merry way. While I'm waiting, I imagine Stacy's face as she opens the box filled with cookies and candy—her small boys reaching in for a taste. I imagine my friend Mel, walking to the mailbox with her dog, Molly, looking in and finding the parcel. When she gets home, she'll make a cup of tea to accompany the shortbread, breaking off a small piece for the dog, too.

With each address I write—especially the ones with destinations so far abroad—I wonder if I will ever see that person again. But those who make a lasting impression on me will always carve themselves into my heart. That's why at Christmas I'll always sit down with a stack of cards and a good pen. While the greeting may be brief, the intention runs deep. The holidays are about hope and blessings and goodwill (and good eats!), but I find I become a bit of a reflector. What I wouldn't give to have every soul I've ever loved in my living room. But at Christmas, in a way, they are. The faraway nearby, indeed.

WHAT I WOULDN'T GIVE TO HAVE EVERY SOUL I'VE EVER LOVED IN MY LIVING ROOM. BUT AT CHRISTMAS, IN A WAY, THEY ARE.

Red Wine and Dark Chocolate Truffles

Red wine and chocolate are two of my favourite food groups, so it seems only fitting that they should have a recipe devoted entirely to themselves. Truffles are pretty self-explanatory. They are those luscious orbs of devilish decadence, packaged up with pretty bows complete with a pretty price tag. There's never a bad time to make truffles, but if you're hoping to score points with a certain someone around the holidays or Valentine's Day, you can't go wrong with these. The chocolate should be the best you can afford, and whatever you do, no chocolate chips, please. They contain stabilizers so they hold their shape while being baked (fun fact!) and you don't want that in your truffles. As for the wine, use whatever red you like to drink. This is a great recipe for those last dregs on the bottom of the bottle you almost, but not quite, finished last night.

MAKES 30–36 TRUFFLES

2½ cups chopped (½-inch pieces) dark chocolate
½ cup + 2 Tbsp whipping cream
½ cup red wine
1 Tbsp unsalted butter
Pinch of flaky salt, such as Maldon
½ cup unsweetened cocoa powder

❄ Place the chopped chocolate in a medium bowl. Heat the whipping cream and red wine together in a medium saucepan over medium-high heat. Bring it just to a simmer and then remove the pan from the heat and pour the mixture over the chopped chocolate. Add the butter and salt. Let the mixture stand for about 5 minutes before stirring from the outside in until the chocolate is completely smooth. Let the chocolate come to room temperature, then cover with plastic and refrigerate until firm enough to roll, at least 8 hours but ideally overnight. Congratulations! You've just made ganache!

❄ Sift the cocoa powder into a shallow bowl and scoop a heaping teaspoon of ganache into your hands. Roll the ganache into balls, about 1 inch in diameter or however large (or small) you want to make them. Toss them gently into the cocoa powder. This is a messy job. If this bothers you, you can wear latex or vinyl disposable gloves. Place the truffles on a baking sheet after you roll them in the cocoa. After you've rolled all of the truffles, put them in an airtight container and store them in the refrigerator until you're ready to serve them or package them up.

❄ Truffles taste best after they've been sitting at room temperature for at least 15 minutes. You may have to dust more cocoa powder on them before serving, as it will absorb slightly the longer they sit. The truffles can be kept in an airtight container in the refrigerator for 2–3 weeks.

Caramel Popcorn with Roasted Nuts

For years and years, my mom would make this caramel popcorn at Christmas. Package it up in pretty tins for her kids, she did. All the times I was driving the hundreds of miles home for the holidays, with a couple of wailing cats in the backseat, this popcorn was my light at the end of the tunnel. Well, that and my mom. This popcorn is buttery. No, it is VERY buttery. And heaving with caramel and roasted nuts. You'll want to go for a hike or a skate or a jog around the block after heavy consumption of this stuff. Making the caramel is like a fun science project and requires your undivided attention. There is tremendous bubbling, especially when you add the baking soda and booze, but don't be afraid. This is all normal. After that, you're almost done, and given that this makes a rather large batch, you can keep some for yourself AND pack it up to give away. Everybody wins! Just between you and me, this has been known to very sneakily find its way into a movie theatre over the holiday season. Shhhh! Don't tell!

MAKES ABOUT 25 CUPS

3 cups nuts, preferably unsalted pecan halves
   and almonds
18 cups freshly popped popcorn
   (¾ cup unpopped popcorn kernels)
2²/₃ cups packed brown sugar
2 cups salted butter, plus more for greasing
   the pans
1 cup golden syrup or dark corn syrup
1 tsp cream of tartar
1 Tbsp rum (white or dark)
1 tsp baking soda

✻ Preheat the oven to 350°F. Place the rack in the centre of the oven. Butter 2 rimmed baking sheets.

✻ Spread the nuts on an ungreased baking sheet and roast for 5 minutes, stirring occasionally and keeping an eye on them so they don't burn. Let them cool completely then mix with your popped corn in a VERY large bowl, or 2 large bowls. Combine the sugar, butter, syrup and cream of tartar in a large, deep saucepan. Cook over medium-high heat for about 5 minutes, until a small amount forms a ball when dropped into a glass of cold water. It's tricky, I know, but trust me, it will be okay. Just stir, stir, stir.

✻ Remove the caramel from the heat and stir in the rum and baking soda. It will bubble up quite a lot, but this is normal. Pour this over the nuts and popcorn. Stir everything really well, and then divide it between the 2 buttered baking sheets. Press the caramel corn into the pans. Let the popcorn cool then tear it into pieces to devour immediately, or pack it into airtight containers.

✻ This keeps well in an airtight container for up to 1 week, or you can freeze it for up to 1 month—just let it thaw for an hour before digging in.

CHOCOLATE-DIPPED PRETZELS

These are a quick and simple treat that you can really have fun with. Use dark or white chocolate and whatever colour sprinkles you like. White chocolate with black sprinkles would look cool, as would dark chocolate and all red or green or blue sprinkles. You get the idea. Use your imagination, and create little edible masterpieces. This is a great way to involve kids, though if they're anything like me, there will be lots of chocolate-dipped fingers, too. These pretzels look festive and fancy when they're packaged in clear cellophane bags tied with a pretty bow.

MAKES 3–4 DOZEN PRETZELS

2¼ cups chopped (½-inch pieces) chocolate
  (white or dark chocolate)
1 cup sprinkles of your choice
36-48 small hard pretzels

❄ Line a baking sheet with parchment paper and set aside.

❄ Place the chopped chocolate in a heatproof bowl. Simmer 2 inches of water in a medium saucepan over medium heat. Place the bowl of chocolate over the pot of simmering water, making sure that the bowl is not touching the water. Stir gently and continuously until the chocolate is melted and perfectly smooth. Remove the bowl from the heat. Dip the pretzels into the melted chocolate, using a couple of forks to retrieve them. Place them on the baking sheet and lightly cover in sprinkles. Alternatively, you can dip the pretzels in the chocolate, leaving one corner undipped, then dip the pretzels in a bowl of sprinkles for heavier coverage. When you're done dipping and sprinkling the pretzels, place the baking sheet in the freezer to shock them, about 5 minutes.

❄ When the chocolate is hard, place the dipped pretzels in an airtight container and store them in the refrigerator for up to 1 week.

NOTE

If you're using white chocolate, add 1 tsp of coconut oil to it as it's melting. White chocolate has a tendency to seize up, and the coconut oil helps alleviate that.

Double Chocolate Peppermint Bark

Chocolate bark is one of my favourite treats to give away at the holidays because it's so darn easy to prepare and everyone loves it. The method is quite simple—just melt some chocolate and top it with your favourite candy; bonus points if you have Halloween candy still around the house and want to use it up. I use both dark and white chocolate here, plus crushed candy cane pieces along with other bits and bobs of candy from last year's gingerbread house extravaganza. You never know what you'll find in the back of my cupboard! Coconut oil may seem like an odd thing to add to chocolate as it melts, but it creates a nice sheen and aids in the melting process, especially with temperamental white chocolate, which has a tendency to seize up. And you don't want that to happen. For the best flavour, use the best chocolate you can afford.

MAKES 1 (8-INCH SQUARE) PAN

1½ cups dark chocolate chunks
1 tsp coconut oil, divided
1 ½ cups white chocolate chunks
½ cup crushed candy cane pieces
Sprinkles and other candy (optional)

❋ Line an 8-inch square baking dish with aluminum foil, pressing down to ensure it is smooth.

❋ Melt the dark chocolate with ¼ tsp of the coconut oil in a small saucepan over low heat, stirring constantly until it's completely smooth. When the chocolate is melted and smooth, pour it into the bottom of the prepared dish and place it in the freezer for 15 minutes. In a separate small saucepan (or wash the one you previously used), melt the white chocolate with the remaining ¾ tsp of coconut oil, stirring until completely smooth.

❋ Remove the dish of dark chocolate from the freezer and pour the white chocolate overtop of the dark, using an offset spatula to spread it evenly. Sprinkle with crushed candy cane pieces, and other candy if you wish. Place the dish in the refrigerator until the bark is set, 30–45 minutes. Break the bark into pieces and serve immediately or package it up to give away.

❋ This keeps for up to 2 weeks in an airtight container in the refrigerator.

NOTES

The chocolate can be melted in a microwave instead of on the stovetop. It takes just a minute or two, including stirring occasionally. Be sure to add the coconut oil here as well.

If you aren't into the whole candy thing, add dried fruit and nuts for a healthier take on chocolate bark. The process and volume remain the same.

Honeycomb

Science was never my favourite subject in school, but this is one science project I can fully endorse as it's tremendously exciting to watch and tremendously delicious to eat. However, I'm not going to lie to you. Making honeycomb is tricky. You need to have a candy thermometer. You have to add the baking soda right at the perfect temperature, otherwise either it will burn and likely set off the smoke detector or there won't be as many bubbles and the candy will be flat and underwhelming. I've experienced both scenarios, and in fact, the photograph here is my third try. So keep at it, because when you add the baking soda at the right second and all goes according to plan, it's candy perfection. The golden goo, as I affectionately call it, bubbles and spurts, and you can't take your eyes off it while it's in action. The sugar continues to cook and the baking soda creates pockets of air, which will melt in your mouth when the whole thing cools down. Older kids, heck, even teenagers, might want to get involved when they see just how cool baking with three simple ingredients can be. Let them dunk the honeycomb in melted chocolate and you've got a friend for life.

MAKES ABOUT 24 SMALL PIECES

1 cup minus 1 Tbsp granulated sugar
½ cup minus 1 Tbsp liquid honey
2 tsp baking soda

❋ Line a 10-inch square baking dish with parchment paper, with an overlap on all sides at least 3 inches high—this will be for the honeycomb to "climb." If you don't have a 10-inch baking dish, use a 9-inch square baking dish and have the parchment about 4 inches high on all sides.

❋ Melt the sugar and honey in a heavy-bottomed medium saucepan over low heat for 5–8 minutes, until the sugar is completely melted and smooth, stirring occasionally. Increase the heat to medium-high and let the mixture bubble away, without stirring it, for about 5 minutes, until it's a dark golden colour and reaches about 290°F on a candy thermometer.

❋ Turn off the heat, toss in the baking soda and beat it very quickly by hand for about 5 seconds. It will be bubbling profusely and foaming up. Pour the honeycomb immediately into the prepared dish and watch as it bubbles away and then gradually deflates. Don't move the honeycomb as it's cooling down. Once it has completely cooled, break it into pieces.

❋ You can store this in an airtight container for up to 1 week.

NOTES

With the addition of honey, this honeycomb is a bit stickier and sweeter than traditional sponge toffee. Still, it's amazing—especially when dipped in dark chocolate. To do this, chop dark chocolate into ½-inch pieces so you get about 1½ cups and either microwave it on low, stirring occasionally, or set it in a small saucepan over low heat and stir constantly until it is smooth. Add ¼ tsp of coconut oil to the chocolate as it is melting.

I used a wooden spoon to stir in the baking soda.

Chocolate Nut Clusters with Fleur de Sel

Candy making does not have to be complicated. Take these chocolate nut clusters as proof of that. Melt chocolate, stir in nuts, drop onto parchment, sprinkle with salt and ta-da! You've got delicious treats to give away to those you love best. Or keep them all for yourself to nibble on while you binge-watch *The West Wing*. I approve of either option. Use good chocolate here—it will shine through in the final product—and do melt it in two steps. This is a bit of a cheater method when it comes to tempering chocolate, but it works well. Toasting the nuts brings out their flavour. And do add the salt. Maldon is a little pricey, but when you see how flakes of it shine on the chocolate, you'll agree that it's completely worth it.

MAKES ABOUT 16 CLUSTERS

2 cups raw, unsalted nuts
2 cups chopped (½-inch pieces) dark chocolate
½ tsp coconut oil
1–2 tsp flaky salt, such as Maldon

❉ Preheat the oven to 350°F. Place the rack in the centre of the oven. Line a rimmed baking sheet with parchment paper.

❉ Spread the nuts onto the parchment and toast for 5 minutes, until they are fragrant. Set the timer! There's nothing worse than burnt nuts. Let the nuts cool completely on the baking sheet.

❉ Melt half of the chocolate in a medium saucepan over low heat, stirring until it's completely smooth. Add the remaining chocolate with the coconut oil and stir again, until fully melted and smooth. Stir in the nuts until they're evenly covered with chocolate. Drop by tablespoonfuls onto the parchment-lined baking sheet you used for toasting the nuts and sprinkle with flaky salt. Allow the clusters to cool completely.

❉ Store the nuts clusters in an airtight container in the refrigerator for up to 2 weeks.

NOTES

Use any nuts you like—whole almonds, pecan or walnut halves, Brazil nuts, cashews, peanuts or a combination.

The chocolate can be melted in a microwave instead of on the stovetop using the same method. It takes just a minute or two, including stirring occasionally. Be sure to add the coconut oil with the second addition of chocolate.

The recipe can be easily doubled.

Vanilla Bean Marshmallows

Have you noticed that all the fancy pastry shops have pretty bags of homemade marshmallows for you to buy? I've bought these ribboned parcels in the name of "research," just to see what the fuss is all about. Now I know. There really is nothing like the magnificence of a homemade marshmallow. Fluffy, yes, but with a toothsome density that's terribly appealing. Once you taste these, you'll never want to buy marshmallows again, unless it's for a batch of beloved rice crispy squares (no, I haven't included them in this book) or for Chocolate Marshmallow Pie (page 184). Those recipes need definitive amounts. But for good ol' snacking and gift giving, make a batch of these. All that is necessary is a stand mixer, some gelatin and various forms of sugar. This is another of those scientific marvels I love about baking. Yay, science! In case you were wondering, these melt exquisitely well in hot chocolate, and your s'more game will be knocked out of the park when you use them. Play around with other flavours. Once you make them, I guarantee you'll be hooked.

MAKES 24–36 MARSHMALLOWS

1½ Tbsp canola or vegetable oil, plus more for hands
1 cup cold water, divided
3 Tbsp unflavoured powdered gelatin (typically 3 pkgs)
1½ Tbsp vanilla bean paste or 1 vanilla bean scraped of its seeds, or 1 Tbsp pure vanilla extract

2 cups granulated sugar
$^2/_3$ cup light corn syrup
¼ tsp salt
1 cup icing sugar
½ cup cornstarch

※ Pour the oil into a 9×13-inch baking dish and spread it evenly around. Be sure that all of the sides, corners and bottom have a thin layer of oil.

※ Pour ½ cup cold water into the bowl of a stand mixer fitted with a whisk attachment. Stir in the gelatin and vanilla bean paste by hand. Continue stirring until there are no large lumps. Let this stand for 15 minutes. Combine the granulated sugar, corn syrup, salt and ½ cup cold water in a medium saucepan. Stir over medium-high heat until the sugar dissolves, brushing down the sides of the pan with a wet pastry brush. Attach a candy thermometer to the side of the pan, being certain it's not touching the bottom. Increase the heat to high and bring the mixture to a boil. Do not stir. Boil the mixture for 7–8 minutes, or until the syrup reaches 247°F–250°F.

※ Take the pan off the heat and remove the thermometer. Turn on your mixer to medium-low speed and slowly pour the hot syrup into the gelatin mixture in a thin stream down the side of the bowl. Try not to get any onto the whisk as it may splash out onto you, and you don't want that. Gradually increase the speed to high and beat until the mixture is very thick, 10–12 minutes.

※ Now the tough part. This marshmallow fluff is VERY sticky. Bring the bowl close to your prepared pan and use a very firm spatula to scrape the marshmallow into the pan. You may need to grease your hands to smooth the top of the marshmallow. Try to get it as even as you can. The marshmallow should come about halfway up the sides of the pan. Let the marshmallow block sit, uncovered, at room temperature for at least 6 hours or overnight.

※ This is the "curing" process. When you're ready to cut the marshmallows, put the icing sugar and cornstarch into a resealable plastic bag. Shake it well. Sprinkle the top of the marshmallow block with some of the icing sugar/cornstarch mixture and smooth it with your hand. Dust some onto your work surface and flip the block of marshmallow onto it. Use a spatula to pry the marshmallow out of the pan if it's stuck. Once it's on your counter, sprinkle more icing sugar/cornstarch mixture

on top of the marshmallow block. Using a very sharp knife, cut the marshmallow into your desired shapes and sizes. I like to dip the knife in hot water between each cut. The marshmallows are very, very sticky! Once they're cut, drop a few marshmallows into the plastic bag and shake to coat them evenly. Tap off any excess coating and serve.

❄ The marshmallows will keep for up to 2 weeks in an airtight container at room temperature. If you're giving them away as gifts, be sure they're sealed up well. This will prevent them from drying out.

NOTES

Play around with flavour extracts. Maple, almond, peppermint, orange or rosewater would all be delicious. If you aren't averse to food colouring, add a drop or two when you add the vanilla.

You'll likely have some icing sugar/cornstarch mixture left over, but you do need to make as much as the recipe says so that the marshmallows can be tossed and covered properly. Consider the leftovers an incentive to make marshmallows again!

Almond and Orange Chocolate Macaroon Truffles

I'm not a picky eater. There are, however, a few things I do run away from. Offal and bugs are two of them. Tripe does not rock my world—just ask those who've had dim sum with me—and the only time I've eaten bugs was on a speeding motorboat while fishing up in Yukon. It was under the midnight sun and we were out past our bedtime. Still. Not a fan of swallowing bugs. Raisins and coconut are also on that list, and their general omission from this cookbook hasn't been unintentional. Perhaps this makes me a weirdo, but I figure I checked that box long ago when I got my fourth cat. No matter. So, these truffles are for the coconut lovers out there who've been neglected up until now. And they are super simple to prepare: make the macaroons, then squish them up and roll them into balls. Dip and drizzle with chocolate. And you know what? I kinda like them! This says a lot for someone who has shredded coconut on the same list as beef tongue.

MAKES 26–30 TRUFFLES

2¾ cups unsweetened shredded coconut
½ cup ground almonds
1 (10 oz) can sweetened condensed milk
1 tsp grated orange zest
1 tsp pure vanilla extract

2 large egg whites, at room temperature
½ tsp salt
½ cup chopped (½-inch pieces) dark chocolate
½ tsp coconut oil

❋ Preheat the oven to 350°F. Place racks in the upper and lower thirds of the oven. Line 2 rimmed baking sheets with parchment paper.

❋ Mix together the coconut, ground almonds, condensed milk, orange zest and vanilla in a medium bowl. In a stand mixer fitted with a whisk attachment, beat the egg whites and salt together until stiff peaks form. Gently fold the whites into the coconut mixture. Use an ice cream scoop (about ¼-cup size) to mound the cookies onto the baking sheets, spacing them about 2 inches apart. Place the baking sheets in the oven and bake for about 20 minutes, rotating their shelf positions halfway through. The cookies should be golden around the edges. Let them cool completely.

❋ You can stop now and eat them as is (except, of course, you won't be able to call them truffles), or you can grind them in a food processor fitted with the steel blade until they are coarse crumbs and stick together when squeezed by hand. If they don't stick together, add a drop or two of water. Scoop a small amount of the macaroon mixture into your hands and roll into balls about 1 inch in diameter. Place these truffles on a baking sheet and refrigerate, uncovered, for 30 minutes. Melt the chocolate and coconut oil in a small saucepan over low heat, stirring constantly until smooth. Line another baking sheet with wax paper or parchment paper and dip the bottoms of the truffles into the chocolate. Place them on the wax paper and drizzle any remaining chocolate on top of them.

❋ Refrigerate, uncovered, until set, then place them in an airtight container and keep refrigerated for up to 1 week. These can also be frozen for up to 1 month.

Maple Pumpkin Seed Brittle

I've never been one for peanut brittle. It's too sweet and it hurts my teeth. It's kinda my philosophy that sweet things shouldn't make your mouth hurt. As my dentist (hi, Eunice!) can attest, my chompers aren't in the best shape and it's best if I avoid anything too caramelly or crunchy—the two combined spell a dental disaster. This brittle is cool because I use maple syrup, so it doesn't set up quite as firm as traditional peanut brittle and the pumpkin seeds are a nice touch for those who have a nut allergy. Spiked with cardamom and salt, the brittle is wonderful when crushed between layers of Carrot Cake (page 140) and it adds a lovely texture to the Butterscotch Pudding Parfaits (page 196). If you want to share the love, you can never go wrong with packaging this brittle up and giving it away at the holidays.

MAKES ABOUT 1½ CUPS

1 Tbsp olive oil, for brushing the parchment
½ cup raw unsalted pumpkin seeds
½ cup pure maple syrup
½ tsp ground cardamom
¼ tsp salt

❋ Preheat the oven to 375°F. Place the rack in the centre of the oven. Line a rimmed baking sheet with parchment paper and brush the parchment evenly with the olive oil.

❋ Stir together the pumpkin seeds, maple syrup, cardamom and salt. Pour this mixture onto the prepared baking sheet (it won't spread to the sides and it will be a funky, uneven shape) and bake for 15 minutes, rotating the sheet 180 degrees at the 8-minute mark. The brittle should be bubbling and golden. Remove the baking sheet from the oven and let it cool completely on a wire rack.

❋ Break the brittle into pieces and store it in an airtight container at room temperature for up to 2 weeks.

Chocolate Peanut Butter Cups

For those of us who are fond of the chocolate/peanut butter combo, these are pretty much a dream come true. If you're like me, you can recall sticking large chunks of dark chocolate into the peanut butter jar and eating it as is. This was an activity best enjoyed when no one else was around, lest they catch onto your secret and force you to share. God forbid that should happen. Perhaps you too have memories of ripping open that famous orange candy bar package containing three chocolate peanut butter cups, eating them in too-quick succession and feeling slightly nauseated afterwards. Whenever someone admits to me that they don't like chocolate and peanut butter together, I give them a look of pity and disbelief. Poor things. More for us, then. And if you don't feel like standing at the counter and making 36 individual peanut butter cups, I have good news! Simply double the recipe and press the peanut butter mixture into a parchment-lined 9×13-inch baking dish. Pour the chocolate on top and refrigerate before cutting into bars.

MAKES ABOUT 3 DOZEN

1 cup + 2 Tbsp graham cracker crumbs
¾ cup icing sugar
²/₃ cup natural smooth peanut butter
   (containing only peanuts)
¼ cup unsalted butter, melted
Pinch of salt
¾ cup chopped (½-inch pieces) dark chocolate
½ tsp coconut oil
Flaky salt, for garnish (optional)

❋ Combine the graham crumbs, icing sugar, peanut butter, melted butter and salt in the bowl of a food processor fitted with the steel blade. Process until smooth and uniform. The mixture should also hold its shape when squeezed gently. Arrange 36 miniature paper cups on a tray or baking sheet. Use a heaping teaspoon to scoop out the peanut butter mixture and press it firmly into the cups.

❋ Melt the chocolate and coconut oil over low heat in a small saucepan, stirring until smooth. (You can do this in the microwave as well.) Pour 1 tsp of chocolate over each peanut butter cup, gently shaking the cup to smooth out the chocolate. Sprinkle each one with flaky salt and refrigerate, uncovered, until the chocolate has set.

❋ These keep well in an airtight container in the refrigerator for up to 1 week.

NOTES

I use miniature foil-lined baking cups by Reynolds, which I found in the baking aisle of my supermarket. They measure 1½ inches in diameter.

If you find your graham cracker crumbs are too coarse, blitz them in a blender or food processor for a bit until they're finer.

If you don't have a food processor, you can still make this recipe. Place the crumbs in a blender to process them a little finer first, then add the remaining ingredients and proceed with the rest of the recipe.

Chocolate-Swirled Molasses Meringues

Meringue is nothing but egg whites and sugar and rules. Lots of rules. But if you abide by them, you'll have light-as-air, melt-in-your-mouth, tiny pillows of confectionary bliss. If you don't follow the rules, you won't have any of that and you'll be sad. The result should be glossy, thick peaks, though don't overbeat the meringue, either. It's always good to stop when you're ahead of the game. I love how these are still chewy in the centre and ever so delicately crispy on the out-side. The molasses flavour is hanging out in the background—subtle and yet seductive—and the coating of cocoa powder and cinnamon is terribly attractive and incredibly tasty.

MAKES ABOUT 16 MERINGUES

4 large egg whites, at room temperature
1 cup granulated sugar
1 tsp molasses
½ tsp vanilla bean paste or pure vanilla extract
1 Tbsp unsweetened cocoa powder
¼ tsp ground cinnamon

❋ Preheat the oven to 215°F. Place racks in the upper and lower thirds of the oven. Line 2 baking sheets with parchment paper.

❋ In a stand mixer fitted with a whisk attachment, beat the egg whites on high speed until soft peaks form. Gradually add the sugar 1 Tbsp at a time, beating until all of the sugar dissolves and the egg whites are thick and glossy, 3–5 minutes. Stop the mixer occasionally and dip your finger into the meringue. Rub your fingers together. When you don't feel any sugar crystals, the meringue is done. With the mixer running on medium speed, beat in the molasses and vanilla until evenly mixed, stopping once or twice to scrape down the bowl. Stir together the cocoa powder and cinnamon in a small bowl and sift over the meringue. Do not stir!

❋ Use a ¼-cup ice cream scoop to gently scoop out meringues, placing them about 2 inches apart on the prepared baking sheets. Place the baking sheets in the oven and bake for about 1 hour and 5 minutes, rotating their shelf positions halfway through. You should be able to lift them off the parchment paper. If they don't release easily, bake them until they do. Turn the oven off, prop the oven door open with a wooden spoon and let the meringues cool inside for another hour. Once they sound hollow when tapped on the bottom, remove them from the oven.

❋ Eat these plain or with whipped cream and berries. They keep well in an airtight container at room temperature for up to 1 week. Do not refrigerate.

NOTES

Humidity plays a major role when baking meringues. My climate is quite dry, so this baking time is what works well for me. If your climate is more humid, it could take anywhere up to 4 hours for the meringues to be done (between baking time and sitting time). The clear sign they are finished baking is when they easily release from the parchment. If they're sticking, they aren't done and need a little longer. Don't turn the oven off until they release from the parchment.

If you don't have an ice cream scoop, dollop the meringues onto the parchment so they're approximately 2 inches wide and 1½ inches high. Try not to stir too much cocoa powder and cinnamon into the meringue as you're scooping, as you want that pretty, marbled look.

Recipes

THE
FREEZER
SECTION

ICE CREAM

I don't have many memories of my dad, which is probably the biggest hurt that my heart has to hold. But there are a few, and I hope they never leave until my last breath has to leave me. I remember us bumbling down the grid roads in our pickup truck, heading towards the tiny hamlet of Cactus Lake. Here we would stop at the only store around for miles, and I remember standing on the well-worn wooden floors, eyeing up the candy section, the cooler of pop and the small freezer full of ice cream. Sometimes I left with a root beer, or the tartan package of Mackintosh's toffee (see Maple Pumpkin Seed Brittle, page 278—this is probably where it all began). And sometimes I left with ice cream, licking it dreamily like kids do. We would then pile back into the truck, making our way south, back to the farm, passing fields of gold and herds of cows. Not a cactus in sight. And that is where the memory ends. But not my love of ice cream.

I remember my mom cooking up a chocolate sauce on the stove, the smell of cocoa and sugar breaking down into something magnificent. Four kids with empty bowls and small spoons sat at the kitchen table, watching her in anticipation. While she let the sauce cool down a bit, two, three scoops of vanilla ice cream filled our bowls and then she would drizzle the still-warm sauce over it. I would watch the chocolate as it came down in a thick ribbon and then, as it pooled in the bottom of my bowl, mixed together with the ice cream it had melted on the short slide down. The swirls of dark brown, light brown, palest brown were so beautiful to watch I didn't want their performance to end. Mom would say, "Renée, eat your ice cream before it's all melted," and I would snap back to reality, eagerly tucking into what was left, spooning up the last of the sauce, licking my lips.

When I lived in Montreal, Ben and Jerry's was just a hop, skip and a jump away from Concordia, and on their free ice cream days, I would line up with the other students, because, well, free ice cream. I'm a bit of a purist and likely got something with chocolate and caramel, and then my friends and I would sit on the sidewalk afterwards, feeling pretty good about our deal, our day, the pure magic of living in a big city when you're young.

Ice cream in Yukon was a luxury, and was seldom brought in because it had to travel so far to reach us, and if it had to stay for any amount of time outside of a freezer, it would arrive in a sad, sad state. But when it did arrive, more or less intact, there were sundaes for the staff, and it was ecstasy. For one or two days out of the summer, we were doing what everyone down south was doing on a much more regular basis. I didn't miss many things those four months I was in Yukon, but I did miss that first spoonful of really good ice cream hitting the tongue, the first crunch of an ice cream cone, the second that hot fudge meets cold ice cream.

Whenever I visit good friends in the summer, they always take me for ice cream. Toronto has no shortage of fine ice cream parlours. Josée, who would line up with me for free ice cream in Montreal, now has two kids who know a thing or two about ice cream. Her son Bram especially has great taste and he never steers me wrong on flavours to try. Salted caramel. Chocolate and cherry. The most perfect raspberry gelato. We sit on a picnic table outside, the kids licking cones, and us, the grown-ups (how did that happen?) eating some of the best ice cream I've ever had. It's a gorgeous moment. The kids. The summer. The friendship. It's more than the ice cream. It's the sum of all of its parts. These sweet moments, with family, with friends, are what linger with me long after the cones have been bitten and the bowls spooned of every last drop. Long after the ice cream has been put back into the freezer and the dishes done. Long after we are buckled in safe and sound and driving along the quiet prairie, listening to Johnny Cash on the radio. We make our way home, thankful for all of the sweet, frozen cream. For all of the sweet things.

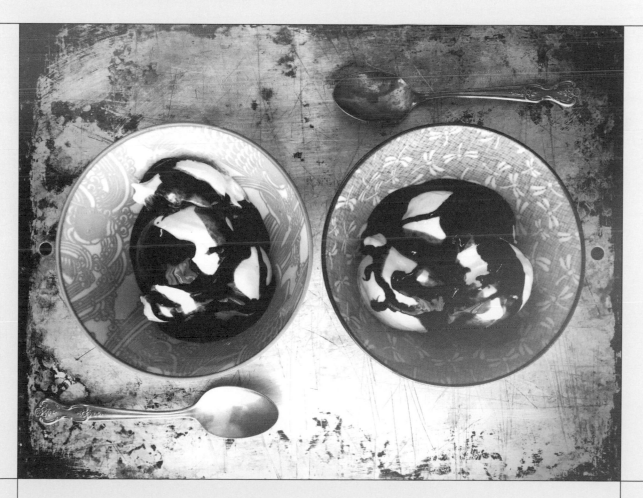

BLACKCURRANT AND VANILLA BEAN ICE CREAM TERRINE

I was never really a fan of currants until I tasted this ice cream. A friend had picked copious amounts, more than she could handle, and asked if I wanted some. Yes, please. It's always good to have friends who will drop fresh fruit off at your house. I could have turned them into a crisp, with some apples or raspberries, but it was summertime and the thought of turning the oven on made me shudder. Thus, this terrine. A simple vanilla base is swirled with a blackcurrant compote of sorts, making a great summertime patio dessert. The currants don't allow it to be terribly sweet, and as the pockets of deep purple swirl into vanilla bean cream, it's sure to please the eyes as well as the palate.

SERVES 8–10

2¾ cups blackcurrants (fresh or frozen)
3 Tbsp granulated sugar
½ tsp pure vanilla extract
2 cups whipping cream
1 (10 oz) can sweetened condensed milk
1 vanilla bean

⁎ Line a 9×5×3-inch freezer-safe container or loaf pan with parchment paper, with the paper overhanging the sides enough that it will meet in the middle when pulled over the pan.

⁎ Remove the stems from the currants and place the currants in a medium saucepan along with the sugar and 3 Tbsp water. Bring to a boil over high heat, turn down the heat to medium-low and simmer, uncovered, for 3–5 minutes, until the liquid is reduced a little. Remove the pan from the heat and let cool completely. Stir in the vanilla.

⁎ In a stand mixer fitted with a whisk attachment, beat the whipping cream on medium speed until soft peaks form, 2–4 minutes. Turn the mixer off. Add the condensed milk. Cut the vanilla bean in half and scrape out all of the seeds into the cream. Discard the pod. Beat on high speed until the cream holds its shape in medium-firm peaks, about 1 minute. The cream should slowly slide from the whisk attachment. Scrape this mixture into the prepared pan. Pour the currant mixture overtop and gently swirl the two together using a butter knife. You want some sections of just currant and just cream, so don't overdo it. Fold the parchment overhang on top of the ice cream and freeze for at least 6 hours. Remove the terrine from the freezer, let it stand for 10 minutes and then remove from the pan. Slice it with a warm, sharp knife and arrange on plates.

⁎ The terrine can be kept frozen for up to 2 weeks, though be sure it is wrapped very tightly in plastic.

Salted Caramel Toffee Chip Ice Cream

I'm convinced that if I had my very own ice cream maker at home, I would never leave my house—unless it was to get supplies to make more ice cream. I concocted this recipe while working as a pastry chef in the summer of 2015 at Riverside Golf and Country Club. As it was churning away, I would stick a spoon in just to "check consistency" as I like to call it. I did manage to save some for the dining room customers, but when Chef Darren wasn't looking, I would sneak a spoonful for "quality control measures." Ahem. While you do need an ice cream maker for this, and there are several steps involved, the end product will be equal to, if not better than, that of the fancy ice cream shops in your town. Note that you have to prep your ice cream maker a day ahead.

MAKES ABOUT 4 CUPS

1 cup granulated sugar
2¼ cups whipping cream, divided
2 tsp flaky salt, such as Maldon
2 tsp vanilla bean paste
1 cup whole milk
3 large eggs, at room temperature
¾ cup Skor toffee bits

❄ Freeze the container of your ice cream maker for at least 24 hours before you plan to make this.

❄ Heat the sugar in a medium saucepan over medium-high heat. Stir with a wooden spoon occasionally until it starts to melt. Stop stirring and let the sugar cook, swirling the pan occasionally, until it's dark amber, 8–10 minutes. Be sure not to let it burn. Turn off the heat.

❄ While the sugar is cooking, heat 1¼ cups of the whipping cream in a small saucepan over medium-high heat until bubbles start to form on the sides of the pot. Remove from the heat. Pour the hot cream into the hot sugar—be careful, as a large waft of steam will come off the sugar—and stir constantly with a wooden spoon until the caramel cooks down and is smooth. If there are any solid bits of sugar, place the saucepan on medium heat and stir until smooth.

❄ Pour the caramel into a medium bowl and then stir in the salt and vanilla. Let it cool to room temperature.

❄ Bring the milk and the remaining 1 cup of whipping cream to a boil in another medium saucepan over medium-high heat, stirring occasionally. Whisk the eggs in a medium bowl, then add half of the hot milk mixture to them in a slow stream, whisking constantly. If the bowl is sliding around, place a damp tea towel under it. Pour this egg mixture back into the saucepan, whisking constantly, on medium heat. Stir constantly with a heatproof spatula until the custard reaches 170°F. Use a thermometer to check the temperature. Do not let it boil or it will curdle.

❄ Strain the custard through a fine mesh sieve into a clean medium-size bowl. Stir the salted caramel into the strained custard and mix well. Chill, uncovered, for 2–3 hours.

❄ Pour the salted caramel custard into the cold ice cream maker along with the toffee bits, let it churn until thick and creamy, and then scoop it into an airtight freezer-safe container.

❄ This will keep well in the freezer for up to 1 month.

NOTE

This recipe was tested in a 2-quart ice cream maker. If yours is smaller, consider making it in 2 batches.

Strawberry Balsamic Ice Cream

I have stacks of cookbooks all around my house. Most of these books are too beautiful to be stuffed away into a cupboard. Now and then I'll cozy up with one of them to read while sipping tea on a lazy afternoon, or when I'm nestled in bed—you know, to encourage sweet dreams. Nigel Slater's *Ripe* is one of my favourite go-to books for such times, as much for the photographs as the writing. Devoted to all things fruit, this book is an education and an inspiration. From that inspiration, I came up with this recipe on a sweltering July day when I had a mountain of strawberries practically bursting with ripeness.

There's no need for an ice cream maker here; all you need is a food processor, a mixer and a handful of ingredients. The result? A fresh, creamy taste, with deep strawberry flavour and just a murmur of balsamic. Simple. Sensational.

MAKES ABOUT 4 CUPS

3¾ cups fresh, ripe strawberries, rinsed
½ cup superfine sugar
2 tsp balsamic vinegar
1¼ cups whipping cream
½ cup finely chopped pistachios, for garnish

❋ Hull and thinly slice the strawberries. Put them in a medium bowl and sprinkle with the sugar. Let them rest, uncovered, for 1 hour at room temperature.

❋ Scrape the strawberries and all of the juices into the bowl of a food processor fitted with the steel blade and process until smooth. Pour this purée into a large bowl and stir in the balsamic vinegar. In a stand mixer fitted with a whisk attachment, whip the cream into soft peaks. Gently stir the whipped cream into the strawberry purée, leaving chunks of white showing. Pour the ice cream into a freezer-safe 6- or 8-cup container, preferably one with a lid, and freeze for 3-4 hours, stirring every hour and bringing the outside edges into the centre. If you don't have a freezer-safe container with a lid, a 9×5×3-inch glass loaf pan will do fine. Just cover the ice cream tightly with plastic wrap.

❋ Remove the ice cream from the freezer about 20 minutes before you want to serve it. It will keep well in the freezer in an airtight container for up to 4 days, though it's best enjoyed the day it's made.

NOTES

I like to use local strawberries for this ice cream.

To make your own superfine sugar, simply grind granulated white sugar in the bowl of a food processor or blender to make the crystals smaller. A mortar and pestle will do the trick, too.

No-Churn Black Forest Ice Cream with Sour Cherry Ripple

I'm fortunate to live in a part of Canada where lovely sour cherries grow. Orchards are scattered throughout Saskatchewan, and if I can't get out to pick my own sour cherries, there is a local supply of frozen ones at the farmers' market for a reasonable cost. Best deal in town, come the dead of winter.

Cherries and chocolate love to be together in ice cream. This no-churn style has a ripple of sour cherry compote running through it, making it kind of tart, kind of sweet and all kinds of delicious. I like to let the ice cream soften a bit before I scoop it into cones. There's nothing better to eat as I sit in my backyard on an August afternoon, watching the dragonflies dance high above the treetops while a thunderstorm rumbles off in the distance.

MAKES ABOUT 4 CUPS

2 cups pitted sour cherries
   (frozen can be used)
¼ cup granulated sugar
2 Tbsp water
2 cups whipping cream
1 (10 oz) can sweetened condensed milk
½ cup unsweetened cocoa powder

❋ Put the cherries, sugar and water in a medium saucepan and bring to a boil over medium-high heat. Turn down the heat to low and simmer, uncovered, for 12 minutes, until syrupy. Remove from the heat and let cool completely. This can be done up to a week in advance—just keep the cherry sauce in an airtight container in the refrigerator until needed.

❋ In a stand mixer fitted with a whisk attachment, beat the cream on high speed until soft peaks form. Add the condensed milk and sift in the cocoa powder. Beat on medium-high speed until stiff peaks form. Scrape down the sides of the bowl occasionally. Scrape half of this chocolate cream into a freezer-safe container or 9×5×3-inch loaf pan. Spoon half of the sour cherry sauce on top and gently swirl the layers together with a butter knife. Repeat with the remaining chocolate cream and cherry sauce, giving it a final swirl. Freeze until set, about 4 hours, then serve.

❋ This keeps well in an airtight container in the freezer for up to 2 weeks—be sure to cover it tightly with plastic wrap if you are using a loaf pan.

NOTES

Sweet cherries can be substituted for the sour cherries, though the ice cream will be sweeter.

Make a double batch of the sour cherry sauce and use it on top of yogurt, pancakes, waffles or cake.

Honey Bourbon Vanilla Ice Cream

There's nothing quite like a spoonful of good vanilla ice cream. I'm not talking about the huge pails of modified milk ingredients mixed with fructose/glucose and other such nonsense ingredients. I don't go near that stuff. I'm talking about real ice cream, made with cream, egg yolks and just a few add-ins you know how to pronounce. Like bourbon. I can pronounce that very well. The neat thing about this recipe is that the flavour depends on the type of honey you use. Buckwheat will produce a bolder ice cream, with a dark, intense flavour. For a lighter route, clover and fireweed will do just fine. I love to buy honey locally, and a jar of it never lasts too long in my house. Winnie the Pooh and I are kindred spirits in that regard. If you make your own espresso at home, do me a favour and pour a shot over this ice cream for the most perfect affogato. You're welcome. Note that you have to prep your ice cream maker a day ahead.

MAKES ABOUT 6 CUPS

3 cups half-and-half cream
1 cup whipping cream
²⁄₃ cup raw, unpasteurized honey
4 large egg yolks, at room temperature
1 Tbsp bourbon
1 vanilla bean
¼ tsp flaky salt, such as Maldon

✳ Freeze the container of your ice cream maker for at least 24 hours before you plan to make this.

✳ Heat the half-and-half, whipping cream and honey in a medium saucepan over medium-high heat just until it is steaming, whisking to dissolve the honey. Do not let it boil. Remove from the heat.

✳ Whisk the egg yolks in a large bowl. Gradually pour in 1 cup of the hot cream mixture in a steady stream, whisking constantly. The yolks should be slightly warm to the touch. Whisk the egg yolks back into the hot cream in the saucepan. Put this mixture back on medium-high heat and cook it for 2–3 minutes, stirring constantly, until steaming but not boiling. A thermometer will read 170°F. Remove the pan from the heat. Stir in the bourbon. Slice the vanilla bean in half, scrape the seeds into the cream and discard the pod. Stir in the salt. Pour the mixture into a clean bowl and let it cool to room temperature.

✳ Refrigerate, uncovered, for 2 hours. Pour the mixture into the frozen container of your ice cream machine and let it churn until thick, about 30 minutes. Scrape the ice cream into a freezer-safe container or a 9×5×3-inch loaf pan (they don't have to be cold when you do this), and freeze until solid. If you're using a loaf pan, wrap the ice cream well with plastic.

✳ The ice cream will last for up to 2 weeks in the freezer.

NOTES

If you don't have a vanilla bean, use 2 tsp of vanilla extract or 2 tsp of vanilla bean paste, but you won't get the lovely flakes of colour if you use extract.

This recipe was tested in a 2-quart ice cream maker. If yours is smaller, consider making it in 2 batches.

Mango Ginger Lime Sorbet

The first time I ate a mango, I was standing over the sink in my friend Ariel's kitchen at the end of summer in 1994. She couldn't believe I'd gone over 20 years without eating a mango and sought to remedy that embarrassing fact. She picked out the biggest, ripest mango, and showed me how to slice it in half, cut the pit out and eat the sweet, ripe fruit all the way down to the peel. Juice ran down to my elbows, perhaps onto my sundress, but who cares? I've been a convert ever since. When mangoes are ripe, they taste like the beach and sunshine. When they are underripe, they taste like chalk. So, be sure your mangoes taste like beach and sunshine before proceeding with this recipe. I blend in ginger, lime juice, a bit of vodka and salt because they also belong with any beach experience, in my opinion. This sorbet is already super refreshing, but if you want more boozy punch, add more booze. Gin or tequila would also be quite good here, but I just love how the mango really shines through, taking me back to that tiny kitchen on a humid night in Montreal. Note that you have to prep your ice cream maker a day ahead.

MAKES ABOUT 6 CUPS

²/₃ cup granulated sugar
1-inch piece fresh, peeled ginger, thinly sliced
4 cups chopped fresh, ripe mango
   (about 4 large mangoes)
¼ cup fresh lime juice
2 tsp vodka
¼ tsp salt
Mint leaves, for garnish

❋ Freeze the container of your ice cream maker for at least 24 hours before you plan to make this.

❋ In a small saucepan over high heat, stir the sugar and sliced ginger with ²/₃ cup water. Bring to a boil, turn down the heat and stir until the sugar has completely dissolved. Let this syrup cool completely then strain it through a fine mesh sieve into a small bowl. Place the syrup in a blender then add the mango, lime juice, vodka and salt. Purée until very smooth. Strain through a fine mesh sieve into a large bowl. Pour the mango mixture into the container of your ice cream machine and let it churn until thick, about 30 minutes. Put it into a freezer-safe 6- or 8-cup container, or a 9×5×3-inch loaf pan (they don't have to be cold), and freeze until firm. Serve with a sprig of mint.

❋ This will keep well in the freezer for up to 1 week—be sure to wrap it tightly in plastic if your container doesn't have a lid.

Mascarpone Soft Serve with Chocolate Sauce

Does anyone else have memories of lining up at a Dairy Queen, ordering a chocolate-dipped cone and watching it come twirling out of the soft-serve machine? *How magical*, I thought, *to have ice cream come out of a machine like that.* The teenager behind the counter would then dip the cone in chocolate sauce and hand it to me, whereby I would proceed to inhale it.

Now that I'm a grown-up, with some mad ice cream–making skills of my own, I'm pretty pumped to pass this recipe for soft serve along to you. The best part is that you don't need an ice cream machine and you don't need to heat cream to a certain temperature. You do need a food processor, though, as that machine is what will break down the cubes of frozen goodness into creamy soft serve. You can pipe it out into swirls if you want to be fancy, but scooping it into bowls is just as fantastic. The chocolate sauce is just like the stuff my mom made when we were kids. It's full of intense chocolate flavour, and it's so easy to make. Let the sauce cool down a bit before you pour thick ribbons of it on bowls full of the soft serve. The gelatin gives the ice cream a velvety, almost mousse-like texture when it's whipped, which is all kinds of wonderful. We've already gone over how much I adore mascarpone, and it, as well as the cream cheese, gives this ice cream added flavour, as well as richness. Oh, mama!

MAKES ABOUT 8 CUPS

MASCARPONE SOFT SERVE
1¼ cups mascarpone cheese, softened
  (see my recipe on page 28)
1 cup full-fat cream cheese, softened
2 tsp pure vanilla extract
3 cups whole milk
1 (10 oz) can sweetened condensed milk
¼ cup granulated sugar
¼ tsp salt
4 tsp unflavoured powdered gelatin
  (just less than 2 pkgs)

CHOCOLATE SAUCE
1 cup unsweetened cocoa powder
1 cup granulated sugar
½ tsp salt
1 cup just-boiled water
2 tsp pure vanilla extract

❋ Line a 9×13-inch baking dish with parchment paper overhanging the sides.

❋ To make the soft serve, in a stand mixer fitted with a paddle attachment, beat the mascarpone, cream cheese and vanilla on medium-high speed until smooth, stopping to scrape down the bottom and sides of the bowl once or twice. Remove the paddle and add a whisk attachment.

❋ In a medium saucepan, whisk the milk, condensed milk, sugar and salt over medium-low heat just until the sugar has dissolved. Sprinkle the gelatin overtop. Increase the heat to medium-high and bring the mixture to a simmer. Cook it for 1 minute, stirring once or twice, to fully dissolve the gelatin. Remove the pan from the heat. With the mixer running on low speed, gradually pour the hot gelatin mixture into the mascarpone mixture. Stop the mixer and scrape down the bottom and sides. Beat on medium speed until the mixture is smooth. Pour the mixture into the prepared pan and let it come to room temperature.

❋ Place it in the freezer, uncovered, and freeze for about 3 hours, until it's almost fully frozen. Take a sharp knife and score the mixture into small blocks. I score it into 35 blocks. Put the pan back into the freezer and freeze completely, covered with plastic wrap, for another 4 hours or overnight. Remove the ice cream from the pan by grabbing the edges of the parchment and lifting them up.

Let the ice cream soften a bit, about 10 minutes, then proceed to cut the pieces fully, using a sharp knife. Place 8–10 pieces at a time into a food processor fitted with the steel blade. They will clang around for a bit, so stop and scrape down the bottom and sides of the processor bowl to break up the clumps. Eventually, they will break down and become creamy. You can keep the blocks of ice cream in a resealable freezer bag in the freezer for up to 1 month, so you can make soft serve whenever you get a craving.

❋ The soft serve is best made to order, but any leftovers will keep well in an airtight container in the freezer for 3 days.

❋ To make the sauce, whisk together the cocoa, sugar and salt in a medium saucepan. Pour in the hot water and then whisk the mixture over medium-high heat. You may need to take a heatproof spatula to scrape the inside edges of the saucepan. Bring the mixture to a boil then turn down the heat and simmer for 3 minutes, stirring constantly with the heatproof spatula. Stir in the vanilla. Let the sauce cool a little, just so it is still warm, then pour it over the ice cream.

❋ The chocolate sauce will keep well in an airtight container in the refrigerator for up to 1 month—just warm it gently before serving with ice cream.

NOTE

The chocolate sauce is equally excellent when whisked into hot or cold milk. You can also serve it with cake, over brownies, or any time chocolate sauce is required. Serve it with the Brown Butter Spelt Brownies on page 82 and ice cream, the Mocha Bundt Cake on page 118, the Chocolate Espresso Date Cake on page 130, the Chocolate-Swirled Molasses Meringues on page 282 and whipped cream, and Angel Food Cake on page 126, or with any other recipe where chocolate sauce may be desirable!

In Gratitude

During the writing of *All the Sweet Things*, I would periodically pinch myself, because I was living out a dream. And now that we are at the back of the cookbook, I get to thank those who helped me reach this tremendous goal.

The bulk of this cookbook was written between November 2015 and March 2016. Although several people (listed below) tested out my recipes, I did not have a team to help me—I did all of the baking, styling, photographing (with my iPhone!) and dish-washing by myself (with no dishwasher, I might add), and for the most part, this was a very solitary process. I left the house just once or twice a week and probably talked to my cats too much, but with that being said, I had fantastic love and support from good friends and family, near and far. I would get phone calls, emails and texts from loved ones, checking in and cheering me on. I was so happy when friends would pop in to say hi, and gladly took pieces of pie or cake or muffins off my hands. Having people around you, who support you, is tremendously motivating, and I've been lucky to have such a crew.

Special thanks to those old, dear friends, who pop up in my stories and have an everlasting place in my heart: Josée Johnston, Stacy Deschamps, Chyanne Kehler, Candus Hunter, Chelsey Bast, Mel Rahm, Tanya Frigault and Grace Thompson. Thank you to my amazing team of recipe testers, who gave such valuable feedback. You're the best! I had chefs, home cooks, experienced bakers and less-experienced bakers helping me out. These wonderful people took the time to test my recipes to make sure they aren't crap: Marie-France Raumel, Marlene Charpentier, Auntie Helen Stang, Leonore Johnston, Catherin Boden, Kim Fehr, Rachel Dyer, Donna Pelech, Stacy Deschamps, Peter Graefe, Jenni Willems, Jenny Jack, Leanne Kohlman, Amy Bronee, Ashley Markus, Jan Scott, Lindsay Janzen, Grace Thompson, Chelsey Bast, and my mom, Lorna Boser. Thank you, Helen Davis, for your kind and encouraging words. Your timing is always perfect. Thanks to my chef, Darren Craddock, for giving me time off to work on the book and for letting me eat a great deal of the salted caramel ice cream when I was at work. Thank you to Bob Deutscher, Gail Vandersteen and Jenni Willems, who lent me props for the photographs when I was getting so tired of looking at my own. Thanks for trusting me with your goods! Huge thanks to *The Western Producer* for allowing me to share the recipe for butterhorns. Thank you, *Chatelaine*, for allowing me to share the dough-nut recipe. Thank you, Dan Clapson, for your friendship, as well as your lemon posset recipe. Thank you, Cinda Chavich, for sharing your sticky toffee pudding with molasses sauce recipe with me. A giant thank-you to Great-Aunt Helen for the big batch bran muffin recipe and for being there when I needed you the most. Much love to Josée and Leonore Johnston for the chocolate marshmallow pie recipe. Thank you, dear Agata, for the cream cheese pistachio twists recipe, and very special thanks to my mom for sharing with me her treasured recipes. It's so nice to see them in print!

Thank you to Aimée Wimbush-Bourque, Julie Van Rosendaal, dee Hobsbawn-Smith and Erin Scott for the blurbs on the book. I love you ladies. You agreed to say a few kind words when this cookbook was just an idea. Thank you for your faith in me.

A special thank you to the readers of Sweetsugarbean. Your kinds words of support and encouragement have filled my heart. Who knew my little blog could amount to so much?

I can't thank the team at TouchWood Editions enough. Thank you, Taryn Boyd, for reaching out to me on that cold February day. You've changed my life, lady. Thanks to Pete, Tori and Renée for working so hard on a cookbook I am so very proud of. One day I'll surprise you all with a basket of baked goods.

Thank you to my editor, Lesley Cameron, for going through all of my recipes and stories, making sure they make sense. You, too, are owed a basket of baked goods! Special thanks also to Tree Abraham for designing this cookbook. It's like you popped into my brain and read my mind! It's so beautiful. Thank you, thank you, thank you.

To my darling Dixon, thank you for your love and support and for making me laugh every day, especially when I was working on the edits and you gently nudged me away from Procrastination Station. You came into my life when I had very nearly given up hope of finding the love of my life, proving that good things really do come to those who wait. I'm so glad we waited. I'm so glad you said yes.

Much love to my sister, Juanita, and her daughters Olivia, Maggie and Lizzie, and to my brothers Arron and Travis and their families.

And lastly, to my dear, sweet mom. Thank you for everything. For letting me make a mess in the kitchen when I was a kid. For letting me go on my adventures across the country. For showing me what strength, courage and kindness look like in times of adversity. This cookbook is as much yours as it is mine.

METRIC CONVERSIONS

VOLUME

IMPERIAL	METRIC
⅛ tsp	0.5 mL
¼ tsp	1 mL
½ tsp	2.5 mL
¾ tsp	4 mL
1 tsp	5 mL
½ Tbsp	8 mL
1 Tbsp	15 mL
1½ Tbsp	23 mL
2 Tbsp	30 mL
2½ Tbsp	38 mL
¼ cup	60 mL
⅓ cup	80 mL
½ cup	125 mL
⅔ cup	165 mL
¾ cup	185 mL
1 cup	250 mL
1¼ cups	310 mL
1⅓ cups	330 mL
1½ cups	375 mL
1⅔ cups	415 mL
1¾ cups	435 mL
2 cups	500 mL
2¼ cups	560 mL
2⅓ cups	580 mL
2½ cups	625 mL
2⅔ cups	665 mL
2¾ cups	690 mL
3 cups	750 mL
3½ cups	875 mL
4 cups	1 L
5 cups	1.25 L
6 cups	1.5 L
8 cups / 2 quarts	2 L
25 cups	6 L

WEIGHT

IMPERIAL	METRIC
1 oz	30 g
4 oz	115 g
8 oz	225 g
12 oz	340 g
1 lb (16 oz)	450 g

CANS

IMPERIAL	METRIC
10 oz	284 mL
14 oz	398 mL

LENGTH

IMPERIAL	METRIC
1/12 inch	2 mm
⅛ inch	3 mm
1/6 inch	4 mm
¼ inch	6 mm
½ inch	12 mm
¾ inch	2 cm
1 inch	2.5 cm
1¼ inches	3 cm
1½ inches	3.5 cm
1¾ inches	4.5 cm
2 inches	5 cm
2½ inches	6.5 cm
3 inches	7.5 cm
3½ inches	9 cm
4 inches	10 cm
5 inches	12.5 cm
6 inches	15 cm
7 inches	18 cm
8 inches	20 cm
9 inches	23 cm
10 inches	25 cm
11 inches	28 cm
12 inches	30 cm
17 inches	43 cm
18 inches	46 cm
20 inches	50 cm

TEMPERATURE

(For oven temperatures, see chart below)

IMPERIAL	METRIC
115°F	46°C
150°F	66°C
160°F	71°C
170°F	77°C
180°F	82°C
185°F	85°C
190°F	88°C
200°F	93°C
240°F	116°C
247°F	119°C
250°F	121°C
290°F	143°C
300°F	149°C
350°F	177°C
360°F	182°C
370°F	188°C

OVEN TEMPERATURE

IMPERIAL	METRIC
200°F	95°C
225°F	105°C
250°F	120°C
275°F	135°C
300°F	150°C
325°F	160°C
350°F	180°C
375°F	190°C
400°F	200°C
425°F	220°C
450°F	230°C

INDEX